TWO HUNDRED YEARS OF AMERICAN
*CLOCKS & WATCHES*

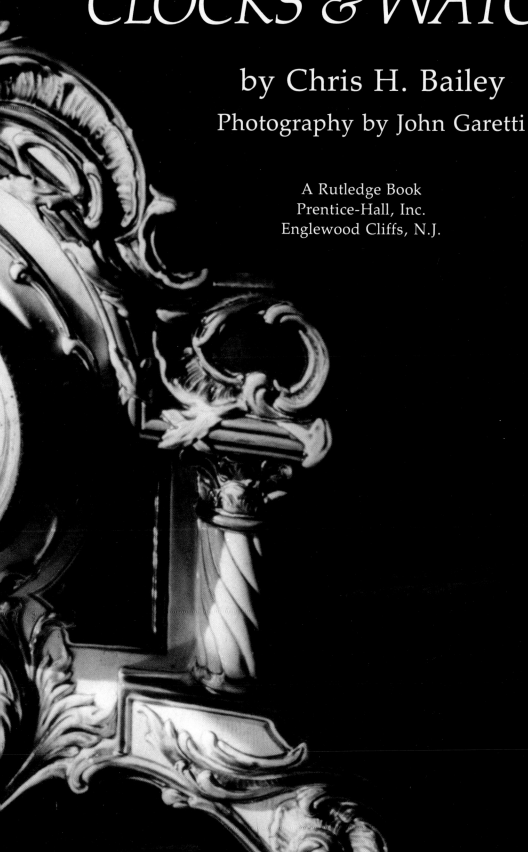

# TWO HUNDRED YEARS OF AMERICAN
# CLOCKS & WATCHES

### by Chris H. Bailey
### Photography by John Garetti

A Rutledge Book
Prentice-Hall, Inc.
Englewood Cliffs, N.J.

Fred R. Sammis *Publisher*
John T. Sammis *Creative Director*
Doris Townsend *Editor-in-Chief*
Allan Mogel *Art Director*
Sally Andrews *Managing Editor*
B. G. Murphy *Associate Editor*
Jeremy Friedlander *Associate Editor*
Mimi Koren *Associate Editor*
Arthur Gubernick *Production Consultant*
Annemarie Bosch *Production Manager*
Elyse Shick *Associate Art Director*
Eric Marshall *Art Associate*
Jay Hyams *Assistant Editor*

ISBN: 0-13-935130-2
Library of Congress Catalog Card
Number: 75-13714

Printed in Italy by Mondadori, Verona

# CONTENTS

# FOREWORD

Can one write a complete history of clockmaking and watchmaking in America? I doubt any person could complete such a task in a lifetime. If he could, the product of his research would fill many volumes. This work, though as factual and comprehensive as possible, is not the complete story. It is a general history of these crafts and of the industries that grew from them. Hopefully the reader will develop an appreciation for the part played by these men in colonial times and in the 200 years that followed the birth of our great nation.

The reader will find the history of American clock and watchmaking filled with men of ingenuity and perseverance in a constant struggle for economic survival. Some businesses lasted for a considerable time; many did not. But the efforts of these men, however lengthy or brief, resulted in the manufacture of hundreds of millions of clocks and watches. Some of these timepieces were made for the wealthy, but not all. Perhaps the greatest contribution of American horology to the industry was the manufacture of time-keeping devices at a cost so low that they could be purchased by almost anyone.

Research into horological history continues to progress daily. In the last decade alone new findings have greatly broadened our knowledge of timepieces and added a wealth of information to their background. No doubt future investigations will supplement, and perhaps in some cases correct, information contained in this history. And so it should be.

Clocks and watches stir the interest of the historian, mechanic, collector, and casual admirer. As Director-Curator of the American Clock & Watch Museum of Bristol, Connecticut, I come in contact daily with a public fascinated by timepieces.

Collectors especially are being drawn more frequently to horological items. The National Association of Watch and Clock Collectors, formed in 1943, has now over 26,000 active members and is growing rapidly. Membership is distributed over the entire country and extends to over forty foreign lands.

Interest and acquisition by the public, and in particular by collectors, has caused an increasing

scarcity of old clocks in the past few years. Handcrafted clocks, because of the small quantity produced, were of course never plentiful, but even the kinds manufactured in great numbers are becoming harder to acquire. American antique buyers have scoured foreign countries to supply the home market; in recent years they have even bought and returned to the United States many of the clocks that were exported from 1840 to about 1920.

Values have escalated sharply, especially in the last ten to fifteen years. Except in rare cases, the days of buying a tall clock for twenty-five dollars or a shelf clock for two dollars and a half have long passed and are only fantasies in the minds of present-day buyers. Values are affected not only by the scarcity of an item, but by its quality and precision, unusual features or gadgetry, beauty, usability (especially for very tall clocks in many of today's low-ceilinged homes), and present condition. The latter is an important factor, for a rare clock is of little value if it is in poor condition or has been seriously abused by a would-be repairman or restorer. Certainly few items survive without the marks of time and use, but once the condition has deteriorated to near ruin, restoration is often so extensive that the individual quality of the original suffers.

Present-day buyers should also be wary of possible fakery. Because many antique clocks command high prices, it has become increasingly profitable for "restorers" to construct complete clocks from parts of useless ones. Restoration is entirely acceptable if the clock is represented as such and priced accordingly when sold, but too often a restored clock is sold as being genuine and in its original working condition.

It is hoped that this volume may prove helpful to those who proudly possess timekeepers, increasing their knowledge of items they have and of the men who produced them. If this is accomplished to some degree, then I feel I have fulfilled my task.

January 1, 1975

CHRIS H. BAILEY

The Watch
with the
Non-Breakable
Crystal
(TRADE MARK)

RADIUM DIAL

Ingraham Company

Conn., U.S.A.

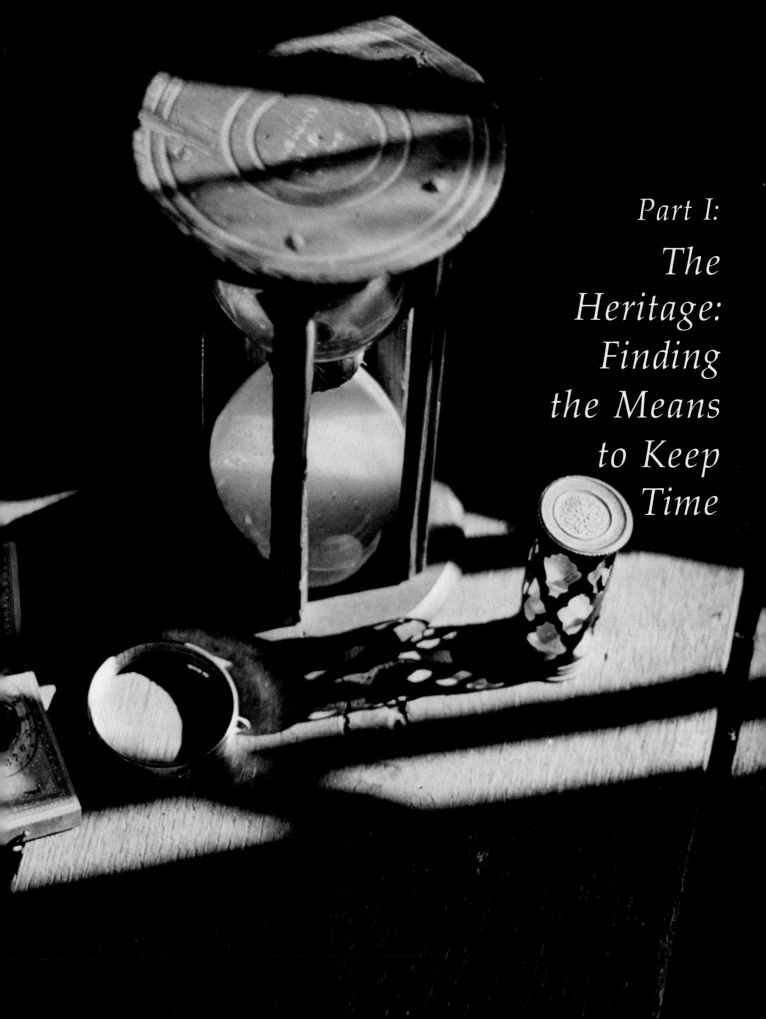

Part I:
*The*
*Heritage:*
*Finding*
*the Means*
*to Keep*
*Time*

$V$ery early in human history man recognized the passing of time and tried by one means or another, throughout the ages, to measure and record it. He first noted the passing of days, cycles of the moon, and seasons. Devices using the sun for measurement—sundials—were used before 1000 B.C. About 450 B.C. the Greek philosopher Herodotus recorded that it was from the Babylonians that the Greeks learned about "the pole, the gnomon, and the twelve parts of the day."

Other devices, such as water clocks, sandglasses, graduated candles, and oil lamps were developed, and some of these were used well into modern times. An egg timer, still in common use, is a sandglass not much different from those in use hundreds of years ago. Man's history has always been a story of striving for refinement and this attitude led naturally to the development of more accurate mechanical time-measuring devices.

Mechanical clocks were probably developed in the latter part of the thirteenth century, but just where or by whom is unknown. Researchers have suggested that the earliest clocks were made by monks in Italy or central Europe to time the call to worship.

In England there is evidence that by 1283 a church clock was made by Austin canons (a position between a monk and secular canon) at Dunstable Priory, Bedford. Thereafter, mention of such clocks occurs with greater frequency in English church records. But, though clocks were being made in England by about 1283, it is believed that most of the timepieces constructed there before 1600 were made by craftsmen brought into England from the continent.

The earliest church "clocks," located within the buildings, were without hands; they indicated time by ringing bells at intervals, striking the hour. Some clocks of this early period were probably elevated into the church belfry to utilize the existing bells. Small dials for indicating time on these clocks probably appeared in the first part of the fourteenth century; approximately a century later large, readily visible dials were placed on the outside of the towers.

Early tower clocks had iron frames and gears and were made and repaired by men—usually blacksmiths—skilled in working iron. By the latter half of the fourteenth century smaller domestic clocks appeared; they were called chamber clocks, and it is likely that locksmiths and gunsmiths constructed them. During the fifteenth century springs were used in some European domestic clocks. Table clocks were beginning to appear too, but they were crude and not generally accepted.

Shortly after 1600, a style of domestic clock emerged in Britain, undoubtedly developed from the European chamber clock, known as the "lantern" clock. This weight-driven lantern clock became extremely popular and was produced extensively after 1630. Because of its popularity many men were induced to learn the clockmaking trade and by August 22, 1631, there were so many clockmakers at work in London that King Charles I granted a charter to a trade union of master clockmakers. The guild controlled the business in the city of London and was commonly called the Clockmaker's Company. Although many exceedingly fine items were made in London under the strict quality standards of the company, technical advancement, mechanical individuality, and inventiveness were often equally prevalent in areas outside the city.

In 1656, Christian Huygens, a Dutchman, invented the pendulum for regulating clocks more

1

accurately. The knowledge of this invention spread rapidly in Europe and within two or three years it was introduced into England by another Dutchman, Ahasuerus Fromanteel. About this time clocks were beginning to be housed in tall, free-standing wooden cases and were generally called tall clocks. The earliest of these had Huygens' short, swinging pendulums; the purpose of the long case was to hide and support the unsightly weights. About 1675, the three-foot-long pendulum with anchor escapement came into general use and the long case also enclosed this extremity.

## CLOCKS IN THE NEW LAND

The earliest domestic clocks brought to the American colonies in the early 1600s by wealthy colonizers or government officials were undoubtedly of the English lantern type or similar types created by the Dutch or the French. The tall clock was probably first brought over in the latter part of the century. From the earliest settlements until about 1700, it is doubtful that there was much clockmaking activity in the colonies. The new land held a much greater appeal for men with abilities to cultivate the land and supply the basic necessities. Too, few people in the early settlements were financially able to own a clock. Imported horological items were available to the few who could afford them, and the idea of procuring a clock of colonial workmanship most likely would have been frowned upon.

Records do exist of men who were capable of attending public clocks, most notably blacksmiths and gunsmiths. It is reasonable to assume that these men were able to repair such clocks, being skilled in working iron. The public clock, because of its size, could not be transported to the mother country for repair as easily as could smaller items.

By 1668, Boston had a town clock and one Richard Taylor was in charge of it. Two years later he was replaced by Thomas Matson, a gunsmith, who was "to looke after the towne clocke and keepe it in good repair"—a job for which he was paid ten shillings a year. After 1673, the clock was attended by Giles Dyer, who was probably a blacksmith. In 1680, Dyer was paid five pounds for setting up a clock in the North Meeting House. It is unlikely that he did more than install a clock that had been imported from England. In 1684, William Sumner, a blacksmith, was responsible for the clock in the North Meeting House and five years later Robert Williams began to attend the one in the old meetinghouse.

The first immigrant who claimed to be a clockmaker was William Davis, who arrived in Boston in 1683. Boston tax rolls of 1687 list a David Johnson as a watchmaker, though he was probably a repairman. Everard Bogardus was a clock-

**1.** English lantern clock made by Henry Webster, London, *c.* 1710. Originally hung on a wall bracket, this single-hand striking clock is similar to those used in the American colonies during the 17th and early 18th centuries. (*American Clock & Watch Museum*) **2.** Pinwheel escapement bracket clock by Frederick Heisely, Harrisburg, PA, *c.* 1815. Though some bracket clocks were made earlier in colonial times, tall clocks were the major American handcrafted timekeepers. (*Courtesy, Edward F. LaFond*)

maker in New York as early as 1698 and, though no names were given, a historical account of Pennsylvania written in 1698 stated that clock and watchmakers were then working in Philadelphia. No examples of signed work by these men are known and it is more likely that they were repairing and marketing imported items than constructing new ones.

Watches of this period were also imported from England and Europe for the very few who could afford them. And though many colonial craftsmen called themselves "watchmakers," they, too, were in fact repairmen and did not construct complete watches. (Watches had been developed about 1510 in Germany. By the seventeenth century the art of watchmaking was well understood. After about 1775 a few watches were probably made in America, but the number was small until after 1850.)

By 1700, the number of clocks and watches in the colonies had grown to such an extent that

**3.** Line drawing of standard tall clock movement to indicate the different parts of the movement. This movement is similar to the majority produced in America from *c.* 1700 until *c.* 1850 (though some areas ceased production shortly after the introduction of mass-produced shelf clocks).

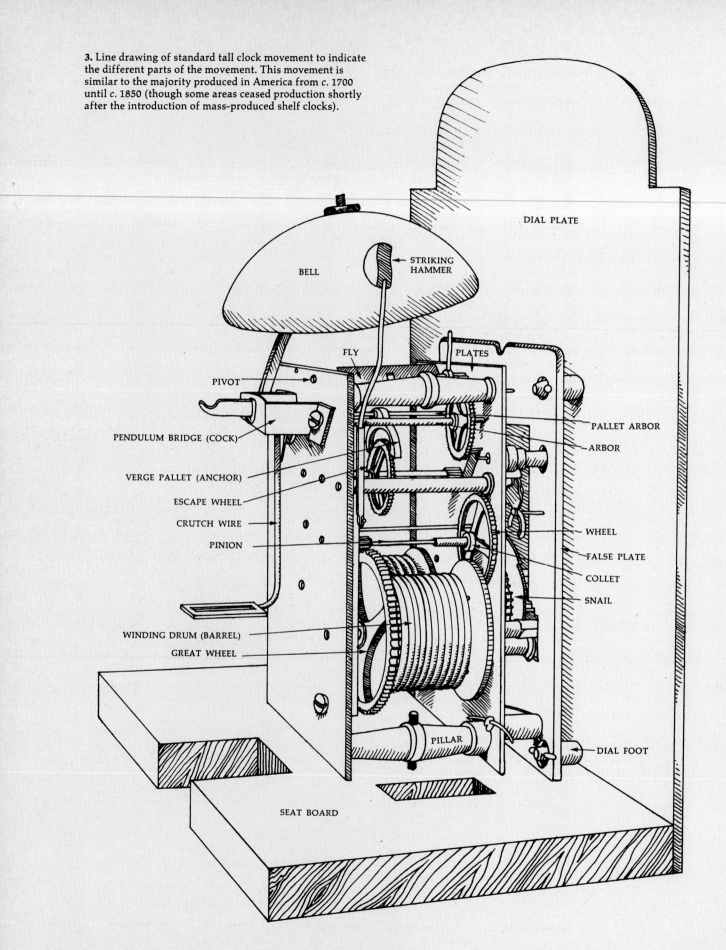

DIAL PLATE

BELL

STRIKING HAMMER

FLY

PLATES

PIVOT

PENDULUM BRIDGE (COCK)

PALLET ARBOR

ARBOR

VERGE PALLET (ANCHOR)

ESCAPE WHEEL

CRUTCH WIRE

PINION

WHEEL

FALSE PLATE

COLLET

SNAIL

WINDING DRUM (BARREL)

GREAT WHEEL

PILLAR

DIAL FOOT

SEAT BOARD

horological artisans, most of them young and recently trained, were attracted to the colonies. Because the majority of clocks and watches were owned by the wealthier class—and the class that had the means to procure new items—the immigrant craftsmen settled in populous centers where the wealthy lived, notably in Philadelphia and Boston. Once craftsmen were established in these centers, other makers set up shop in places such as New York; Newport, Rhode Island; Charleston, South Carolina; Baltimore, Maryland; and New Haven, Connecticut.

Handcrafting of clocks continued and grew until 1825 in most areas, and in many instances until 1850. After 1800 less expensive wooden tall clocks were manufactured in quantity and their lower price found a new buying public. About 1815 the wooden shelf clock was introduced; by 1825 it was mass produced and sold by peddlers east of the Mississippi River. The brass shelf clock, developed in 1838, eventually supplanted other styles of clocks in popularity. Its success opened the way for smaller, more portable clocks.

From 1840 to 1870 the clockmaking industry enjoyed considerable expansion and development; in that time seven companies evolved as giants of manufacturing. From 1870 to 1920 the companies enjoyed a ''golden age'' of constant development, high profits, and quantity production. Beginning with the Great Depression of the thirties, the industry went into decline—a decline that, aided by the disruption and consequences of World War II, resulted in the demise of one of the great American industries.

## THE AGE OF HANDCRAFTING

During the latter part of the eighteenth century, the majority of clocks made in the colonies were handcrafted in the English manner for the wealthy and upper-middle class. Though there was some European influence, it was minimal in most parts of the country. The majority of colonial craftsmen had been trained in England or had been apprenticed to an English immigrant, so it is safe to assume that American clockmaking at this time was an adaptation of English skills and methods.

Early domestic clocks were almost exclusively tall clocks, now commonly called grandfather clocks, though some production of table or bracket clocks was carried on in Boston and Philadelphia and in some smaller centers. After 1775, wall and shelf clocks were introduced by the Willard family in Boston, and after 1800, the demand for smaller clocks increased while that for old-fashioned tall clocks declined. By 1820, Connecticut manufacturers were producing shelf clocks in numbers greater than any other type; this remains a major production style to the present day.

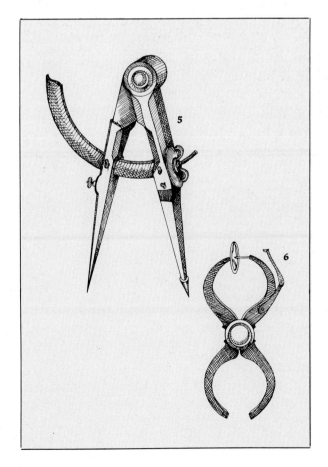

4. Ancient church clock of Salisbury Cathedral, Wiltshire, England, installed in 1386. Restored and operating, this is the earliest mechanical clock surviving in its original state. Having no dials, the clock indicated time by striking on the hours. *(Courtesy, Salisbury Cathedral)* 5. Dividers, or compass, measuring tool. 6. Calipers to measure thickness.

## CLOCK COMPONENTS

A clock consists of a movement, a case, and appurtenances—accessories which include such items as the dial, hands, winding key, weights, pendulum bob, case hardware, and decoration. During the era of handcrafting, the clockmaker was primarily concerned with the construction of the clock movement and perhaps some appurtenances. When possible he purchased the case and other appurtenances.

An early clockmaker had to be skilled in forging, casting, turning, and engraving, all of which were part of his apprenticeship training. In times of good trade relations, he could import rough wheel and plate castings and steel rod or pinion wire for making arbors and pinions and other basic movement components to finish and assemble himself, but for much of the period—and certainly in times of trade embargoes or war with Britain—the clockmaker had to rely almost totally on his own skills.

Because he was skilled in forging and casting metals as well as engraving, the clockmaker usually carried on other small businesses to supplement his income. Goldsmithing, silversmithing, and jewelry making were common sidelines, as was the production of surveying instruments and small tools. Many small metal items such as buckles and hardware were made as well. Repairing clocks, watches, and metal items was often an equally important part of a clockmaker's business.

## PARTS OF A CLOCK

**Anchor (verge)**—a device that regulates the speed of rotation of the escape wheel.

**Arbor**—a steel shaft or rod on which wheels and pinions are affixed.

**Boss**—an attachment to a dial, usually round, on which the clockmaker's name and town is shown.

**Bridge (cock)**—a bracket from which the pendulum suspends.

**Bushing**—an insert of hard material in a clock plate at the point of arbor pivot to allow for added wear. In watches, bushing is usually a mineral substance known as a jewel.

**Chapter**—the ring on the dial plate on which are painted or engraved the hour numerals and minute graduations.

**Collet**—a brass collar that holds a wheel on an arbor.

**Count wheel**—a wheel with spaced slots that indexes the correct number of blows the hammer makes on the bell when the clock is striking.

**Crutch wire**—a wire that carries the impulse from the escapement to the pendulum.

**Dial arch**—the arched portion at the top of many dials (some dials are square). It may contain a boss, a moon dial, or decoration.

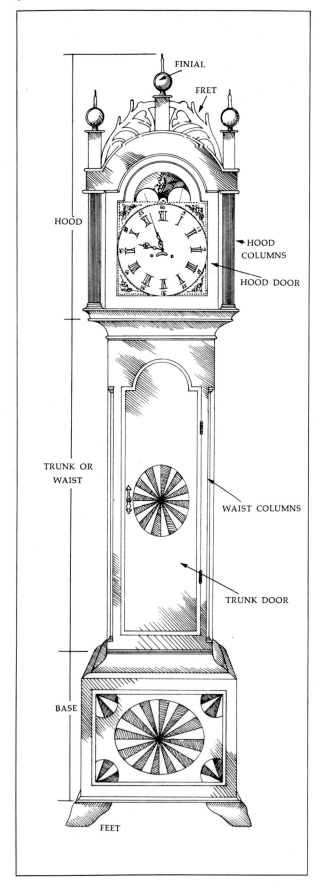

## COUNT WHEEL STRIKING SYSTEM

LIFTING PIECE

COUNT WHEEL

9 8 7 12 6 10 11 5 4 1 2 3

NUMBER OF TIMES CLOCK WILL STRIKE
WHEN ACTUATED NEXT

## MECHANISM FOR MUSICAL OR CHIMING CLOCK

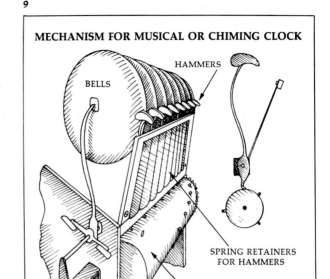

BELLS

HAMMERS

SPRING RETAINERS
FOR HAMMERS

PIN DRUM

FAN (SPEED REGULATOR)

## DEPTHING TOOL

PINION

WHEEL

ARBOR

10

**Dial foot**—a pillar on the back of a dial for attaching the dial to a false plate or movement.

**Dial plate**—a plate, usually brass, iron, or wood, on which the dial is engraved or painted.

**Escapement**—a device by which the pendulum controls the rate of time keeping. It consists of an anchor and an escape wheel.

**Escape wheel**—a wheel at the end of the wheel train that is engaged by the anchor to regulate the clock's running.

**False plate**—an intermediate plate between the movement and dial on some clocks to aid fitting the dial to the movement.

**Fly**—a wind-resistant fan that regulates the speed of striking or chiming.

**Great wheel**—the first wheel in a train to which is usually attached the winding arbor and drum.

**Moon dial**—a dial, often found in the arch portion of a clock dial, that indicates the cycle of the moon.

**Motion train**—a series of wheels that regulates the rotation of the hour and minute hands.

**Pallets**—the two projections from the ends of the anchor that engage with the escape-wheel teeth and allow one tooth to pass with each complete swing of the pendulum.

**Pendulum**—a swinging device attached to the escapement by means of the crutch that controls the rate of time keeping.

**Pillar**—a turned post of metal or wood that connects to the front and back plates and establishes a fixed distance between them.

**Pinion**—a small wheel with twelve or less teeth, called leaves, that meshes with a larger wheel.

7. Representation of a tall case, or grandfather clock, with components noted. 8. Count wheel system of indexing the number of times a clock will strike when actuated at the hour. 9. Musical clocks have the addition of a system of bells, hammers, and a regulating mechanism that are actuated by clock. Barrel has pins so placed that tripped hammers produce a recognizable tune. Some play hourly, some only every four hours. 10. Depthing tool, a device whereby two arbors are placed and correct wheel and pinion mesh is determined. Pointed ends can then scribe brass clock plates to locate position to drill arbor pivot holes.

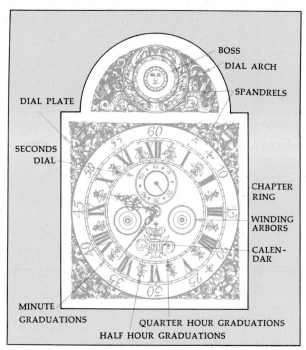

BOSS
DIAL ARCH
SPANDRELS
DIAL PLATE
SECONDS DIAL
CHAPTER RING
WINDING ARBORS
CALEN-DAR
MINUTE GRADUATIONS
QUARTER HOUR GRADUATIONS
HALF HOUR GRADUATIONS

**11.** Engraved brass dial similar to those used in America, with components noted. Clockmakers often did their own casting and engraving. Chapter, spandrels, and boss were sometimes cast from pewter, though usually on country-made clocks only. **12.** Painted or "japanned" iron dials with colorful spandrels came into popularity in America after 1780. Though some American firms produced "white dials," most were imported from England. *(Author's collection)*

**Pivot**—a hole in a clock plate in which an arbor end rotates.

**Plates**—two parallel pieces of metal or wood between which the wheels, pinions, and arbors are fitted.

**Rack and snail**—an indexing system for striking that sets itself for correct striking shortly before striking begins.

**Seat board**—a wooden board on which a clock movement sits when in a case.

**Spandrels**—painted or cast-metal decoration for dials.

**Train**—a series of wheels and pinions through which power is transmitted from its source (usually weights or springs) to the escapement.

**Wheel**—a circular piece of metal on the perimeter of which are cut teeth.

**Winding drum (barrel)**—a cylinder onto which the cord holding the weight is wound.

### THE MOVEMENT

The striking, weight-driven clock made to run eight days without rewinding was the most common type of brass clock produced in America before 1800. A number of thirty-hour clocks were made in Pennsylvania, a few in New England, but the eight-day clock was the standard. Though the thirty-hour movement was less costly to produce—thereby reducing the price by about five

dollars—the eight-day clock proved more popular, for the greater price was overshadowed by the greater appeal of a clock that had to be wound only once a week.

In any case, the handcrafted brass clock was expensive. In 1800, a tall clock and case could cost forty dollars or more and was often the owner's most valuable household possession.

The usual eight-day tall clock movement consists of two brass plates, approximately five inches by seven inches, held together by four or more posts. Arranged between these plates are nine arbors, or shafts, on which are two cord barrels, seven wheels, six pinions, one fly for regulation of striking speed, and escapement pallets for time-keeping regulation. On the exterior of the front plate are two wheels and two pinions, which are called the motion work or motion train, and which regulate movement of the clock's hands. Outside the plates is an additional mechanism to index the correct number of striking blows on the bell mounted above the movement. Two basic striking mechanisms are used, the count wheel system and a more elaborate self-setting and self-correcting system known as the rack and snail.

Occasionally early clocks were constructed so as to chime quarterly or had musical attachments for which more elaborate systems were necessary, but these were not common. The chiming clock is one that sounds a portion of a musical strain on several bells at intervals, usually every fifteen minutes. A musical clock is capable of playing a tune as well as striking. Sometimes a clock was fitted with an alarm mechanism that would cause multiple blows on the clock bell at a time set by the owner.

To construct the mechanism the clockmaker took rough plate and wheel castings and hammered or "planished" them to harden the metal. Once the hardening was accomplished, the parts were filed to smoothness and to the size needed and laid aside to be finished later.

Wheel blanks were first centered with a compass or dividers and drilled for the arbor. The teeth were then cut on the wheels. In order to be accurately spaced, they were cut on a wheel-cutting engine, a mechanical device with a circular cutting blade powered by a hand crank. The wheel blank was temporarily fastened to a rotating shaft, which then was attached to the circular indexing plate. On this plate were engraved a number of concentric circles; along the circumference of each circle were differently spaced indentations, the various number of indentations corresponding to the numbers of teeth needed for different clock wheels.

Different numbers of teeth are required on different wheels to produce gear reduction so that motive power is not used up too rapidly. For

**13.** Roxbury-style tall clock by Simon Willard, made *c.* 1800. Finely veneered cases with delicate fretwork were characteristic of Boston area. *(Courtesy, Charles S. Parsons)*

**14.** Norwich-style tall clock by Thomas Jackson, Preston, CT, *c.* 1790. "Whale's tails" fretwork and escallion show maritime influence. *(Courtesy, Arthur S. Liverant)*

example, in a clock having a gear train with an escape wheel that turns once per minute, the train is so geared that the great wheel, which is attached to the motive power, turns only once in twelve hours. Thus, in one week the escape wheel makes 10,080 revolutions while the great wheel makes only 14. Were the great wheel to turn faster, the weights would fall too rapidly or the springs would uncoil too quickly and the clock would not run the full week.

Once attached to the indexing plate, the blank was rotated so that the correct number of teeth could be cut. The early engines cut only a series of rectangular slots, so ends of the teeth had to be rounded afterward with a special file or rounding-up tool.

The wheels were mounted on steel rods known as arbors, and fastened to them with small metal collars called collets. An arbor was formed by turning a steel rod down to correct size by means of a turn, a treadle, or a hand-bow-driven lathe. Part of this arbor was usually a pinion, a small steel wheel with less than twelve teeth, called leaves, that meshed with the brass teeth. A pinion had to be cut on a device especially made for cutting pinions, filed by hand, or made from pinion wire. Pinion wire was steel rod that had been drawn through a series of hardened forms to give it the shape of the leaves.

After the wheels, arbors, and pinions were finished, the position of the pivot holes on the plates was determined by either mapping out the positions with dividers or by using a locating device known as a depthing tool. Once the correct pivot-hole positions were found, the plates were drilled with a treadle or bow-drawn drill.

Escapement pallets were filed to final shape from steel castings, then the miscellaneous parts were finished and assembled. After the pendulum was made, the movement was set up, run, and inspected for flaws that might hinder accurate and reliable operation.

Completely assembled and finished movements could be imported—for installation in locally made cases—and perhaps some such movements were imported in areas where there were few clockmakers. But it is doubtful that this practice was prevalent in areas where locally made movements were plentiful. The belief that prominent clockmakers imported a portion of their movements is probably a myth precipitated by the common use of English painted dials. Clock owners often have noted dial plates marked with an English dial maker's name and place of manufacture and have erroneously assumed the entire clock movement was made by the English firm.

## THE APPURTENANCES

Appurtenances to the clock movement or case

**16.** Inlaid marquetry case English clock by William Troutbeck, Leeds, *c.* 1710. Such sophisticated cases were rare in the colonies. (*American Clock & Watch Museum*)

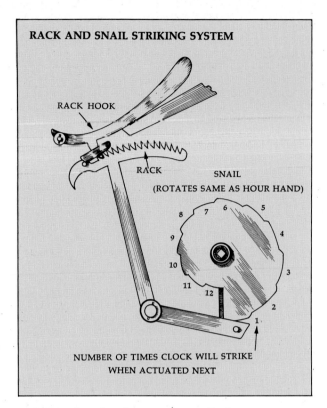

**17.** Rack and snail striking system: a self-adjusting system that would always correlate with time indicated by clock.

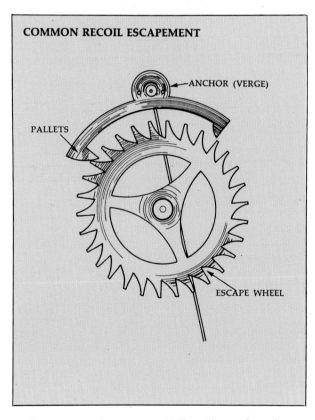

**18.** Common recoil escapement. Pallets allow each tooth to "escape" at a common rate, thereby achieving accuracy.

could be made by the clockmaker, but more often were purchased from American merchants who were supplied from England. Such items included dials, pulleys, weights, keys, and decorative items such as dial spandrels, case hardware, metal column capitals, and finials.

Dials are divided into two basic categories, brass and painted. Brass dials, which were often engraved by the clockmaker, were used almost exclusively in America until about 1780. About that time white-painted dials with hand decoration were imported from England in increasing numbers. Though the brass dial was still used in some areas, especially in Connecticut, as late as 1800, painted dials predominated; they could be purchased more cheaply than the clockmaker could produce his engraved brass ones. Some painted tall-clock dials were made in America after 1800, but most continued to be imported.

Roman numerals were popularly used on dials of this early period. English clocks made as early as the sixteenth century are occasionally seen with Arabic numerals, but these are rare. The widespread use of Roman numerals was probably a result of the traditional use of Latin in documents or formal script until nearly 1700. Many English and European clockmakers also engraved their names on their dials in Latin. The formality and tradition of using Roman numerals continued until almost 1800, when the use of Arabic numerals became widespread. Both styles have been used to the present day, and though Roman numerals were more often used on clocks before 1800, they do not necessarily indicate that the clock is older than another with Arabic numerals.

## THE CASES

During the age of handcrafting, the clock case was considered a separate item and expense and had to be purchased from a local cabinetmaker, some of whom specialized in clock cases. The buyer might order the case himself or have the clockmaker do it for him. Often the buyer purchased a clock without a case and simply hung it on a wall bracket.

Cases often reflect traits of cabinetmaking periods and styles, but it is hard to classify a case in regard to time through styles such as Chippendale, Sheraton, and Hepplewhite, among others. Though current styles were more closely adhered to in larger centers, cases made in country areas often display features of styles and time periods that defy their classification.

Mahogany was usually considered the most elegant wood for cases, though it had to be imported. But native woods were often utilized, walnut and maple being commonly used in Pennsylvania and the southern areas, and cherry and pine in New England.

**20.** Dwarf tall, or "grandmother," timepiece by Thomas Claggett, Newport, RI, made *c.* 1740. Less than 5 ft. tall. (*Edward Ingraham Library*)

During the mid-eighteenth century a style of painted case came into vogue in England and spread to the colonies. Cases were painted, then decorated with an Oriental motif, a process that became known as "japanning." Some japanned cases are found in America, but they are rare.

The painting of cases became popular after 1800 as a means of cutting the cost of construction. To avoid using expensive veneers, cases were often painted and hand-grained to simulate expensive wood. Though many of these look unlike any wood known, their primitive artistic value has made them important today.

In ordering cases, clockmakers often dealt with only a few cabinetmakers, which explains why cases housing a particular maker's movements may have similar characteristics. On the other hand, some areas had numerous cabinetmakers who constructed cases for several different clockmakers. In areas such as Boston; Philadelphia; Newport, Rhode Island; and Norwich, Connecticut, distinctive schools of cabinetmaking developed and, though exceptions do occur, cases from these areas are often identified by the styles that flourished there.

## APPRENTICESHIP—LIFEBLOOD OF THE CRAFT

Clockmaking by handcrafting involved many processes that could only be learned under the direction and supervision of a master. As in other crafts, the period of apprenticeship was a necessary and vital part of attaining skill as an artisan. The earliest clockmakers in America served apprenticeships in their native countries and thereafter emigrated to the colonies, bringing with them a variety of backgrounds and knowledge. So it was with such clockmaking notables as Benjamin Bagnall, William Claggett, Gawen Brown, Thomas Harland, Abel Cottey, and Peter Stretch. But by 1710, men such as Benjamin Chandlee, Isaac Pearson, and Ebenezer Parmele were completing apprenticeships in this country under English-trained masters and beginning the first of many generations to the craft in America.

As an apprentice, a youth—of about fourteen years of age—was bound by a contract to a tradesman, normally for seven years, though sometimes for less. The master agreed to teach the youth all aspects of his trade or trades; in return the youth would assist in completion of work being carried on in the shop. A trainee first was assigned simple tasks; then, as he became more proficient, he was graduated progressively to more complex work until be became skilled in the art. Although paid no wages, the apprentice was usually given room and board in the master craftsman's home.

The system benefited the clockmaker as well as the youth. Because of the free labor provided by the apprentice, many were able to conduct large businesses, taking on more work than they could do alone and thereby bringing in more revenue.

At the end of the youth's apprenticeship, the master usually gave him a letter of recommendation as proof of his training. Such a letter has survived in the case of Daniel Munroe of Concord, Massachusetts. His letter of recommendation was dated July 13, 1796:

> This is to certify that Daniel Munroe, Jun. has served an Apprenticeship of seven years with me the Subscriber, that he has been uncommonly faithful, honest, and industrious, and that I hereby acknowledge him capable of making any work that I manufacture and that I do pronounce him as one of the best workmen in America. (signed) Simon Willard

The apprenticeship was not always successfully completed. Early newspapers often carried notices about runaway apprentices. In some cases the master had failed to fulfill his obligation and could be held liable. One example was the case of Richard Huntington, who was bound to Thomas Harland of Norwich, Connecticut, on October 15, 1802. Harland died before young Huntington's training was completed and his estate was compelled to pay a thirty-five dollar penalty to John Huntington, Richard's father.

Following is an existing indenture drawn in Lancaster County, Pennsylvania, of John Erb to Joseph Bowman (1799–1892) for five years and two months from June 26, 1830.

> THIS INDENTURE WITNESSETH,
> That John Erb aged fifteen year & ten months on the 2nd Day of August 1830 Son of Joseph Erb of Lampeter township, Lancaster County, & by and with the advise & Consent of his father hath put himself and by these presents doth, voluntarily, and of his own free will and accord, put himself Apprentice to Joseph Bowman of the Borough of Strasburg County of Lancaster Clockmaker to learn clockmaking art, trade, and mystery; and, after the manner of an Apprentice, to serve five years and two months from the day of the date hereof, for and during and to the full end and term of five years and two months . . . next ensuing. During all which term, the said Apprentice his said Master faithfully shall serve; his secrets keep, his lawful commands every where readily obey. He shall do no damage to his said Masters goods, nor lend them unlawfully to any. He shall not commit fornication, nor contract matrimony, within the said term. He shall not play at cards, dice, or any other unlawful game, whereby his said master may have damage. With his own goods, nor the goods of others, without license from his said Master he shall neither buy nor sell. He shall not absent himself day nor night, from his said Masters service, without leave; nor haunt alehouses, taverns, or playhouses; but in all things behave himself as a faithful Apprentice ought to do, during the said term, of five years and two [months].

And the said Master shall use the utmost of his endeavors to teach or cause to be taught or instructed, the said Apprentice, in the trade or mystery of Clockmaking . . . and procure and provide for him sufficient meat, drink, lodging, and washing, fitting for any Apprentice, during the said term of five year & two months & said Master shall give said Apprentice within said apprenticeship Six Months Schooling in an English Day School and at the expiration of said term said master shall give said Apprentice twenty-five Dollars Good and Lawful Money Which is to be in Lue of his freedom Suit.

And, for the true performance of all and singular the covenants and agreements aforesaid, the said Parties bind themselves, each unto the other, firmly by these presents.

IN WITNESS whereof, the said Parties have, interchangeably, set their hands and seals hereunto. Dated the twenty sixth day of June in the year of our Lord, one thousand eight hundred and thirty.

Sealed and delivered
in the presence of     William Black
                         John Markley
                         John Erb
                         Joseph Erb
                         Joseph Bowman

The above indenture was satisfied on August 26, 1835, and John Erb (born 1814) set up business at Conestoga Centre, Lancaster County, where, until 1860, he made serveral clocks and did repair work.

## THE DAWNING OF MASS PRODUCTION

Once mass production was introduced into manufacturing, the craft of clockmaking changed considerably. Shelf clock makers built their own case-making shops, operating them as part of the factory. Manufactured clocks were usually smaller than handcrafted ones. Cases were constructed at the least expense and clocks were sold complete with the case. Appurtenances were usually purchased from specialized firms.

Mass-produced machine-made clock movements were also produced at a minimum of expense. Rolled brass could be purchased and casting of rough blanks was not usually necessary. Through the use of machinery, wheel blanks and other components could be made in great numbers at low cost. Whereas a clockmaker of 1760 could produce perhaps only twelve to twenty tall clocks a year, a large manufacturer a hundred years later could produce more than a hundred fifty thousand shelf clocks.

Though the first mass-produced clock was usually inferior to the handcrafted type in construction and durability, it was inexpensive both to make and to buy. And it was the very clock that spurred the great American clockmaking industry to growth.

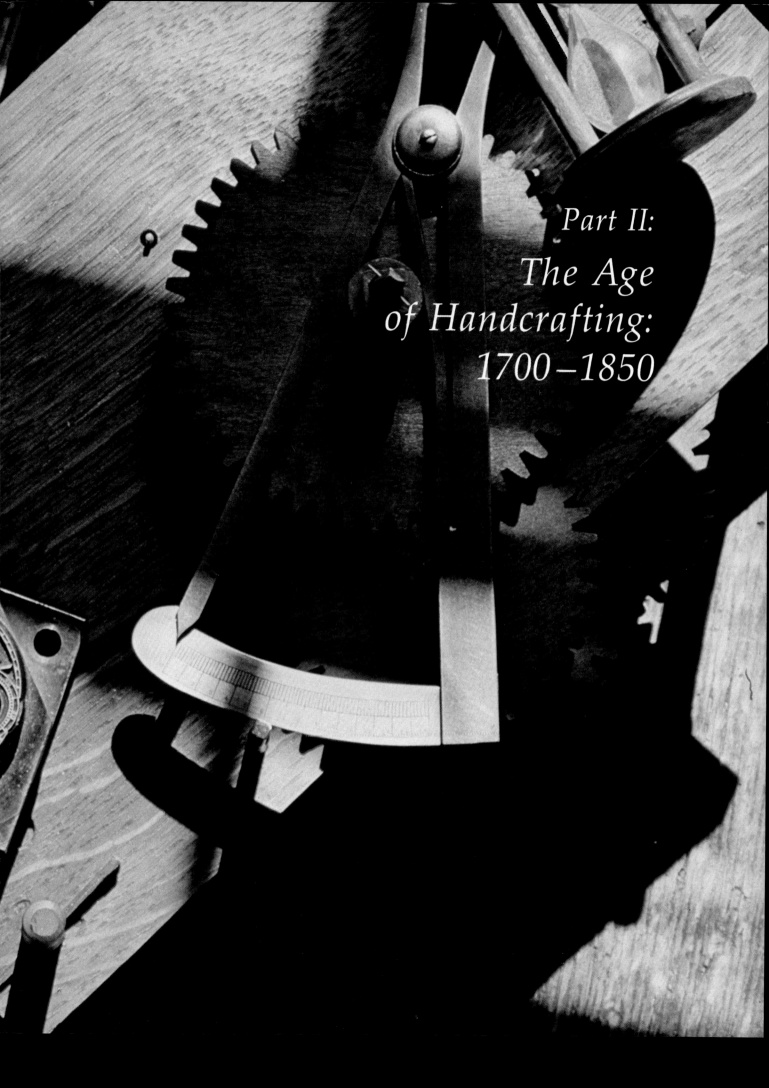

Part II:
The Age
of Handcrafting:
1700–1850

$A$s the American colonies developed and became more and more self-sufficient, clockmakers began to emigrate to the new land and to supply the needed time-keeping devices. They initiated an age of handcrafting skills in America, using the methods of the craft that had been known in Britain and Europe for centuries.

**21.** Superb cherry-cased tall clock by Anthony Ward, made *c*. 1730 in New York, though possibly before 1724 in Philadelphia. *(Courtesy, Edward F. LaFond)*

*Preceding pages:* Clockmakers' tools and equipment.

**22.** Country Pennsylvania tall clock marked "C. Cret, Orwigsburg," made *c*. 1825. Unusual dial has day, date, and month indicators. *(Courtesy, Frank S. Schwarz & Son)*

## THE PHILADELPHIA SCHOOL

Philadelphia and Boston were the cultural, social, and economic centers of the colonies during the eighteenth century and also the centers of the earliest clockmaking activity. By about 1700, Samuel Bispham, Abel Cottey, and Peter Stretch had settled in Philadelphia and their activities inspired the training of young men in the trade and drew new residents who had already acquired the skills. By 1750, the town was considered a focal point for fine craftsmanship in the arts of repairing clocks and watches, constructing clock movements, and building fine cases for them. Philadelphia cabinetmaking, considered among the most superb in America, was exemplified in many of the Philadelphia-made clock cases.

At the same time, the work of the Philadelphia school began to influence the craft in surrounding and southern colonies. Moving westward into Pennsylvania, clockmaking was affected somewhat by German craftsmen, but this was perhaps more prevalent in the art of case making. Their cases often seemed less graceful and well-proportioned than those made by Philadelphia cabinetmakers. The western Pennsylvania influence had spread into Ohio by 1800 and into Indiana by 1825.

Philadelphia's influence radiated eastward into New Jersey and New York. Isaac Pearson, who was working in Burlington, New Jersey, by 1710, had probably received his training in Philadelphia, as had Anthony Ward, who left Philadelphia in 1724 to become one of New York's earliest clockmakers. Benjamin Chandlee was also trained in Philadelphia; he and his sons carried their skills into Maryland, Delaware, and Virginia.

The main products of the Philadelphia school were tall clocks, though a few table or bracket clocks were made. They were not mass produced; artisans adhered to the strict tradition of fine handcrafting and used the apprenticeship system to perpetuate time-honored methods of clockmaking. The craft declined severely in Philadelphia after 1830, though rural areas carried on the tradition for several more years. But by 1850, it is doubtful that many timekeepers were made by the old-fashioned methods.

## IN PENNSYLVANIA

Pennsylvania drew immigrants from many European countries, especially Germany and Switzerland, and among them were clockmakers. Examples of European techniques have often been noted in movement design and also in construction and design of cases by local craftsmen.

David Rittenhouse was the most noted Pennsylvania clockmaker of the eighteenth century, and he was renowned as a great mathematician and astronomer. Jacob D. Custer was probably the most inventive maker of the nineteenth century; his experimentation in the design and construction of clocks and watches was unsurpassed.

Except for a few bracket or table clocks, the major timekeeper produced in Pennsylvania until about 1825 was the brass tall clock. After 1825, there was, for the next twenty years, some production of shelf clocks in an attempt to compete with inexpensive Connecticut shelf clocks that were being brought into the state by peddlers. Unfortunately, the Pennsylvania craftsmen were unable to adapt their handcrafting methods to mass production; their shelf clocks remained relatively expensive and thus could not compete with the Connecticut clocks. By 1850, the clockmaking craft had nearly ceased in Pennsylvania.

## IN PHILADELPHIA: THE CENTER

Although there were men in other colonies before 1700 who claimed to be clockmakers, it is probable that the first clocks actually constructed in America were made in Philadelphia. An Englishman, Samuel Bispham, who purchased land in the town in 1696, was probably the earliest maker. Though one fine tall clock of his survives in a private collection, little is known about him.

Another early English clockmaker was Abel Cottey, son of John Cottey of Tiverton, Devonshire. Abel was born in 1655, was trained in England and worked there in the town of Devon before moving with his family to Philadelphia. Several examples of his work in England survive in the form of lantern clocks.

The date of Cottey's arrival in Philadelphia is uncertain. Although the year 1682 has frequently been suggested, this is almost certainly in error. Records of Cottey exist in Philadelphia from 1700 and it is generally supposed that he arrived at that time. Cottey continued to work in Philadelphia until his death in August, 1711. One Philadelphia-made tall clock, dated 1709, survives as the earliest-known dated American clock.

Benjamin Chandlee is the only known apprentice of Abel Cottey. Son of William Chandlee, he was born in 1685 at Kilmore, County Kildare, Ireland, and emigrated to Philadelphia in 1702. Soon after his arrival he began training under Cottey and finished his apprenticeship about 1710. On April 28 of that year he married Sarah Cottey, daughter of Abel.

Upon his father-in-law's death, Chandlee inherited land in Nottingham (originally a part of Chester County, Pennsylvania, but later Cecil County, Maryland) and on September 26, 1712, he and his wife and mother-in-law requested that their Quaker meeting allow them to move to Nottingham. Here Benjamin Chandlee continued his clockmaking business until 1741; he then moved

to Wilmington, Delaware, where he died prior to 1750.

His son, Benjamin Chandlee, Jr., (1723–91) trained in the art by his father, continued the business at Nottingham for forty-five years. He in turn trained four sons: Goldsmith (c. 1751–1821), Ellis (1755–1816), John (1757–1813), and Isaac (1760–1813). Goldsmith, Ellis, and Isaac produced brass tall clocks; John conducted a watch repairing and silversmithing business at Nottingham.

Another early Philadelphia maker was Peter Stretch (1670–1746), who came from Leek, Staffordshire, England, before 1702. His training was probably with his uncle, Samuel Stretch of Leek. Stretch produced tall clocks, some with only one hand, and one musical clock of his is known.

Joseph Wills (1700–59) worked in Philadelphia after 1725; his thirty-hour clocks were of an English-style posted movement, which was not normally used in America, though some Massachusetts makers employed the design.

John Wood advertised his clock business as early as 1734 and made a number of handsome tall clocks until 1761, the year of his death. His son John Wood, Jr., (1736–93) carried on his business. In 1791, Ephraim Clark advertised as successor to John Wood, Jr. Clark had been active as early as 1780 in merchandising clocks and watches, most of which were imported. Some Custom House clearance records show that Wood and Clark were importing boxes of watches and cases of painted clock dials from Liverpool by 1790.

In 1708, Dr. Christopher Witt (1675–1765), a native of Wiltshire, England, settled in the Germantown section of Philadelphia. Witt was an astronomer, physician, and clockmaker. Among his apprentices was Christopher Sauer (1693–1758), a native of Wittgenstein, Westphalia, Germany, who settled in Germantown in 1731.

Augustine Neisser (1717–80), a Moravian, came to Germantown about 1740 and worked there until his death. In 1746 he built a tower clock for the Moravian congregation at Bethlehem, Pennsylvania.

## DAVID RITTENHOUSE

In Montgomery County, just outside Philadelphia, several important men were carrying on clockmaking activities. The most noted clockmaker from that area—and one of the most renowned in the country—was David Rittenhouse (1732–96). He was a respected mathematician, surveyor, and clockmaker, and a pioneer astronomer. By 1749, he had established himself as a clockmaker and surveyor at Norriton, now Norristown. In 1763, he surveyed the boundary lines between the states of Delaware and Pennsylvania, and in 1786, those between New York and Pennsylvania. He also designed instruments to be used for surveying.

In 1770, Rittenhouse moved to Philadelphia and set up a shop on Seventh and Arch Streets. He built an astronomical observatory nearby, the only one in the country at that time. His accomplishments were numerous: he was treasurer of the state of Pennsylvania (1777–89); professor of astronomy at the University of Pennsylvania (1779–82); director of the United States Mint at Philadelphia (1792–95); and president of the American Philosophical Society (1790–96), succeeding his friend, Benjamin Franklin.

Little is known of Rittenhouse's clockmaking training, though he probably received some instruction from a cousin, Jacob Gorgas (1728–98), who lived in Germantown. Many of his clocks are of normal styles, but some are classified among the most complicated pieces of horological machinery ever developed.

The most noted of these, which is often referred to as the Rittenhouse masterpiece, is now at the Drexel Institute in Philadelphia. It was made for Joseph Potts in 1774, and originally cost $640. Its dial, housed in an elegant case over nine feet tall, shows the hours, minutes, and seconds by a sweep center indicator; the positions of six planets with respect to each other and with the signs of the zodiac in a planetarium at the top of the dial (three planets had not been discovered at that time); the positions of the sun and moon in the zodiac; the current sign of the zodiac; the moon's orbit around the earth; the equation of time (the difference between solar and actual time); the current month and date; and the phase of the moon. The clock also played ten musical tunes on fifteen bells, and could be adjusted so that up to four tunes could be played at one time.

Rittenhouse's genius was recognized during his lifetime. Even Thomas Jefferson tried to persuade Rittenhouse to pursue his talents and not become further involved in politics. He said, in a letter written from Monticello on July 19, 1778:

> Writing to a Philosopher, I may hope to be pardoned for intruding some thoughts of my own, though they relate to him personally. Your time for two years past has, I believe, been principally employed in the civil government of your country. Though I have been aware of the authority our cause would acquire with the world from it being known that yourself and Doctor Franklin were zealous friends to it, and am myself duly impressed with a sense of the arduousness of government, and the obligation those are under who are able to conduct it; yet I am also satisfied there is an order of geniuses above that obligation, and therefore exempted from it. Nobody can conceive that nature ever intended to throw away a Newton upon the occupations of a crown. . . . I doubt not there are in your country many persons equal to the task of conducting government: but you should consider that the world has but one Rittenhouse, and that it never had one before.

23. David Rittenhouse's finest example, made in 1774. Standing 9½ ft. tall, it has a case of finest Philadelphia craftsmanship. (*Courtesy, Drexel University*)

**24.** Banjo clock by James Doull, Philadelphia, *c.* 1830. Doull left Boston *c.* 1825 but continued to produce styles to which he was accustomed. (*Courtesy, Frank S. Schwarz & Son*)

In his personal notes, Jefferson also wrote, "Rittenhouse is second to no astronomer living. That in genius he must be first because he is self-taught. As an artist he has exhibited as great a proof of mechanical genius as the world has ever produced."

Rittenhouse, a frail man who suffered considerably from what would today be called stomach ulcers, died in Philadelphia on June 26, 1796. On his death, his clockmaking tools went to a nephew, John J. Parry (1773–1835).

Rittenhouse's brother, Benjamin (b. 1740), conducted a clockmaking business after 1760 in Montgomery County. He worked in Philadelphia during the first and second decades of the nineteenth century, making mathematical tools.

## OTHER PENNSYLVANIA ARTISANS

Jacob Godschalk worked first in Towamenein Township, and after 1769, in Philadelphia. Some of his thirty-hour clocks have standard brass movements; others have German-style movements with wooden frames and brass gears. In 1770, Jacob married a widow, Elizabeth Owen, and later trained his stepson, Griffith Owen, who became a prominent Philadelphia maker from 1790 to 1814.

Jacob Detweiler Custer (1805–72) was an inventive artisan who worked in Montgomery County after 1825. Custer constructed tall clocks and shelf clocks—some with striking mechanisms of his own design—tower clocks, and even some watches. He was granted a clock patent in 1830 and one for watches in 1843. His brother Isaac had some interest in the clock business, but moved to Missouri about 1838 and did not pursue a career as a clockmaker.

Three other counties west of Philadelphia—Chester, Berks, and Lancaster—had considerable clockmaking activity. Chester County had at least fifty clockmakers working there at different times. Besides the Chandlee family, who were the earliest in the area at Nottingham, five other men worked there before the Revolution: Isaac Thomas (1721–1802), Isaac Jackson (1734–1807) and his cousin John Jackson (1746–95), Joshua Humphrey, and Eli Bentley (b. 1752).

Isaac Thomas was noted as a clockmaker in Willistown as early as 1768. Thomas was also a joiner and probably constructed his own clock cases. He was a fairly prolific maker and was still making clocks at the age of seventy-five. His son Mordecai Thomas received his clockmaking and joiner's tools on his death and continued the family business.

Isaac Jackson worked in New Garden and London Grove townships. In 1755, he received a certificate of removal to the Quaker meeting at Nottingham, and in that town received instruction from Benjamin Chandlee. Jackson's grandson, Joseph J. Lewis, described him as "exceedingly skillful and ingenious as an artisan, and made himself, the greater part of the tools and implements he needed. He had two shops—one suited for blacksmith work and one for clockmakers' work and when he could do nothing out of doors, employed himself in one or the other in some handicraft labor." Jackson also trained Elisha Kirk, who worked in York from about 1780 to 1790.

John Jackson, cousin to Isaac, worked in London Grove. Because of his loyalist views he was disowned by his Quaker meeting and by 1787 had moved to a loyalist settlement in Canada and continued to make clocks. The family later returned to this country and lived in Baltimore, where Jackson died in 1795.

Joshua Humphrey worked in Charlestown as early as 1764 and later at East Whiteland. He then worked in Chester County until about 1773; no record exists of him after that date.

Eli Bentley worked in West Whiteland after 1774, but sold his farm in Chester County in 1783 and moved to Taneytown, Maryland. Eli's brother, Caleb, carried on similar clockmaking activity in York, Pennsylvania, and Leesburg, Virginia.

After the Revolution, many other makers were active in Chester County; among the most prominent were Joel Baily and his son Emmor Baily of Bradford, Abraham Corl of East Nantmeal, Thomas Dring of West Chester, Jacob Fertig of Vincent, and Benjamin Garrett of Goshen.

Benedict Darlington of Chester County marketed clocks after 1810. His son Abel noted that his father brought three men from Connecticut—Jonathan N. Hatch, Russell Vibber, and Thomas DeWolf—who "fitted up the wooden works or movements, and my father made the cases—about seven feet in height, and peddled them around the country."

Valentine Urletig came to Berks County in 1754 and by 1758 was working in Reading, where he was active until his death in 1783. As Reading's first clockmaker, he constructed the clock for the town's first courthouse. John Keim (1749–1819) was working in Reading by 1779 and Daniel Rose (1749–1827) had a successful business there after the Revolution. Christian Bixler, Jr., an apprentice of John Keim of Reading, set up business in Easton in 1785 and continued there until 1830.

Christian Forrer (1737–83) settled in Lancaster County in 1754 after his arrival from Switzerland, where he had been trained. He first lived in Lampeter, but in 1774 moved to Newberry Township in York County.

The Gorgas family worked in the town of Ephrata after Jacob Gorgas (1728–98) settled there from Germantown before 1763. His son, Solomon Gorgas (1764–1838), carried on the business for a short time, but about 1800 moved to Cumberland County and apparently gave up clockmaking.

George Hoff came to America in 1765 from Germany and settled in the town of Lancaster, where he made clocks until his death in 1816. A son, John Hoff, carried on the business and on his death in 1822, John's widow, with the help of several workmen from Philadelphia, continued the business. Movements by the Hoffs utilize lantern-style pinions (in the manner of German clocks) rather than English-style cut pinions.

Christian Eby had a successful clockmaking business in Manheim after 1799, working until 1837 or perhaps later. Two of his sons, George and Jacob, also engaged in the business.

The Solliday family was active in Bucks County for many years. Frederick Solliday came to America from Basel, Switzerland, about 1750 and settled in Bedminster, Bucks County, where he made clocks. His son Jacob and grandson Peter continued in that town and worked well into the nineteenth century. Another son, Benjamin, worked in Sellersville. Benjamin's son, Samuel, worked in Doylestown until 1833.

John Scharf, another Swiss, settled at Selinsgrove, Snyder County, about 1836; there he made shelf clocks with well-made brass movements. Some of his cases have a Connecticut appearance, but on close examination are definitely Pennsylvania-made.

Scharf supplied some clocks to distributors, one being William Leach of Easton. Leach was apparently only a clock dealer and marketed some Connecticut-made clocks as well as Pennsylvania ones. One interesting example of a Leach clock has a paper label with instructions in both English and German; the clock had a wooden movement and was made in Torrington, Connecticut.

A group of clockmakers worked in the area near Allentown, Pennsylvania, producing a number of unusual shelf clocks with pillar and scroll-

**25.** Country Pennsylvania tall clock movement made *c.* 1785. Note unfinished front plate and latches, which are used to attach plate to posts. (*Author's collection*)

**26.** Magnificent musical movement from David Rittenhouse's masterpiece, made in 1774. Note extensive gearing for planetarium and auxiliary dials. *(Courtesy, Drexel University)*

**27.** Pennsylvania-style pillar and scroll probably made by Jacob D. Custer, Norristown, and sold by Osborn Conrad, Perryville. (*Courtesy, Edward F. LaFond*)

**28.** Unmarked Pennsylvania shelf clock similar to those produced in Montgomery County, PA. (*Edward F. LaFond*)

type cases. The names of these men have not yet been learned, though it is suspected they were working there about 1830. Some of their cases are very similar to Connecticut ones, while others show German influence and are somewhat out of proportion. The movements in these clocks are of several styles, but all have the common characteristics of wooden plates and brass wheels and German-type lantern pinions. At least two examples are known with similar arrangements and brass plates.

In York County, to the west, John Fisher was one of the most important makers. Fisher came from Germany in 1749 and settled in the town of York in 1759. He was a successful clockmaker and wood carver, and is said to have painted portraits; he was a skillful mechanic and had the ability to make astronomical clocks. The *Maryland Gazette* of September, 1790, carried the following article about an astronomical timepiece completed by him in May of that year:

This Timepiece performs the office of a common eight-day clock, but runs thirty-five days. It exhibits the time of the Sun's rising and setting, its destination, the longest and shortest days in the most distant parts of the world, all of which is clearly elucidated by a globe, affixed about three inches from the centre. It has the moon circulating round the verge of the globe, which makes all the different vicissitudes that the real moon seems to make to us in the Heavens. The dial . . . plate is elegantly engraved, and is by no means void of taste; round the verge it is ornamented with the twelve signs of the Zodiac, the seven Planets, and

twelve months, with the exact number of days in each month in a year.

Rudolph Spangler (1738–1811) and his son Jacob (1767–1843) worked in York for many years, and also in Hagerstown, Maryland. Jacob Hostetter (1754–1831) and his master, Richard Chester, were active at Hanover in York County.

At Harrisburg, now the capital of the state, Samuel Hill (1765–1809) was one of the first clockmakers. Hill came to Dauphin County in 1785, having learned his trade in London. After 1790, he trained his brother-in-law, George Beatty (1781–1862). Beatty worked with Hill until 1808, then established his own business.

Frederick Heisely (1759–1843), apprentice of George Hoff of Lancaster, moved from there to Harrisburg about 1811. Heisely, an ingenious mechanic, produced a bracket clock with pinwheel escapement and some interesting shelf clock movements housed in Connecticut-made cases. He also made surveyors' instruments, and from 1783 to 1793 had carried on that business in Frederick, Maryland. His son, George Jacob (1789–1880), continued in the clockmaking business; a second son, Frederick Augustus (1792–1875), made surveyors' instruments in Harrisburg and, after 1836, in Pittsburgh.

In Carlisle, Cumberland County, William Campbell advertised as a clockmaker as early as 1763, but little else is known of him. Jacob Hendel, an ingenious artisan, also worked in that town. Charles Young, John Scott, and Alexander Scott worked in Chambersburg, Franklin County.

**29.** Pillar and scroll made near Allentown, PA, *c.* 1830. Wood-plate, brass-wheel movement reflects Germanic influence. *(Courtesy, Edward F. LaFond)*

**30.** Eight-day striking dwarf tall clock marked "W. Hough, Bridgeport," possibly Pennsylvania, though case shows Ohio influence. *(Courtesy, Connecticut Historical Society)*

Clockmaking was not common in the northern and western parts of the state, but some makers were active in Pittsburgh and Greensburgh in Westmoreland County. Samuel Davis was working in Pittsburgh prior to 1797 and until 1826. James Thomson set up business there in 1812, having come from Chambersburg, and continued working until about 1825. Alexander Cooke was working in Canonsburg, Washington County, before 1802. He used white-painted dials on his clocks, and often inserted a circular brass piece, with his name engraved on it, on the dial. Why he adopted this peculiar practice instead of simply having his name painted on the dial is unknown.

## THE PHILADELPHIA SCHOOL IN NEW YORK

During the eighteenth century the town of New York had several makers of brass-movement tall clocks, but fewer men were engaged in the craft than in other towns in the colonies. This was probably because of the ready availability of imported items.

The Dominy family worked in East Hampton, Long Island, from about 1768 until about 1830, constructing clocks and cases of their own unique design. But they weren't the only ones to break with the traditional English styles. The clockmakers of the Shaker religious sect, who were active at New Lebanon and Watervliet, New York, from about 1785 to 1840, created clocks and cases reflecting the simplicity and modesty of possessions characteristic of the group.

Some attempts were made during the nineteenth century to achieve mass production. About 1820, Asa Munger and his associates, of Auburn, New York, began to manufacture brass shelf clocks in quantity, and during the following decade even contracted for cheap prison labor to further reduce their manufacturing costs.

When the Dutch settled at Fort Orange, now Albany, on the Hudson river in 1624, colonization of New York State began. A year later a settlement was established at New Amsterdam, now New York City. In 1664, the colony came under English rule. The earliest mentioned clockmaker was Everardus Bogardus, of Dutch descent, who became a freeman in New Amsterdam in 1698 at the age of twenty-three. If Bogardus produced signed clocks, they apparently have not survived.

New York clockmakers in the eighteenth century included Anthony Ward, who arrived from Philadelphia in 1724, and John Bell, who advertised eight-day tall clocks with jappanned cases in 1734. Bartholomew Barwell, from Bath, England, advertised his business from 1749 to 1760. After 1750, several others conducted business in the town, but some stayed for only a short time, then moved to more active centers. Such a workman was Isaac Heron, who settled in Philadelphia about 1763, and shortly after moved to New Jersey. About 1765, he settled in New York and conducted his business until tensions with Britain increased. In 1778, he returned to Ireland.

The latter part of the eighteenth century and the beginning of the nineteenth saw many clock businesses set up in New York City. Some of these men were probably making clocks, but most were undoubtedly importing clock movements and watches and conducting repairing businesses.

The mid-nineteenth century also brought to the city some firms that dealt in marine chronometers and other precision timekeepers. One was Bliss & Creighton, who were in business before 1839 at 42 Fulton Street. They imported rough parts from London and finished them in their shops. The original firm was dissolved in 1853 and continued as John Bliss & Son. Successors of the firm continued until about 1899.

Not all clockmaking activity in the state took place in the city. Other larger towns—Poughkeepsie, Albany, Rochester—also had clockmakers. Prior to 1795, Andrew Billings was working in Poughkeepsie, producing tall clocks and some bracket clocks. Connecticut-trained men, such as Jedediah Baldwin, apprentice of Thomas Harland, and Ela Burnap, nephew and apprentice of Daniel Burnap, brought their skills to Rochester.

### THE DOMINYS

An interesting clock- and furniture-making family lived in East Hampton, Long Island, producing clocks from about 1768 to 1830. Nathaniel Dominy (1737–1812), his son Nathaniel (1770–1852), and grandson Felix (1800–68) were active in producing brass-movement tall clocks, many of curious design. Many were timepieces in one- and two-hand varieties, others were striking models, and some had alarms. All were very individualistic and interesting. The Dominys also made cases of their own design; though not unknown, it was unusual for makers in the handcrafting period to construct cases for their clocks, as this family did.

### THE SHAKERS

Some colonies of the religious sect known as the Shakers were established in upstate New York after the Revolution and a small amount of clockmaking was carried on by them. Shakers believed in great simplicity in items they owned and produced and their clocks reflect this philosophy. Most have simple cases without fancy embellishments or decoration and usually without striking features, though alarm mechanisms were often used.

The earliest known Shaker clockmaker was Amos Jewett (1753–1834) of New Lebanon. He made wood tall clocks with printed paper dials. He adopted the uncommon practice of numbering his clocks. Number 12 was dated 1789; number 38, dated 1796, is also extant.

At Watervliet, another Shaker community was active. About 1806, Benjamin Youngs (1736–1818), son of Seth Youngs of Hartford and Windsor, Connecticut, joined the order. Benjamin made a few clocks in the later years of his life; one that is known is dated 1809. Clockmaking was carried on in Watervliet by Benjamin's nephew Benjamin Seth Youngs (1774–1855) and in Mt. Lebanon by another nephew, Isaac Newton Youngs (1793–1865). Brass and wood clocks were made, some as late as 1840. Calvin Wells (1772–

1853) also made a few clocks at Watervliet after 1815.

Though the Shakers' production of clocks was not large, their movement styles and simple casings are an interesting study. After 1840, some manufactured Connecticut clocks were purchased and dials and cases were altered according to the desires of members of the community.

## ASA MUNGER

One of the most successful clock-producing businesses in New York was that of Asa Munger of Auburn. Munger was one of the earliest to venture into the making of brass clocks in quantity so that they could be sold at prices cheaper than those of his competitors. His venture was also important because it was an early attempt to lower production costs by the use of cheap prison labor. The venture was not actually one of handcrafted clocks, nor was it true manufacturing, for it employed aspects of both methods.

Asa Munger was born October 14, 1777, at Granby, Massachusetts, and was the eldest of fifteen children. He had two brothers, trained as silversmiths, who carried on watch- and clock-repair and jewelry businesses. Perley Munger (1788–1870) worked at Rochester, New York, and Sylvester Munger (1790–1857) at Ithaca. Sylvester was also in business during the 1830s with a Mr. Pratt; they marketed Connecticut-style clocks with labels of Munger & Pratt, Ithaca. It is supposed that Mr. Pratt was Daniel Pratt, who was buying Connecticut movements and casing them at his shop in Reading, Massachusetts.

Asa Munger was probably apprenticed about 1791 and learned clockmaking as well as gold- and silversmithing. As his home was then in Ludlow, Massachusetts, his master was probably one of the clockmakers of nearby Springfield.

In a Ludlow deed of 1801, recording Asa's purchase of land, he was called a "goldsmith." On November 26, 1803, he sold the land and subsequently moved to Herkimer, Oneida County, New York. Munger's production in Ludlow included some brass clocks, one dated 1799, as well as some curious wood clocks similar in appearance to Dutch brass movements; one of the latter is dated 1801. After moving to Herkimer, Munger continued producing clocks; one made there in 1817 plays seven different tunes.

In 1818, Munger settled in Auburn, Cayuga County, New York, where he designed a shelf-style clock. The earliest had timepiece movements with pewter plates bushed with brass at the points of pivot. Munger shelf clocks were usually housed in cases resembling various styles of Empire mirrors, though a few were put into large pillar and scroll-style cases.

Sometime after 1820, Munger was in partner-

32

ship with a Mr. Gillmore; many of the pewter-plate clocks are labeled "Munger and Gillmore's Patent Timepieces." No patent has been found issued to either of these men, though Munger's claim of a patent was carried on labels throughout the remainder of his clockmaking career. Munger's timepiece movement was later produced with standard brass plates, as was a striking model. The partnership of Munger and Gillmore was dissolved about 1825 and Asa continued in business alone.

In 1831, Munger went into partnership with Thaddeus Benedict of Auburn. Benedict was a successful financier and businessman, though probably not a clockmaker. Born about 1800 at Milton, New York, Benedict had moved to Auburn by 1824.

In May of 1833, Munger and Benedict were joined by another partner, a tailor named Clark Beers Hotchkiss (1796–1857), and the firm name of Munger & Benedict was changed to Asa Munger & Company. At that time the partners contracted with the State Prison at Auburn for the employment of convicts to make clocks, a practice they continued until August, 1836. In regard to this, Hotchkiss testified in 1834 that he was

> . . . one of the firm of Hotchkiss & Benedict who are the contractors for the labor of convicts in the business of brass clock making . . . he and his partner, Thaddeus Benedict, have now in their employ 25 convicts in the prison, in the business of making brass clocks; they pay 32 cents a day for each convict employed, and have the necessary water power to be used in the business; they turn out about three clocks a day, finished complete, on an average; the clocks are held by them at wholesale at 18 dollars each; they rely on making market for most of them in Ohio and the southern and western states; the business commenced a year ago last November, and the deponent bought in about a year ago; Mr. Munger, one of the contractors, has since sold out to his other partner; they paid him a small bonus for his interest in the contract; whether it will prove a profitable business or not they are as yet unable to determine; it will depend on their success in selling them.

By November of 1833, Munger had sold his interests in the firm. He remained in Auburn and died there on March 2, 1851. During the time of prison production, the firm adopted a newly designed movement, which was undoubtedly developed by him.

Benedict sold out his interests in 1836, and the following year moved to Russellville, Logan County, Kentucky, where he died in April, 1845, a very wealthy bachelor.

## THE NEW YORK GLOBE CLOCK

Globe clocks were also manufactured on a small

**31.** Theodore R. Timby's patent globe clock manufactured by Lewis E. Whiting of Saratoga Springs, NY, c. 1865. (*American Clock & Watch Museum*) **32.** Eight-day single-hand timepiece movement made by Nathaniel Dominy, East Hampton, NY, c. 1790. Note unusual anchor and sparing use of brass for plates. (*Courtesy, Hershel B. Burt*) **33.** Empire mirror shelf clock by Asa Munger, Auburn, NY, c. 1830. Munger is noted for his early use of cheap convict labor to attempt competitive brass clock production. (*Courtesy, Edward F. LaFond*)

scale in New York after 1860 by Theodore R. Timby and Lewis P. Juvet. Except for a brief attempt by a concern known as the Globe Clock Company of Milldale, Connecticut (c. 1883), the production of this style of clock was confined to upstate New York.

These unusual clocks incorporated globes of the earth or, in rare cases, of the heavens. On the Timby clock, the globe was perhaps more of a decoration; time was shown by a ring—upon which the numerals were placed—that appeared in a window above the globe. The Juvet clock had a globe that revolved as does the earth. The clock dial appeared above the polar regions and a ring with hour graduations circled the equator, allowing the observer to determine at a glance the time in other parts of the world.

Theodore Timby of Baldwinsville, New York, first patented his globe clock in 1863 and in subse-

quent years received three additional patents for improvements. The clocks were manufactured at nearby Saratoga Springs by Lewis E. Whiting and then shipped to Boston, where Gilman Joslin, a globe maker, would add his patent globe of the world. Timby's solar timepiece was not well received by the public, and manufacture ceased about 1870. It is believed that only about six hundred of the clocks were made.

A more complicated style of globe clock was invented by Lewis P. Juvet of Glens Falls, New York, in 1867. He formed a partnership with James Arkell of Canajoharie, New York, in 1879, and the following year they built a factory and began production. In 1886, the factory was destroyed by fire and production of the "Time Globe," as they called it, was never resumed. Juvet's clocks usually had a terrestrial globe, but a few were made with celestial globes, which mapped the heavens.

**34.** Large Empire shelf clock made by Abner Jones, East Bloomfield, NY, c. 1830. This clock numbered "90" on pendulum bob. *(Courtesy, Edward F. LaFond)*

**35.** New York pillar and scroll clock made by Joseph Burritt of Ithaca, c. 1825. Striped and bird's-eye maple case. Eight-day brass movement. *(Courtesy, Edward F. LaFond)*

## THE PHILADELPHIA SCHOOL IN NEW JERSEY

New Jersey was a very active clockmaking state. Numerous handcrafted tall clocks were made there between 1710 and 1840. Isaac Pearson, one of the earliest clockmakers in America, initiated considerable activity in the town of Burlington. His son-in-law, Joseph Hollingshead, and Hollingshead's three sons conducted the majority of the business in that town during the eighteenth century.

At Elizabeth Town (now Elizabeth), Aaron Miller set up business before 1750 and his apprentices, including his son-in-law Isaac Brokaw, supplied the area with clocks for the remainder of the century. Miller's clocks are a departure from the standard English style with their wooden, rather than brass, winding drums, a feature adopted by Brokaw and others that was discontinued soon after 1800.

New Jersey clockmaking was in decline by the third decade of the nineteenth century, but at about that time Aaron D. Crane of Caldwell, New Jersey, invented several clocks of considerable merit. The most noteworthy was a clock with a rotary or torsion pendulum. The clock had an escapement that was actuated by a rotating pendulum ball, suspended on a thin wire, rather than by a swinging pendulum. The rotary pendulum was apparently original with Crane and he deserves much credit for it. Modern examples of Crane's principle can be found in the 400-day or "anniversary" clocks still made in Germany.

Isaac Pearson (1685–1749) was the earliest clockmaker in New Jersey. A Quaker, he was probably trained in Philadelphia, though no records exist of his early years. Pearson's career as a clockmaker probably began between 1706 and 1710. In November, 1732, he advertised a runaway apprentice in the *American Weekly Mercury*: "Run away from Isaac Pearson of the Town of Burlington, the 4th of this Instant November, a Servant man named Aaron Middleton, a Clock Maker by Trade. . . ."

On his death, Pearson bequeathed his clockmaking tools to a former apprentice, Joseph Hollingshead, who was by that time his son-in-law and partner. Some examples of clocks by Pearson & Hollingshead are known. (Hollingshead's birth date is not known, but he worked as a clockmaker from 1740 to 1775.)

After 1749, Joseph Hollingshead continued the business alone. By a second wife he had three sons whom he trained in clockmaking: Joseph, Jr., (b. 1751) worked in Burlington; John (b. 1745) worked in Burlington and later Mt. Holly; and Jacob (b. 1747) worked in Salem.

Other members of the Hollingshead family

**36.** New Jersey tall clock by Joseph Yates of Trenton, *c.* 1810. New Jersey clocks of this era often had finely inlaid cases. *(Courtesy, Charles S. Parsons)*

were making clocks in the latter part of the eighteenth century, though their exact relationship to Joseph has not been determined. Hugh Hollingshead (1753–86) worked in Mt. Holly and Morristown. Morgan Hollingshead (b. 1732) worked in Morristown, and his son George (1771–1820) had a business in Woodstown. George followed the practice of sequentially numbering his tall clocks; number 284 was sold about 1817.

A second group of New Jersey makers trace their training to Aaron Miller of Elizabeth Town. Miller's apprenticeship is uncertain, but he produced movements of basic English style, except that they often had wooden winding spools, or drums. This feature was sometimes seen in Ger-

**37.** Eight-day weight-driven clock utilizing Crane's patent, made by the Year Clock Co., New York, *c.* 1845. James R. Mills & Company noted on dial.

**38.** Aaron D. Crane's torsion or rotary pendulum clock, patented in 1841, was a radical departure from the traditional swinging pendulum. (*Courtesy, Edward F. LaFond*)

man-made clocks and it is possible he adopted it from the Germans in his area or in neighboring Pennsylvania.

Miller was at work in Elizabeth Town by 1747. He was a capable mechanic, bell founder, and instrument maker. On occasion, he produced musical clocks. Miller trained his son, Cornelius, and was also the master of Isaac Brokaw (1746–1826), who later became his son-in-law. It is believed that he had a third apprentice, Lebbeus Dod of Mendham, as Dod's clocks are similar.

Aaron Miller and his son Cornelius both died in 1779; their business in Elizabeth Town was continued by Isaac Brokaw. About 1790 Isaac moved to Bridge Town—later known as Rahway—and left the former business to his eldest son, John (b. 1767). Isaac retired in 1816 and turned his Bridge Town business over to his second son, Aaron (1768–1853). A younger son, Cornelius (1772–1857), carried on a small business in Bridge Town.

Joakim Hill (1783–1869) of Flemington was one of the more prolific clockmakers of the early nineteenth century. Hill's clocks are often found in handsome, delicately proportioned and inlaid Hepplewhite-style cases. These were supplied to him by John Tappan, John Scudder, and Oliver Parsell. Scudder also supplied cases to the Brokaws, who purchased cases from Mathew Egerton of New Brunswick and his son, as well.

Aaron Dodd Crane (1804–60), a native of Caldwell, New Jersey, was an inventive horological mechanic. In March of 1829, at the age of twenty-five, he received his first clock patent. It was for an improved clock having only two wheels. On February 10, 1841, he was granted a patent for a torsion pendulum clock that ran for a year with one winding. Crane produced these and similar torsion clocks of eight- and thirty-day duration. Many were marketed by the firms of James R. Mills & Company and the Year Clock Company of New York.

Crane deserves respect as a great inventor; his torsion pendulum clocks utilized a revolutionary concept. About 1858, Crane moved to the Boston area, and became interested in the manufacture of tower clocks. He died of consumption at Roxbury, Massachusetts, on March 10, 1860.

Other notable New Jersey clockmakers were William Crow (1715–58) of Salem; Moses Ogden (1736–1814) of Newark; Benjamin Reeve (1737–1801) of Greenwich; Lebbeus Dod (1739–1816) of Mendham, and his sons, Stephen (1770–1853) and Abner (1772–1847), both of Newark; Aaron Lane (1753–1819) of Elizabeth Town and Bound Brook; Benjamin Norton Cleveland (1767–1837) of Newark; Jacob Bonnel (1767–1841) of Elizabeth Town; Smith Burnet (1770–1830) of Newark; Daniel Dod (1778–1823) of Mendham and Elizabeth Town; and Stephen Tichenor (about 1760) of Newark.

44

# THE BOSTON SCHOOL

Boston rivaled Philadelphia as an important clock-making center throughout the handcrafting period. Men such as Benjamin Bagnall and Gawen Brown were prolific makers of tall clocks of elegant English style that were available to those of the colony with the means to buy them. In the rural areas around Boston, men such as Richard Manning of Ipswich and David Blaisdell of Amesbury designed tall clocks of far less elegance and style, but made to sell for a price closer to the purchasing abilities of rural customers. Manning and Blaisdell gave impetus to clockmaking activities in Essex County, especially at Newburyport and Bradford, in the latter part of the eighteenth century.

At the time of the Revolution, the Willard family of Grafton and later Roxbury began their rise to prominence. Though the Willards produced tall clocks, which had been the standard in the colony's production during colonial times, Simon Willard introduced wall and shelf clock styles and initiated their production. It was the first successful move away from production of the traditional tall clock, and helped pave the way for the acceptance of shelf and wall clocks when they were introduced half a century later by Connecticut manufacturers.

Though most of Boston's clockmaking influence and activity had greatly diminished or ceased entirely by 1850, Edward Howard and his associates continued to manufacture wall clocks in the Willard style through the nineteenth and into the twentieth century. Small-scale manufacturing of these Howard clocks was the only survivor of handcrafting methods in Bostonian clockmaking.

James Batterson advertised in Boston in October, 1707, that he had arrived "lately from London." Previous to this, on September 29, 1707, Batterson had attended a meeting of the Boston selectmen to state that he, a clockmaker, had come to Boston from Pennsylvania, having arrived in August of 1707. Batterson did not remain long in Boston; he later worked in New York City and Charleston, South Carolina.

Joseph Essex of King Street, Boston, advertised in 1712 that he had recently arrived from Great Britain and that he "performs all sorts of new clocks and watch works, 10-hour clocks, week clocks, quarter clocks, turret clocks, and new pocket watches, new repeating watches, guaranteed for 12 months." A business that boasted such a variety of merchandise must have been comprised mostly of imported goods, as items by Essex do not seem to have survived. A possible partner, Thomas Badely, advertised in 1712 as being "with J. Essex in Boston." He died eight years later, insolvent.

In 1711, John Brand of Anne Street advertised as a watchmaker from London who "maketh and mendeth all sorts of clocks and watches." In 1713, he advertised that his servant had run away. The following year he offered for sale new London-made pocket watches. In 1714, he advertised that he had "designs for a time to go to England." As he did not advertise further, it is probable that he did not return.

Benjamin Bagnall, an English Quaker, arrived in Boston before 1712 and set up the most successful business of the day. Born about 1689, Bagnall probably completed his apprenticeship in England and settled in the colonies shortly after. He trained two of his sons—Benjamin, Jr., and Samuel—who followed the trade, but their clocks appear less frequently than those of their father.

On August 13, 1717, a committee of Boston selectmen was directed to approach Bagnall concerning the construction of a tower clock. The clock was constructed and remained in the old meetinghouse until 1839, when it was sold at auction.

Bagnall carried on business in Boston for more than half a century and several examples of his tall clocks, made in the typical English fashion, have survived. Bagnall died on July 11, 1773, and four days later this obituary appeared in the *Boston News-Letter*:

> Last Sunday died after a short illness Benjamin Bagnall, watchmaker of this Town, aged 84 years,

**39.** Dial of primitively cased one-day pull-wind timepiece by Daniel Balch, Bradford, MA, *c.* 1756. Numbered "2." *(Courtesy, Edward F. LaFond)*

one of the people called Quakers. He came from England to America early in life and has always resided in this place. He was a good husband and a good Parent; honest and upright in his Dealings; sincere and steadfast in his friendship; liberal to the Poor, and a good citizen; he acquired the Regard and Esteem of all who had the Pleasure of his Acquaintance.

At the time of Bagnall's activity, there were several minor businesses established in the area. James Bichault advertised in 1729 as having recently arrived from London and in business to "make and mend."

James Atkinson was actively working in the town from 1744 until 1754. On January 2, 1744, he appeared before the selectmen of Boston to state that he "desired to be Admitted an Inhabitant & to open a Shop in this Town, which is hereby granted, he having brought with him upwards of Five Hundred Pounds Sterling & being a Gentleman of Good Character...." Atkinson advertised in 1745 and again in 1748, but he apparently left Boston prior to his death in 1756.

Other clockmakers advertised in the years before the Revolution. One was Thomas Clark "from London," who in 1764 claimed to warrant clocks and watches of his own make. Another was James Ashby, who came to Boston from County Cumberland, England, and established a business in 1769 as watchmaker and finisher. He imported numerous items and advertised until 1773. Being a loyalist, Ashby returned to England when trouble between the two countries became critical. Charles Geddes advertised in 1773 as a "clock and watch maker and finisher from London," and at least one bracket clock is extant on which his name is engraved.

Gawen Brown, a maker of a prolificacy to equal Bagnall's, had a large business in Boston from 1749 until his death in 1801. On January 16, 1749, Brown advertised in the *Boston Evening Post*:

> This is to give Notice to the Public, that Gawen Brown, Clock and Watchmaker lately from London, keeps his shop at Mr. Johnson's Japanner, in Brattle-Street, Boston, near Mr. Cooper's Meeting House, where he makes and sells all sorts of plain, repeating, and astronomical Clocks, with Cases, plain, black walnut, mahogany or Japann'd, or without; likewise does all Sorts of Watch Work in best Manner and sells all sorts of Clock Strings, London Lacker, and white Varnish for Clocks, a great variety of Files for Clock Works, Glasses or Crystalls, Keys, Strings, Pendants for Watches, &c.

Brown later moved his shop to King Street, where he did business until 1797, and finally to George Street.

Brown was interested in making and repairing tower clocks, and in 1767 appeared at a meeting of selectmen and offered to repair the clock in the Old Brick Church in Boston, which had been constructed by Benjamin Bagnall about 1718. On March 21, 1768, the *Boston Gazette* carried an article—about an exhibit by Brown at a town meeting—that indicates his quality workmanship:

> At the said Meeting was exhibited the Frame and principal Movements of a superb stately Town-Clock, made by Mr. Gawen Brown, of this Town: The two great Wheels took near 90 lb. weight of Brass; it is calculated for eight Days to shew the Hours and Minutes; will have three grand Dials, and a machanic lever to preserve the Motion during the winding up. The Pendulum Wheel and Pallets to perform the dead Beat. The Works are nicely executed. The steel Pinions and Teeth of the Wheels are finely polished, which must greatly abate the Friction, add to its Regularity and Duration. It will have a curious mathematical Pendulum, that may be altered the 3500th Parts of an inch while the clock is going. From the exquisite finishing of the Parts already done, good Judges are of Opinion that it will be a Master Piece of the Kind, and do Honor to America.

This interesting clock apparently incorporated the special features of maintaining power while winding and a dead-beat escapement, the latter being a precision method introduced by George Graham of London about 1715. It is probable that this was the clock installed in the Old South Church on Marlboro Street about 1769; in April of 1770, a newspaper item stated that the clock had lost only two minutes since the beginning of the new year. For two years, between 1772 and 1774, Brown had to struggle with the town selectmen, trying to get them to purchase the clock. He originally asked one hundred pounds sterling for it, but later settled for eighty pounds, paid on April 4, 1774.

Brown died at eighty-two. His funeral was held at his George Street residence on August 8, 1801. Besides the numerous brass-movement tall clocks he produced, some watches with his inscription are in existence. However, it is doubtful that he actually produced the watches. More than likely he imported English watches and engraved his name on them.

## IN MASSACHUSETTS

In the eighteenth century, Boston was not the only center of clockmaking activity in the state. The area to the north, comprising Essex County, had early and important activity. The first workman here was probably Richard Manning, son of an Ipswich gunsmith, Thomas Manning. Richard was born about 1710 in Ipswich. Besides clockmaking, he carried on business as a gunsmith and blacksmith. To whom Manning was apprenticed as a clockmaker is unknown, but from the similarity of Manning's clocks to thirty-hour English country-style posted movements with brass wheels and iron frame, it is certain his master was trained in the provinces rather than in London.

Manning's career spanned many years. A one-hand clock, dated 1741, is known, as are two-hand examples dated 1767 and 1773. When Manning died in Ipswich in April, 1774, his inventory included two unfinished clocks, one timepiece, and the following interesting tools: engine to cut clock wheels; lathe; wooden patterns; screw plate, vice, hammer, "chizzels,"

**40.** Dwarf tall, or "grandmother" clock, about 4 ft. tall, made by Joshua Wilder, Hingham, MA, *c.* 1820. Probably stood on shelf. (*Courtesy, Charles S. Parsons*)

tongs, punches, pliers, saw, compasses, burnishers; and clock wheels, bells, and chains.

A few miles north in the town of Amesbury, near the New Hampshire border, David Blaisdell (1712–56) worked. Though their work differed in some respects, Blaisdell was producing a thirty-hour posted-design clock movement very like Manning's, which suggests that the men had similar training. Fortunately, Blaisdell often followed the uncommon practice of dating his crudely engraved dials, many of which have mispellings of his own name and town. One clock is dated 1735 and another reportedly 1741, though its whereabouts is not now known. A number of examples have dates ranging from 1744 to 1756, the year Blaisdell died at the age of forty-four.

Blaisdell's clockmaking skills did not die with him, however. He had trained two of his sons, Isaac (1738–91) and Nicholas (1743–*c.* 1800), in the art. His son David, Jr., (1736–94) may have made a few clocks, but was not a prolific producer. Isaac moved to the town of Chester, New Hampshire, in about 1762 and worked there for many years. Nicholas moved to Newmarket, New Hampshire, and later to Falmouth, Maine, and carried on a small clockmaking business. None of the sons, however, surpassed the father in production. Blaisdell's brother, Jonathan (1709–1802), made clocks in East Kingston, New Hampshire.

The Mullikens and Balches were two other families prominent in clockmaking in this area. Samuel and Nathaniel, sons of John Mulliken, a blacksmith, were born in Bradford in 1720 and 1722 respectively. They were most likely trained by Jonathan Mulliken, a relative who worked in Bradford and later in Falmouth, Massachusetts.

Some Mulliken clocks were of the thirty-hour style with rope-pull wind and, often having a single hand, were reminiscent of the Blaisdell style. Their eight-day clocks were of the standard English style, usually having brass dials. In the latter part of the eighteenth century, the family made early brass-dial examples of the Massachusetts-style shelf clock, though the cases used were often crude in comparison to the ones made a few years later in the Boston area.

Samuel Mulliken first worked in Bradford; after 1740 he moved to Newburyport, where he died in 1756 at thirty-six. Besides a wheel-cutting engine and turning lathes, his inventory listed two partially finished clocks, valued at £7 1s. 4d., and many smaller clockmaking tools. His business was carried on in Newburyport by his son Jonathan (1746–82), and by his grandsons Samuel (b. 1769) and Nathaniel (1776–1847) at Hallowell, Maine. After Jonathan's death in 1782, his widow married Samuel Mulliken (1761–1847), Jonathan's nephew, who ran the business in Newburyport and later worked in Salem and Lynn.

The second branch of this active family was headed by Nathaniel Mulliken (b. 1722), who left Bradford in 1751 and set up a shop in Lexington, Massachusetts. After Nathaniel's sudden death in 1767, his business was continued by two of his sons, Nathaniel, Jr., (1752–76) and Joseph (1765–1802). A third son, John (b. 1754), made clock cases.

The *Boston Evening Post* of December 4, 1767, stated:

> Monday, Mr. Nathaniel Mulliken of Lexington, clockmaker, who to all appearances had been as well that day as any time, as he was coming in the door of his house, instantly fell notwithstanding all possible Endeavors for Relief, expired in a few moments to the Grief of his disconsolate widow and children. His remains were interred on Thursday.

Nathaniel, Jr., kept the shop in Lexington and continued to produce brass-dial tall clocks, but just after the battle of Lexington and Concord, April 17, 1775, the British burned his home and clock shop. Soon afterward, he moved to Concord, Massachusetts, where he died in the winter of 1776 at the age of twenty-four, unmarried.

Joseph, since he was only two years old when his father died and eleven when Nathaniel, Jr., died, apparently received his training from other relatives. He produced white-dial tall clocks in Concord from about 1785 until his death in 1802.

The Balches were the fourth family of Essex County to gain prominence in the field. Daniel Balch (1735–89) was a native of Bradford, where his father, Rev. William Balch, had moved in 1727 to become minister of the East Bradford parish. Daniel made clocks in Bradford and also in Newburyport, where he had moved in about 1757. One timepiece, engraved "No. 2," is a single-hand thirty-hour example with a posted movement and rope-pull wind, which suggests he received his training from Manning, Blaisdell, or perhaps the Mullikens. His later eight-day style was of the standard English type. His sons Daniel, Jr., (1761–1835) and Thomas Hutchinson Balch (1771–1817) continued his business. His brother married Rebecca Bailey, a relative of the author, and family papers state that their son, Benjamin, who was born November 9, 1774, was a "watch and clockmaker in Salem, where he has been since 1796." Benjamin was still in Salem when the papers were written (*c.* 1850) and died there on June 6, 1860.

Another early workman in Essex County was Henry Harmson of Marblehead. Harmson had come to Marblehead about 1733, for by September of that year he had purchased a dwelling house in the town. He had probably come from Newport, Rhode Island—a watchmaker with that surname had been working there about 1725. He was active in Marblehead only a few years; he died in 1737.

His inventory, however, substantiates his clockmaking and watchmaking activities. Among the tools and items listed were a "clock with seven bells," a "Time Piece," and a set of works. One of Harmson's tall clocks, made for Joseph Cogswell, is on display at the Essex Institute in Salem.

Toward the end of the eighteenth century, the Essex County area became very active, especially the larger town of Salem. Probably the most prolific maker of this period was a Newburyport man named David Wood. Wood was born in 1766 and probably was apprenticed to Daniel Balch, Sr. He advertised in 1792 that he had set up a shop in Market Street, Newburyport, and for several decades he carried on extensive business activities there. He moved into the former shop of Thomas Hutchinson Balch after the latter's death in 1817, and there worked until 1824, when an advertisement stated he had recently moved to a shop on the west side of Market Square. From the number of clocks surviving, his output must have been large. Besides tall clocks, he also dealt in Massachusetts-style shelf clocks and banjo clocks.

Other notable Essex County clockmakers include Michael Carleton (1757–1836) of Bradford and Haverhill, John Osgood (1770–1840) of Andover, and Paine Wingate (1767–1833) and Frederick Wingate (1782–1860) of Haverhill.

South of Boston, in the Plymouth County town of Hanover, the Bailey family achieved some prominence as clockmakers. The majority of clocks they produced were of the normal eight-day style with either brass or, more commonly, white dials. Some examples are known with unusual skeletonized movement plates or unusual gearing arrangements. Some thirty-hour wood movements with brass dials marked "John Bailey, Hanover" are known. These wood movements more closely resemble the large, crude style made by the Cheney family of East Hartford, Connecticut, in the latter half of the eighteenth century than the mass-produced style made by Eli Terry and others after 1800. The Bailey family also appears to be the earliest producers of the dwarf tall clock, or "grandmother" clock.

John Bailey (1730–1810) was a Quaker, as were many other early makers. He set up shop in Hanover after 1750, carrying on business until after the Revolution. His son John, Jr., (1751–1823) worked on Curtis Street in Hanover after 1770 and later in Lynn, where he produced tall, shelf, dwarf tall or grandmother clocks, and surveyors' instruments. The younger John trained his two sons, John III and Joseph, as well as David Studley. Studley worked in Hanover and after 1834 in North Bridgewater with his brother Luther. John Bailey III (1787–1883) worked in Hanover for a time, but about 1824 moved to New Bedford. In March of that year he sent a letter to Eli and

**41.** Gilt French figurine clock made for American markets by Jean Baptiste Blanc of Paris, in 1816, with likeness of George Washington. (*American Clock & Watch Museum*)

42

43

**42.** Finely painted Pennsylvania one-day clock by Samuel Schneck. Case dated 1804 and probably made near Reading, PA. (*Courtesy, Edward F. LaFond*) **43.** Unsigned tall clock, probably made in south-central Pennsylvania. Case shows strong Philadelphia influence. Dial shown in illus. 12; movement in illus. 25. (*Author's collection*)

Samuel Terry of Plymouth, Connecticut, asking them to consider him as a sales agent for their pillar and scroll shelf clocks. He wrote: "I have heretofore carried on the Manufacture of Brass Clocks pretty largely . . ."

John III built an observatory in New Bedford and imported astronomical instruments to rate chronometers for ships, a business which is said to have brought in five thousand dollars a year. Bailey had conscientious abolitionist views and because of them was at odds with the Whigs, who owned all but two ships in New Bedford. When he would not change his views, the Whigs hired another man to set up business in the town and Bailey was ruined. His unmarried brother, Joseph, carried on a clock business in Hingham, New Bedford, and in Lynn from about 1800 to 1840.

Calvin Bailey (1761–1835), the second clock-making son of John Bailey, Sr., kept a day book, which gives some insight into his activities. Calvin did not consider clockmaking his foremost profession—farming was first. In 1809 he was doing very little clockmaking, but the book does have entries such as one for carting 600 pounds of clock weights from Easton, where they apparently were cast. His records also show the cost of clocks in his day: in 1799 the plain eight-day tall clock cost thirty-five dollars; a clock with a moon dial sold for forty-one fifty. About eight years later moon clocks cost forty dollars and clocks with alarms, fifty dollars; cases cost another twenty.

Lebbeus Bailey (1763–1827), a third son of John Bailey, Sr., worked in Hanover after his training; in 1791, he sold his land to his brother Calvin and moved to North Yarmouth, Maine,

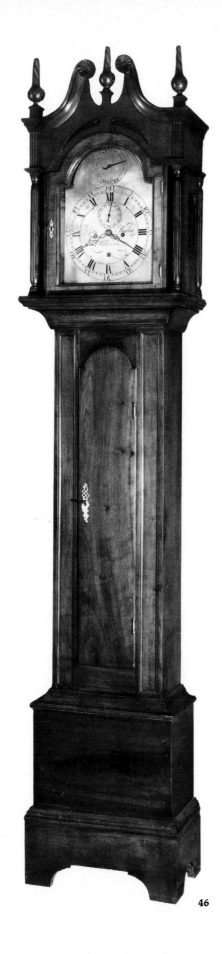

**44.** Primitive cherry-cased tall clock probably made near
Greenfield, MA, *c. 1780.* One-day wood movement with
brass dial, pewter spandrels, boss, and chapter ring.
*(Author's collection)* **45.** One-day wood-movement tall clock
in pine case made by Alexander T. Willard, Ashby, MA,
*c. 1810. (American Clock & Watch Museum)* **46.** Eight-day
brass-movement tall clock by John Bailey, Hanover, MA,
*c. 1780.* **47.** Simon Willard (1753–1848), famed inventor of
the "banjo" clock, became one of America's most respected
clockmakers. *(46 and 47, courtesy, Old Sturbridge Village)*

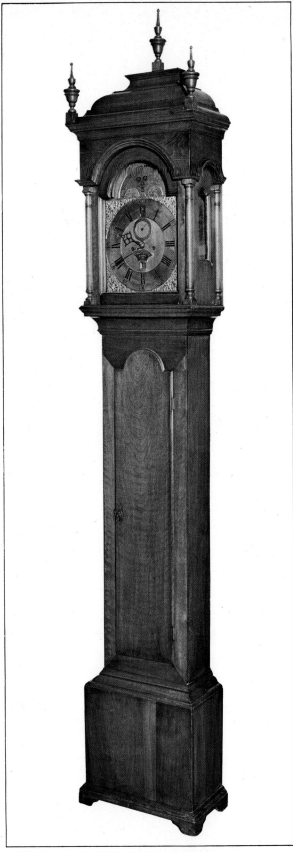

**48.** Walnut-cased tall clock by David Rittenhouse, Norristown, PA, dated 1769. Rittenhouse moved to Philadelphia the following year and there continued to make superb timekeepers. *(Courtesy, Frank S. Schwarz & Son)*

where he continued business until his death.

Joshua Wilder (1786–1860) of Hingham, Massachusetts, was apprenticed to a member of the Bailey family, probably John, Jr. Also a Quaker, Wilder was one of the last men to make the types of clocks considered to be handcrafted. Although he marketed some wood clocks, as an advertisement from a Hingham newspaper shows, the majority of his clocks were styles that had been discontinued by most makers before 1843.

Not only did Joshua and his son Ezra manufacture timepieces after 1843, but on September 18, 1860, less than one month before his death, Joshua transferred to his son all his tools and equipment and "all partially manufactured clock work." Ezra had been married in 1841 to Rebecca Tower, and the name of his father-in-law, Reuben Tower, is occasionally seen on dials, notably on dwarf tall clocks.

Western Massachusetts was generally considered the frontier before the Revolution, but there were occasional makers who moved into the area. Preserved Clapp (b. 1731) of Amherst, for example, who was considered an ingenious mechanic and inventor of his time, produced a limited number of brass clocks and timepieces.

Asa Munger, a native of Granby who was trained as a silversmith and clockmaker, moved into the western Massachusetts town of Ludlow, where he worked until about 1803. He then moved to Herkimer, New York, and later Auburn. In Ludlow, Munger made some handsome brass tall clocks as well as some curious thirty-hour wood tall clocks with a movement design somewhat similar to those made by the Dutch.

Wood clocks were produced in several other rural areas in Massachusetts. Besides those made by John Bailey of Hanover and Asa Munger of Ludlow, they were produced in some quantity in the north central part of the state. Jonas Fitch (1741–1808), a native of Bedford, Massachusetts, was one of the earliest of this group. He started making wood tall clocks in Pepperell before the Revolution.

Less than fifteen miles west of Pepperell is the town of Ashby; it was from there that most of the wood tall clocks made in the state came. Some might object to calling the Ashby-style tall clocks "handcrafted," as they were produced in considerable numbers, but studies of the movements show that they were made by hand-sawing and hand-finishing methods. Though some mass-production techniques may have been used, the movements were basically handmade.

It is thought that Jonas Fitch trained the first Ashby makers, Abraham Edwards (1761–1840) and his brother Calvin (1763–96). The brothers worked in partnership from about 1785 until Calvin died in 1796. Their clocks, marked "A. & C.

Edwards," were sequentially numbered and early examples had sheet tin dials covered with a gilt wash to give them the appearance of brass. Pewter was used for the chapter ring and circular nameplate, or boss, and spandrels were pressed out of thin metal so they would appear to be cast. Numbers 121 and 122 have this type of dial. Before number 200, however, the dials were changed to wood plates painted white and decorated by hand, giving them an appearance similar to the popular painted iron dials commonly imported from England for brass clocks.

Clocks by the brothers that are numbered as high as 532 exist, and perhaps 600 or more were made before Calvin died. An appraisal of the business for his estate showed the stock and tools in the shop to be valued at over twelve hundred dollars. One new clock was valued at fifteen dollars and eighty dollars' worth of unfinished clocks was in the shop.

Abraham Edwards continued the business alone until about 1820. His son John made some clocks, perhaps working only four or five years. Another son, Samuel, worked in Ashby about four years, but moved to Gorham, Maine, about 1808 and worked there until his death in 1830.

Two Willard brothers from the neighboring town of Ashburnham also became involved in wood clock making in Ashby after 1801. The men were distant relatives of the Willard clockmakers in Boston, but it is doubtful whether the Boston men even knew of their existence.

Alexander Tarbell Willard (1774–1850) trained for a time under Abraham Edwards. Numerous of his clocks with painted wooden dials are known, some of which were designed to simulate the astronomical-type dials used on precision clocks. With a small chapter and hands and an unusually large seconds bit and seconds hand, the clock dial looked like a precision regulator, although it was not more precise than any other wood tall clock.

Willard continued to make clocks after 1820. In 1829, he wrote in a small almanac: "Made one improved small clock—took about eight days." Another entry in March of that year stated: "Put up another improved small clock and made it in five days." Willard apparently made clocks—although in diminishing numbers—until his death on December 4, 1850. An inventory of stock and tools in his shop included:

| | |
|---|---|
| 3 Clock Engines and Measuring Machine | $1.00 |
| 1 Lathe and Turning Tools | 2.50 |
| Watch Lathes and Tools | 3.00 |
| Lot of Files, Shears, Awls | 1.00 |
| 3 Wooden Clocks and Cases | 3.00 |
| Clock Cases and Parts of Clocks | .25 |
| 1 Brass Clock and Case | 4.00 |
| 1 Marble Clock | 6.00 |
| 1 Clock | 1.80 |

**49.** Celestial time globe made by Lewis P. Juvet, Glens Falls, NY, c. 1885. Usually made with a terrestrial globe, Juvet's unusual timepieces were produced from 1879 to 1886. *(Courtesy, Henry C. Wing, Jr.)*

| | |
|---|---|
| 1 Wooden Timepiece | 1.50 |
| 4 Clock Cases | .50 |

Philander Jacob Willard (1772–1840), Alexander's brother, moved to Ashby in 1825 and assisted Alexander in the business. He is said to have produced some brass clocks.

Jonathan Winslow (1765–1847) made wood clocks in a number of Massachusetts towns, including Warren, New Salem, Worcester, and, after 1820, Springfield. Some wood-movement dwarf tall clocks, or grandmother clocks, by Winslow are known. They have reverse painted glass dials and Winslow's name impressed in the wooden seat board.

Wood tall clocks by Taylor & Edwards, Worcester, are known. Their movements are of the style made in Ashby, and Abraham Edwards or one of his sons may have been in partnership for a short time with Samuel Taylor of Worcester. One of these clocks has the date 1801 penciled under the count wheel.

# SIMON WILLARD'S BANJO CLOCK

The Boston school of clockmakers has not a name better known than that of the Willard family, which became prominent in the Boston area after the Revolution. The styles of clocks they developed, adopted, or improved upon injected new life into the craft. Their influence spread throughout New England and was felt to some degree in areas such as Philadelphia and Baltimore.

Of the eight sons of Benjamin and Sarah Willard of Grafton, Massachusetts, to live to maturity, four of them—Benjamin, Simon, Ephraim, and Aaron—became known clockmakers. The activities of these four men spanned nearly seventy-five years, from the time of Benjamin's initial work after 1764 until the retirement of Simon in 1839. Their influence, however, was felt through another century of production. They contributed new styles of clocks to the Massachusetts area, which helped to sever ties with the old-fashioned traditional tall clock. Benjamin and Ephraim produced mainly tall clocks; Simon and Aaron produced wall and shelf clocks as well, especially after 1800.

Benjamin, Jr., born on March 19, 1743, was ten years older than the next of the surviving sons. Who trained him in the craft remains a mystery. There were certainly masters in Boston, but perhaps there were men located closer to Grafton with the ability to teach him.

If apprenticed at the normal age of fourteen, Benjamin would have started his apprenticeship in 1757 and completed it in 1764. This seems a reasonable assumption, for on May 18 of that year he purchased from his father two lots of land, with a house, in Grafton. A young man not yet trained in a skill would probably have avoided such financial obligations.

A Benjamin Willard "from Boston," advertised in the December 3, 1764, edition of the *Connecticut Courant* that he was setting up a "Last Making" business at East Hartford at the home of Benjamin Cheney, wood and brass clockmaker of that town. No mention was made of clockmaking, but this appears to be the same Benjamin Willard, for the clockmaker did construct these shoemaking forms, or lasts, and was described as a lastmaker in another Grafton deed of 1764. Although there has been one clock reported with a Cheney-style wood movement and a dial engraved "Benjamin Willard," it is doubtful that Willard spent much time training with Cheney.

Some studies of clockmaking advance the theory that Benjamin Willard may have been apprenticed to Nathaniel Mulliken, Sr., of Lexington, Massachusetts; this could be the case, since Willard lived in Lexington for a time. On December 17, 1771, the *Boston Evening Post* carried notice that "Benjamin Willard Clock Maker, Hereby

informs the Publick, That he has removed from Lexington to Roxbury . . ." Later parts of the advertisement state that he had a shop in Roxbury Street "near Boston" and that business was also carried on "by his Workman at Grafton." Later advertisements show he manufactured many types of clocks, including musical ones, at shops in Roxbury and Grafton. Willard produced many tall clocks in these two towns, as well as in Lexington, but he is not known to have produced shelf or wall clocks.

About the time of the Revolution, Willard returned to Grafton, where he carried on his clockmaking business. In 1784, he stated in an advertisement in the *Massachusetts Spy* that "he has finished and sold two hundred and fifty-three eight-day clocks, chiefly in this State." By 1790, he had moved to Worcester. He became involved in a legal suit about 1798 that ended in a judgment against him for over nineteen hundred dollars and a short jail term. By 1800, he had been released from jail and was back in Grafton. In 1803, he made a trip to Baltimore, Maryland, and while there died. Boston's *Columbian Sentinel,* September 28, 1803, stated: "Deaths. At Baltimore, Mr. Benjamin Willard of this Town, where he has left a wife and four children." Willard died nearly penniless, his estate being valued the following year at $75.09.

Simon, the second of the Willard brothers, was born at Grafton on April 3, 1753, and became one of the most famous clockmakers of his day. Much investigation has been done in this century in an attempt to discover the source of Simon's training, but nothing conclusive has been found. In 1857, historian Edward Holden stated in the *Boston Transcript* that Willard was apprenticed to a Mr. Morris, "an Englishman then engaged in the manufacture of clocks in Grafton."

Willard's own great grandson, John Ware Willard, researched this point but was unable to find proof. He published his findings in 1910 in the book *A History of Simon Willard, Inventor and Clockmaker*. The book stated that "Simon Willard himself was heard to say that the man to whom he was apprenticed knew little or nothing of the art himself, and that his teacher was his brother Benjamin." The statement seems to have merit, for some clocks are known that have cast-lead pendulum bobs with raised lettering and with the names John Morris and S. Willard and the dates 1770 and 1771. (Unfortunately, little else is known of John Morris.) One clock having this unusual bob has an engraved dial that reads: "Benjamin Willard, Roxbury, Fecit" and "Warranted for Mr. James Mears, 1772." Engraved on the movement of the clock, which is numbered 131, is "Made by Simon Willard in his 17th year—Cleaned by him in his 81st year, August 10th 1833." This inscription

**50.** Miniature shelf clock by Aaron Willard, Roxbury, MA, *c.* 1780, stands just over 15 inches. *(Hershel B. Burt)*

**51.** Willard's patent alarm timepiece or "lighthouse" clock, inscribed: "Made by Simon Willard in 1833 in his 80th year." *(Old Sturbridge Village)*

**52.** Kidney-dial shelf clock by Aaron Willard, Boston, MA, *c.* 1795. Mahogany case is elegantly simple. *(American Clock & Watch Museum)*

tends to substantiate the statement that Simon Willard at least completed his apprenticeship under his brother Benjamin.

About the time Simon finished his training, the American Revolution had become a reality and he, along with three of his brothers, marched during the Lexington alarm. After the war ended, he continued to manufacture tall clocks, thirty-hour wall timepieces, and some eight-day shelf clocks, on which he inscribed: "Simon Willard, Grafton."

In 1783, he settled in Roxbury, where he had a shop on Roxbury Street—possibly the same shop Benjamin had occupied some years before. About this time, Simon was also involved in the development of a clockwork roasting jack for the constant rotation of meat while it cooked. In 1784, he was given exclusive right by the General Court of Massachusetts to make and sell the item.

After his establishment in Roxbury, Simon continued making tall clocks—adopting the popular white-painted dial—and the eight-day shelf timepiece or Massachusetts shelf clock, but it appears that he discontinued making the thirty-hour wall timepiece. Before 1800, however, he had developed an eight-day brass timepiece housed in

a wall-style case that was completely different from the thirty-hour clock case. On February 8, 1802, a patent was granted, and Willard's "Improved Timepiece" became one of the best-known American clocks. It brought him acclaim during his lifetime and immortality in the field of horological history. Today it is generally called a "banjo" clock.

Willard claimed nine improvements in his 1802 patent. Eight of these concerned the movement; the ninth concerned the shape of the case. His classic design has been improved upon little, if at all, since that time.

The basic shape of the clock rarely varied, but the finish often did. Early standard Willard cases were simply banded inlay work with an acorn finial. Clocks made for special presentations had twisted rope-like gilded trim encompassing the door and throat panels. The "presentation" clocks often had gilded brackets and fancier finials. The gilt-style cases were rarely made by Simon Willard, though his younger brother Aaron produced them in considerable numbers. Some presentation clocks were made to be given to brides; these were often finished in white to symbolize purity.

Decorative glasses for the Simon Willard

**53.** Cherry-cased clock by Isaac Doolittle, New Haven, CT, *c.* 1750. He produced a great many tall clocks until his death in 1800 at 79. *(Courtesy, Hershel B. Burt)*

timepieces were well done; they were usually in geometric patterns, with "S. Willard's Patent" in gilt on the lower door glass. They were probably supplied by John R. Penniman, an ornamental painter in Boston from 1806 to 1828, and by Charles Bullard, who worked there from 1816 to 1844. William Fish (1770–1844), a Boston cabinet-maker, supplied Willard with many cases after 1800.

As with most successful items, it was not long before other makers in the Boston area were copying the Willard-style clock. "Willard's Patent" became a phrase commonly used by them and was often painted on the throat glass. In August, 1822, Willard cautioned the public in a newspaper advertisement:

CAUTION

I believe the public are not generally aware, that my former Patent Right expired 6 years ago; which induces me to caution them against the frequent impositions practiced, in vending spurious Timepieces. It is true, they have "Patent" printed on them, and some with my name, and their outward appearance resembles those formerly made by me: Thus they are palm'd upon the public. Several of them have lately been brought to me for repairs, that would certainly put the greatest bungler to the blush. Such is the country inundated with, and such, I consider prejudicial to my reputation; I therefore disclaim being the manufacturer of such vile performances.

S. WILLARD

After the timepiece, or banjo, became successful, Simon Willard apparently discontinued manufacturing tall clocks and shelf clocks, except on special order. In 1819, he was granted a patent for an alarm clock, stating that "when let off, it strikes on the top of the case of the clock, and makes a noise like someone rapping at the door, and it will wake you much quicker than to strike on a bell in the usual way." Cases of these clocks resemble a lighthouse, the clock face being under a glass dome on the top of a circular case. Willard advertised his patent alarm timepiece (now usually called a "lighthouse" clock) in August of 1822, stating that Thomas Richards of New York and J. B. Jones of Boston were authorized sales agents. Willard also produced the design without the alarm, but the style was not well received, judging from the rarity of examples today.

Willard also produced public clocks on order. In 1791, he took charge of the clock in the First Church of Roxbury and in April of 1806, he set up a new one for the church at a cost of $858. In 1801, he made a large clock for the United States Senate in Washington and eventually had to travel there to set it running. Willard's bill for the clock, dated

**54.** Early Connecticut tall clock by Abel Parmele, New Haven, made *c.* 1735. Painted graining on case probably redone in last century. *(Courtesy, Connecticut Historical Society)* **55.** Inlaid cherry tall clock by Abner Burnham, Sharon, CT, *c.* 1800. Painted dial, without decoration, has "up and down" indicator showing the number of days until it is necessary to wind clock again. *(Frank S. Schwarz & Son)*

November 21, 1801, shows he charged $750 for the clock and an additional $20 to pack it for shipment. The clock was destroyed in 1814, when the British burned Washington. In 1826, Willard constructed a turret clock, on the order of Thomas Jefferson, for the University of Virginia. Jefferson never saw the clock, for he died one month after sending Willard final details on how the clock should be constructed to fit the tower. The clock was eventually installed in the rotunda and remained in use until 1895, when the building was destroyed by fire.

In 1837, Willard was commissioned to make two more clocks for the capitol at Washington. One was put in the Senate Chamber; the second was a movement to be placed in a sculptured case (made by Carlo Franzoni in 1819) in Statuary Hall. In about December of 1839, at the age of eighty-

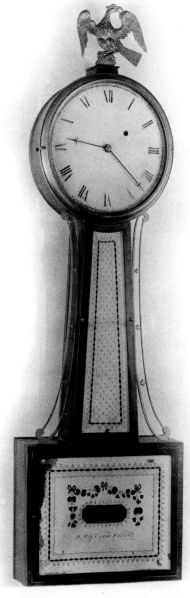

**56.** "Improved timepiece," now commonly called banjo clock, made by Simon Willard, Boston, MA. Design patented by him in 1801. *(Courtesy, Hershel B. Burt)*

five, Simon retired from active business and spent the remainder of his life with his children. He died at the home of his son-in-law, Isaac Cary, on Washington Street in Boston on August 30, 1848, at the age of ninety-five.

Simon Willard's apprentices included his sons Simon, Jr., and Benjamin F. Willard. Simon, Jr., (1795–1874) did not immediately go into the manufacture of horological items. He first attempted to establish a crockery business, but it failed in 1824. In his own writing, Simon, Jr., stated:

> After my failure in 1824, went into my Father's clockmaking establishment and remained until 1826. In July, 1826, at the age of 31, I went to New York and apprenticed myself to Mr. D. Eggert, a very ingenious mechanician, to learn the Chronometer and Watch business. Mastered the business and returned in 1828 and set up for myself at No. 9 Congress Street, Boston, where I remained till January 1, 1870, a period of 42 years.

After the year 1850, his son and apprentice, Zabdiel Adams Willard, was admitted into the business, which then became known as Simon Willard & Son.

Benjamin Franklin Willard (1803–47), second son of Simon, Sr., carried on a small clockmaking business and, like his brother, favored astronomical regulators and precision instruments. Benjamin was granted a patent in 1839 for a lighthouse signal light. Over a decade before, he had been given a contract by the United States government to build such a device, which on completion was installed at the entrance to Boston Harbor.

Ephraim Willard (b. 1755), brother of Benjamin and Simon, worked in Medford, Roxbury, and from 1801 to 1805 in Boston. After 1805, he went to New York City, apparently giving up the clock business. White-dial tall clocks made by him are seen occasionally, but are scarce in comparison to the number made by his brothers.

Aaron Willard, the youngest brother, was born in Grafton on October 13, 1757, and died in Boston on May 20, 1844, at the age of eighty-seven. In 1780, he settled in Roxbury and set up a shop on Washington Street, a short distance from his brother Simon's establishment. In the 1790s, Aaron opened a factory, considered to be quite large for the time, just across the Boston town line. By the turn of the century his production was greater than most makers in Boston. He produced the "half clock," or Massachusetts-style shelf clock, in greater quantity and for several years longer than Simon. Those found that are made by Aaron are often of a later style with painted glass fronts. About 1823 he retired, leaving the business in the hands of his son, Aaron, Jr.

Aaron, Jr., (1783–1864) had been trained by

his father. From about 1804 to 1806, he was in partnership with his brother-in-law, Spencer Nolan, in a business that produced painted and decorated metal clock dials. Nolan continued in business after November, 1806, with Samuel Curtis (1788–1879), brother of Lemuel Curtis.

After the younger Willard took over his father's business, he continued to manufacture timepieces as well as gallery clocks and regulators. He is generally credited with the development of the lyre version of the wall timepiece. His banjo clocks often have wood bezels and wood panels in throats and lower doors—this version produced a simpler, often pleasing appearance, but is generally considered to be a sign of decline in the quality of the style. The decision to change the style was probably prompted by the fact that the product of decorative glass painters had declined in quality after 1830. When Aaron Willard, Jr., retired in about 1850, the factory was sold and business discontinued.

His brother Henry (1802–87) was apprenticed to William Fish in the cabinetmaker's trade. He specialized in the making of clock cases and supplied them to his father and brother, as well as to William Cummens, Elnathan Taber, and the firm of Simon Willard, Jr., & Son.

Several important clockmakers of the period had been apprenticed to Simon Willard, Sr. The list includes Levi Hutchins (1761–1855) and his brother Abel (1763–1853), who moved to Concord, New Hampshire, in 1788; William Cummens (1768–1834) of Boston; and William Lemist (1791–1820). Elnathan Taber (1768–1854) produced many fine items after Willard's styles.

An important apprentice to Simon Willard, Jr., was John Sawin (1801–63), who set up shop in Boston with George W. Dyer in 1822. The partnership was dissolved in 1828; Dyer moved to Utica, New York, but Sawin remained in business in Boston for some time afterward.

To recount the activities of all the makers of banjo and shelf-style clocks would be impractical, but there were several important makers in the area of Concord, Massachusetts, whose work should be considered.

Daniel Munroe, Jr., (1775–1859) settled in Concord after completing his apprenticeship under Simon Willard. In Concord, Munroe produced clocks under his own name, with the designation "D. Munroe & Company." Munroe returned to Boston in 1809, where he set up a business that he conducted until retiring in 1858, the year before his death at the age of eighty-four.

Two of Munroe's brothers, Nathaniel and William, conducted clock businesses. Nathaniel (1777–1861) was apprenticed to Abel Hutchins of Concord, New Hampshire. With the completion of his training in about 1798, he conducted a business, working first alone and after 1808 in partnership with Samuel Whiting, as Munroe & Whiting. About 1816 he moved to Baltimore, Maryland, and continued in business there until 1840. Examples of clocks made by him in that city are known. William (1778–1861) was more interested in cabinetmaking than clockmaking. Having learned the cabinetmaking trade from Nehemiah Munroe of Roxbury, he made clock cases from about 1800 until 1819.

After Nathaniel Munroe left Concord, Samuel Whiting (b. 1778) continued in business alone at least another twenty years. Some of his clocks have the simple black and gilt glasses usually associated with the banjo clock after 1840.

**57.** Massachusetts diamond-head timepiece marked "Munroe, Concord." An unusual banjo variation, made ʳ. 1810. *(Courtesy, Old Sturbridge Village)*

## THE CONNECTICUT SCHOOL

Though Connecticut was a small, rural colony, it became an area of extensive clock production. Some of the earliest artisans may have been trained in the Boston or Philadelphia areas, but the clockmaking activity in Connecticut remained fairly isolated and grew internally during the eighteenth century.

Brass clocks especially were produced from the early part of the eighteenth century until 1800. Their production declined sharply after that time—because of the mass manufacture of the wood tall clock—and ceased by 1825.

Thomas Harland of Norwich was a forerunner of mass production in Connecticut. From the number of clocks produced by Harland, there is indication that he was making an effort to standardize parts in order to increase production. His methods were undoubtedly carried on through his apprentice, Daniel Burnap, and through Burnap's apprentice, Eli Terry.

Connecticut also saw extensive production of wood clocks, which was unique in colonial America. The Cheney family of East Hartford produced wood clocks of a crude nature for over fifty years and laid the foundation for their ultimate refinement and mass manufacture by Eli Terry after 1800.

Ebenezer Parmele (1690–1777), born in Guilford, Connecticut, is the earliest native American known to have engaged in clockmaking. From whom Parmele received training is not known, for he may have been working as early as 1712. Clockmaking was not his major occupation. He was usually spoken of as a ship builder, a business in which he was still engaged when he gave his son interest in a sloop called the *Aliane* in 1761.

On December 20, 1726, members of the church in Guilford decided to have a clock set up in their meetinghouse. Parmele made the clock and was still keeping it in order in 1741. On December 12, 1742, the selectmen of the town of Milford were authorized to buy the clock from him and pay for it from the town's treasury. Though no domestic clocks by Parmele are known, this public clock has survived and is now displayed at the Henry Whitfield Museum in Guilford.

Abel Parmele (1703–*c.* 1766), a nephew who was probably apprenticed to Ebenezer, worked in New Haven as a clockmaker and bell founder. Abel had moved to Branford, where he carried on a successful business, by 1741.

Macock Ward (1702–83), a native of Wallingford, was probably another of Ebenezer Parmele's apprentices. About 1724, Ward established a shop in Wallingford and there carried on his business in clockmaking and bell founding. In 1738, he built

**58.** Connecticut tall clock in striped maple case, brass dial engraved "Hosmer, Hartford." Made *c.* 1750, perhaps earlier. *(Courtesy, Connecticut Historical Society)*

a public clock for the Wallingford meetinghouse. Ward was very active in the public affairs of his town and was a noted Tory. At his death in 1783, Ward's inventory contained numerous clock-making tools.

Ward was probably the master of Isaac Doolittle, Hezekiah Hotchkiss, and Silas Merriman, who were the major clockmakers in the New Haven area before the Revolution. Isaac Doolittle (1721–1800), a Wallingford native, set up a shop on Chapel Street in New Haven about 1742. He made clocks and surveyors' instruments, cast bells, and repaired watches. He was an able mechanic and, in 1769, constructed a printing press, which he said was of the most approved construction and "is allowed to be the neatest ever made in America and equal, if not superior, to any imported from Great-Britain."

About 1785, Doolittle's health failed and he was forced to discontinue business for a few years. In January, 1788, he announced:

> This is to give notice to the Public in General and to my former Customers, that I, the subscriber, hath so far recovered my health, that I carry on the repairing of Watches, making of Clocks, Screws for Clothiers; also the Casting of Bells, and every other kind of business that used to be carried on before my late illness, at my shop in Chapel Street. All favours will be gratefully received by the Public's humble Servant, Isaac Doolittle.

Doolittle continued in business for nearly ten years, when his health failed again. The *Connecticut Courant* of February 20, 1800, carried the notice:

> Died in this city, after a long and distressing illness of several years continuance, Mr. Isaac Doolittle, in the 79th year of his age; a very worthy and respectable character.

A son, Isaac Doolittle, Jr., (1759–1821) continued the business in New Haven. On May 22, 1799, prior to his father's death, he advertised:

> The subscriber having commenced business at the shop lately occupied by Mr. Isaac Doolittle, in Chapel Street, where he repairs watches, makes and repairs Surveyors' Compasses and Chains, Brass Amplitude, plain brass and common Ship's Compasses, Gauging Rods, Quadrants, repair'd &c. every favor gratefully received by the public's humble servant. Isaac Doolittle, jun.

It is interesting to note that the advertisement does not mention the making of clocks, though he did mention the making and repairing of them in a previous advertisement in 1781.

Hezekiah Hotchkiss (1729–61) had set up a shop in New Haven by 1748, though he was not yet twenty years old. Besides clocks, he made metal items, including buckles, spoons, buttons, nails, and tools. His death, at the age of thirty-two, was supposedly from a smallpox innocula-

**59.** Handsome Connecticut tall clock by Thomas Harland, Norwich, c. 1790. Solid cherry case with concave escallion and "whale's tails" fretwork displays superb Norwich cabinetmaking. (*American Clock & Watch Museum*)

tion. The inventory of his estate included many clockmaking tools. Most notable was the tremendous number of files he owned: besides fifteen pounds of old files, some 338 usable ones were inventoried. Also included was an engine, clockhand patterns, two partially made clocks, and one case.

Silas Merriman (1734–1805), another native of Wallingford, established his home and clock shop on State Street in New Haven. At Merriman's death, the estate inventory included clock patterns, parts of a new clock, two completed clocks, and tin-cased clock weights. Some of Merriman's clock movements had unusual skeletonized plates, a feature also used by Phineas Pratt (1747–1813) of Saybrook.

Two other prominent New Haven makers, Nathan Howell and Simeon Jocelin, are believed to have been apprenticed to Isaac Doolittle, Sr. Nathan Howell (1740–84) established a shop after 1760, and was still engaged in the business at the time of his death. Simeon Jocelin (1746–1823) set up a shop before 1771, when he advertised that he made clocks of all kinds as well as repairing all sorts, "however damaged they may be."

Jocelin was granted a patent on March 8, 1800, for a silent moving timepiece. In October of that year he advertised his invention:

Clock Factory—The Subscriber intending to carry on the Clock making Business more extensively than heretofore, and being unwilling to go upon uncertainties, respectfully solicits encouragement by subscription. Those who are in want of his Clocks or Timepieces, and subscribe accordingly, shall be supplied at ten percent below the retailing prices, provided twenty are subscribed for within three months after date. Subscriptions will be taken at public houses, in this and most of the adjacent towns, & by the subscriber. The retailing prices are as follows, viz.  Dolls.

| | |
|---|---|
| Eight Day Clock with Jappann'd | |
| Moon Face | 45 |
| Ditto, Ditto, Plain Face | 40 |
| Eight Day Time Piece | 20 |
| Thirty-Two Day (Patent) Silent | |
| Moving Time-Keeper | 30 |
| Eight Day (Ditto) Silent Moving | |
| Clock with Moon Face | 50 |
| Ditto (Ditto) Ditto, Plain Face | 45 |

The above described, to be well finished, with elegant faces, without cases, and warranted, and those not equal to expectations, subscribers will not be holden to take. Steeple Clocks, House Spring Clocks, and Chamber Time-pieces of various descriptions, will be made according to orders and warranted. Wanted, a good Boy, for the Clockmaking and Watch-mending business, 13 or 14 years old, from the country. The Silent Moving Time-keeper, on trial of six months, fully answers expectation; when its principles are gen-

erally known, no other recommendation will be necessary.

Simeon Jocelin

It is unfortunate that the exact specifications of Jocelin's patent have not survived, but it is known he claimed that this type clock had fewer wheels and pinions and less friction and that it would run with much less weight than a normal clock, five pounds driving the thirty-two-day model. Jocelin's death in 1823 ended the career of one of the most important and inventive clockmakers of the handcrafting period in Connecticut.

Southwest of New Haven, in the towns of Stratford and Fairfield, a few makers were active.

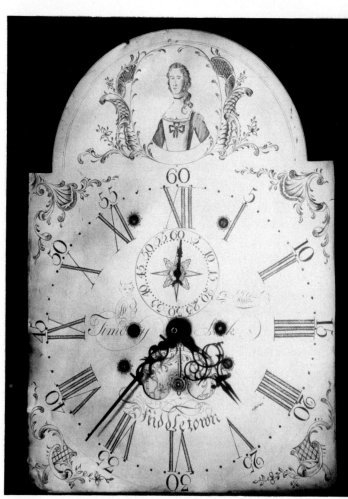

**60.** Single-piece engraved brass dial by Timothy Peck, Middletown, CT, c. 1788. Dial attaches to movement with four screws. (*Courtesy, Connecticut Historical Society*)

John Whitear was the first clockmaker in Fairfield. He may have been trained in New York, but it is more probable he worked under Ebenezer Parmele of Guilford. Whitear carried on business as a clockmaker and bell founder until his death in 1762 and was succeeded in business by his son, John, Jr., (1738–73). The younger Whitear, on his death at the age of thirty-five, had an extensive inventory of clockmaking tools.

John Whitear, Sr., was possibly the master of both Richardson Minor (1736–97) of Stratford and John Davis, who was working about 1750 in Stratford and Fairfield. John Whitear, Jr., was probably the master of Joseph Buckley (1755–1815), who became a noted clockmaker in Fairfield after Whitear's death.

William Burr was working in Fairfield after 1760 and the firm of Whiting & Marquand was doing business there from about 1790 to 1800. This firm, a partnership between G. Bradford Whiting (1764–1844) and Isaac Marquand (1766–1838), was dissolved shortly after 1800, when Marquand moved to Rye, New York.

John Clark came from New York before 1777 and set up a business in Danbury. He stayed in Danbury until 1811, then returned to New York. Clark probably trained Comfort Starr Mygatt (1763–1823), who worked in Danbury from about 1783 to 1807, and Ziba Blakeslee (1768–1834), who worked in nearby Newton after 1790.

There was some activity inland in Middletown on the Connecticut river. One of the more prominent makers there was Samuel Rockwell (1722–73). Though a native of Middletown, Rockwell carried on business in Providence and Philadelphia before returning to Middletown about 1760. He was still actively producing clocks at the time of his death.

Several makers were active after 1735 in the town of Hartford. Seth Youngs (1711–61), who was probably apprenticed to Ebenezer Parmele, moved to Hartford in 1735 and conducted a business there until 1742, when he moved to Windsor, then finally settled in Torrington in 1760. He was most likely master to Benjamin and Timothy Cheney of East Hartford.

On Youngs' death his working tools and utensils were willed to his sons Benjamin, Joseph, and Seth. Benjamin (1736–1818) continued his father's business in Windsor until about 1766, when he moved to Schenectady, New York. Late in life he and his family joined the Shakers at Watervliet, New York, and he made some clocks for the group.

Enos Doolittle, nephew and apprentice to Isaac Doolittle of New Haven, set up business in Hartford in 1772. Doolittle made clocks until the time of the Revolution; afterward he became more involved with watch repairing, bell casting, and the making of mariners' compasses. Ebenezer Balch (1723–1808) was a native of Boston and trained there, but came to Hartford about 1744, where he worked until 1756, when he moved to Wethersfield. Jacob Sargeant (1761–1843) was a clockmaker and goldsmith at Mansfield, but went to Springfield, Massachusetts, where he worked from 1787 to 1795. He settled in Hartford in 1796 and carried on a successful business there for many years.

The town of Litchfield, a prosperous social center in the western part of the state, had several clockmakers, the earliest being Timothy Barnes, Jr., (1749–1825) and Miles Beach (1743–1828). Some evidence suggests these men were trained by Macock Ward of Wallingford. Barnes was engaged in the making of both brass- and wood-movement tall clocks and Beach manufactured brass clocks and metal items. Beach worked in Litchfield from about 1765 to 1785 and then in Hartford, in partnership with Isaac Sanford, an engraver, from 1785 to 1788.

Benjamin Hanks (1755–1824) moved from Windham, Connecticut, to Litchfield about 1780; in 1783, he petitioned for a patent concerning a remarkable clock that was said to be wound automatically—by air. The Connecticut General Assembly granted a patent, and this curious invention, the air clock, was mentioned in a newspaper advertisement of 1787, but examples do not seem to have survived. The clock was apparently not as functional as Hanks claimed. Hanks left Litchfield in 1790 and returned to Mansfield; in later life he moved to Albany, New York.

East of the Connecticut river, in the northern town of Woodstock; Peregrine White (1747–1834) and Asa Sibley (1764–1829) worked. White produced white-dial and engraved brass-dial tall clocks, some of them musical. Sibley worked in Woodstock after 1785; in Walpole, New Hampshire, after 1800; and finally in Rochester, New York. He had been preceded to Walpole by Gurdon Huntington (1763–1804), who had, from 1784 to 1789, worked in Windham, Connecticut. Though some New Hampshire-made Huntington clocks are extant, none made by Sibley after he left Connecticut has been found. Sibley and Huntington must have been well acquainted, however, because Sibley administered the latter's estate in 1804.

John Avery (1732–94) began work after 1750 in Preston, Connecticut. Avery undoubtedly conducted the largest business in western Connecticut before Thomas Harland established his business in Norwich. He trained his sons William and Christopher in the art, but clocks by them are rare. William became a noted silversmith in Stonington, Connecticut.

Another John Avery (1762–1843) worked in

Plainfield, Connecticut, and made a few clocks. He was, however, more active in the manufacture of surveyors' instruments. About 1796 he moved to Bridgewater, New York, where he made instruments and worked as a silversmith.

Thomas Jackson settled before the Revolution in a part of Preston, Connecticut, now known as Griswold. He was supposedly an Englishman, born in 1727, and was working by 1760 in Portsmouth, New Hampshire, and in neighboring Kittery, Maine. Prior to 1775, he had settled in Preston, where his son, Thomas, Jr., (1775–1853) was born in February of that year. Jackson is mentioned in the accounting records of the Portsmouth and Kittery area from 1778 to 1781, but whether he returned to the area or had long-range business dealings from Preston is not known. His clocks are quite handsome and have nicely engraved brass dials. It is not known who constructed cases for him, but they are among the most handsome made in Connecticut.

In August, 1875, an article was carried by the *Norwich Weekly Courier* that sheds some light on Jackson's activities:

> His residence and shop were situated at the east end of what is now known as Pachaug plain in Griswold. He is remembered by several of the oldest inhabitants of that part of the town. One of them says when he was a boy he loved to go to Mr. Jackson's workshop occasionally to see him work on clocks. A few of his cheaper clocks struck only one strike when the hour came round for striking. He made a clock that was quite a curiosity for those days. On a small shelf attached to the clock was a metallic image of a bull, and when the clock warned a few minutes before the regular time for striking the hour, the bull rose on his feet, and when the time for striking came, there appeared a butcher with an axe raised with which he knocked the bull down, in which position he remained until the time for warning again, when he rose to his feet as before. Another of the old residents says he remembers attending Mr. Jackson's funeral and thinks he was buried in the cemetery on Pachaug plain, but if he had any tombstone it is so overgrown with moss that the inscription cannot be read.

Thomas Jackson died in Preston on November 22, 1806, at the age of seventy-nine. His son, Thomas, Jr., did not continue the clockmaking business.

Reuben Ingraham (1743–1811) worked with Thomas Jackson for a time at Preston, and was possibly an apprentice. Ingraham settled at Plainfield, Connecticut, before 1790 and made a limited number of tall clocks. He was a descendant of the Ingraham or Ingham family of Saybrook, Connecticut, and was in no way related to the Ingraham family of Bristol, who became prominent in the age of manufacturing.

**61.** Striped maple Norwich-style tall clock made by Thomas Jackson, Preston, CT, c. 1790. (*Courtesy, John S. Walton*)

64

## THE FORERUNNER OF MANUFACTURING— THOMAS HARLAND

Although he began work before the Revolution, Thomas Harland of Norwich, Connecticut, must be considered the forerunner of the era of manufacturing. His career in America spanned less than thirty-five years and yet he probably produced more tall clocks than any artisan in Connecticut—perhaps even in the country—up to that time. He kept several apprentices busy at work in his shop throughout his career, and in his years of production trained more than fifteen men. To have achieved the production he did, he undoubtedly contributed to the progress made in standardizing parts for tall clocks. It is also probable that he was the first man to construct watches in America.

Harland was born in England in 1735. Having learned his clockmaking skills in his native land, he came to the American colonies in 1773, at a time when tensions were mounting between the colonies and the mother country. A family story, related by Harland's grandson in 1872, says he came over on one of the ships carrying the tea that was later dumped into the Boston harbor during the Boston Tea Party.

Finding the tensions in Boston not to his liking, Harland remained only briefly. He traveled south to Norwich, Connecticut, a manufacturing center of about 7,500 inhabitants, and set up a shop. On December 9, 1773, in the *Norwich Packet*, he advertised:

> Thomas Harland, Watch and Clockmaker from London, begs leave to acquaint the public that he has opened a shop near the store of Christopher Leffingwell in Norwich, where he makes in the neatest manner and on the most approved principles, horizontal, repeating and plain watches in gold, silver, metal or covered cases. Spring, musical and plain clocks; church clocks; regulators, &c. He also cleans and repairs watches and clocks with the greatest care and dispatch, and upon reasonable terms.
>
>     N.B. Clock faces engraved and finished for the trade. Watch wheels and fuzees [fusees] of all sorts and dimensions, cut and finished upon the shortest notice, neat as in London, and at the same price.

It is unfortunate that research into Harland's life has yet to reveal just what his English training and background was. His advertisement stated that he was "from London," but it should be remembered that London was considered the focal point of fine clockmaking and watchmaking in England, and most immigrant artisans attempting to establish themselves in the colonies would have wisely claimed London training.

In any case, it is important to note that Harland's initial advertisement claimed he was not only adept at making and repairing watches and clocks, but also at making musical and spring-driven clocks, as well as church or tower clocks and regulators. In 1773, English-style spring-driven table clocks were rare in the colonies. A few were imported from England and a limited number were manufactured domestically, mostly in Boston and Philadelphia.

Since Harland had gear- and fusee-cutting machinery for clocks and watches, it is apparent he brought these and probably other tools from England. For, with growing tensions between England and the colonies, a trade boycott was effected, and as the Revolution neared, it became increasingly difficult, if not impossible, to import tools, watches, or the various castings, dials, or case embellishments for clocks. The artisan had to rely almost totally on his manufacturing skills.

Harland occupied the Leffingwell shop for about five years. On April 30, 1778, he purchased land and a shop from David Nevins of Norwich and most likely moved his business into it soon after. By 1787, his business was flourishing, and on August 3 of that year he purchased land just to the north of his recently built home, and either built a new shop there or, more probably, moved into an existing building. Here he remained until one fateful Friday—December 11, 1795—when a fire totally destroyed the property. The *Norwich Packet* of the following Thursday reported:

> Between the hours of eleven and twelve on Friday evening last, the valuable clock and watch manufactory belonging to Mr. Thomas Harland of this city, was discovered to be on fire; the destructive element was raging with such fury before it was discovered as to render all exertions for preserving any part of the building totally abortive. Attempts were made to get out some of the most valuable articles but it was found wholly impracticable to save any thing whatever. — the building had a small insurance upon it; but the loss at a low valuation is computed at 1,500 dollars! through the calmness of the night and the spirited exertions of the citizens the flames were prevented from communicating to any of the adjoining buildings.

After this disaster, Harland reestablished his trades in the old shop to the south of his house, which he still owned, and continued business until his death.

It is ironic to note that seven years earlier, in 1788, Harland had been employed by the town of Norwich to build a new fire engine.

Harland was not only an accomplished clockmaker, watchmaker, and mechanic, but also excelled as a gold- and silversmith and engraver. Numerous fine pieces of silver have been found, usually marked with an eagle and bearing his name enclosed within a rectangular border.

Engraving, especially of clock dials, must

have been an important part of the business, because Harland advertised this service on occasion. The dial of one of his clocks, probably an early example, has applied spandrels and chapter, with an elaborately engraved center. A boss, engraved "Thos Harland, Norwich," is in the arch. In England this style of dial was popular after 1760. Most of Harland's dials, however, were single-piece sheets of brass that were completely engraved, including the spandrels and chapter. The latter style was becoming popular in England about the time of his emigration; Harland apparently found it extremely popular with his American customers, for he used it beyond 1800, long after the style had become obsolete in England. One feature of Harland's dials was the use of four visible screws for attachment rather than the more elaborate nonvisible method. It was an unusual method, even for English makers, and it is thought that Harland initiated its use in America.

Harland passed his engraving skills on to his apprentices, the most notable being Daniel Burnap, and they, in turn, supplied dials to makers less skillful in the art of engraving. At least two makers, Joseph Carpenter of Norwich and John Avery of Preston, are known to have used Harland's style of dial on some of their clocks, although they began clockmaking before Harland arrived in the country. However, as both of the men were in business after 1773, it is believed they either adopted the style in their later careers or purchased the engraved dials they used from him.

At least two clocks known to have been made by Harland have painted white-enameled dials. This type of dial was being imported as early as 1780, but it was not especially popular in Connecticut until the nineteenth century. One of Harland's white-dial clocks has a musical mechanism and plays six tunes.

In a history of Norwich published in 1866, Miss Frances Caulkins states that Harland produced forty clocks and two hundred watches annually, but it is likely that the passage of seventy-five years had inflated these figures. Even though Harland was the most prolific clockmaker in Connecticut before 1800—with the possible exception of Daniel Burnap—it is doubtful his production was more than twenty or twenty-five clocks a year.

It is possible that he sold as many as two hundred watches a year, but he did not make the majority of them. There are, however, at least two examples known with "T. Harland" engraved on them. During the war with England, Harland advertised that he made watches, but in peacetime, he indicated he was marketing imported examples.

In his declining years, Harland turned over

**62.** Musical bracket clock with moon-phase dial made by Thomas Harland, Norwich, CT, *c.* 1780. Movement removed in photo. *(Courtesy, Mrs. Rose P. Brandt)*

most of his business to his oldest son, Thomas, Jr. By 1802, when the younger Harland turned twenty-one, his father was nearing seventy and undoubtedly was looking forward to the day when he could retire and leave the business to Thomas, Jr., and a younger son, Henry. But his hopes were cut short. Four years later, on November 27, 1806, Thomas, Jr., died.

His estate included twenty-four gold-cased and ninety-three silver-cased watches of English, Irish, and French manufacture. His sixteen-year-old brother, Henry, cleaned and prepared a number of them for sale, and charged the estate $5.13 for the service. The one hundred seventeen watches were appraised at $1,618, but brought only $1,256.24 at auction.

The elder Harland paid Bliss Corning one pound ten shillings for a good coffin and had his son laid in an unmarked plot in the Norwich burying ground, across the meadow from the homestead. Four months and fourteen days later, the master craftsman followed his son to the grave.

Many of the larger Connecticut newspapers carried a death notice, but the most interesting of them was the one in the *Connecticut Gazette*, which stated: "Died at Norwich, Mr. Thomas Harland, aged seventy-two, Goldsmith; he is said to have made the first watch ever manufactured in America."

Mrs. Hannah Harland paid Caleb Huntington twelve dollars to prepare a sandstone marker to carry the following epitaph:

> This monument perpetuates the memory of Thomas Harland and Thomas Harland Junr. Thomas Harland departed this life March 31st 1807 aged 72 years. Thomas Harland Junr died Nov. 17th 1806 aged 25 years.
>
> *Here age & youth a common doom have found.*
> *And both be mingled in this hallow'd ground.*

The monument, greatly deteriorated, its verse almost illegible, still stands.

Harland's estate was appraised at $3,585.36, a total that included $57.67 worth of tinware, $385.74 worth of clocks, watches, and jewelry, and $286.82 worth of tools for making these products.

Finished eight-day clocks were valued at $40, uncased movements at $25, and cases at $15.

Of Harland's six children, only Henry is known to have carried on the business after his father's death. By 1813, he had moved to Boston, where he conducted a watch-repairing and jewelry business with William Adams. By 1822, he had returned to Norwich, but soon after moved to New Orleans, where he continued business until about 1830. He then returned to Norwich, residing in the Harland homestead until his death in 1841. None of the grandchildren is known to have pursued the business.

Harland trained many men over the thirty-four years he was active in Norwich, and they in turn spread their talents throughout New England. The first of these apprentices—and the most renowned—was Daniel Burnap, who settled at East Windsor, Connecticut.

Others of importance were Nathaniel Shipman (1764–1853) of Norwich, David Greenleaf, Jr., (1765–1835) of Hartford, and Ezra Dodge (1766–98) of New London.

**63.** Movement of Harland musical bracket clock. Note unusual type of pinwheel escapement. *(Courtesy, Mrs. Rose P. Brandt)*

## DANIEL BURNAP

During Burnap's active twenty-five years of clock-making, he, like his master, produced a considerable number of clocks. He probably also utilized an early method of standardization and interchangeability of parts, which he passed on to Eli Terry, his most noted apprentice.

Burnap, a native of Coventry, Connecticut, was born on November 1, 1759. He was apprenticed to Thomas Harland about 1774, when he was fourteen years old, and had completed his training by July of 1780. Soon after, Burnap moved to East Windsor, Connecticut, and before 1786 had established himself in a shop near Bissell's Tavern as a clockmaker, watch repairer, silversmith, and brass founder.

A survey of Burnap's accounting records still in existence shows that by 1790 his business consisted of watch repairing and production of brass hardware, with occasional orders for clocks or engraving of brass clock dials. Occasionally he received orders for surveyors' instruments. Gold and silver jewelry, silver spoons, and buckles of many styles were also a significant part of his business. For fifteen years after he left Harland, his business continued to flourish; he produced a greater number of tall clocks than any of his local contemporaries.

In April of 1785, Burnap acquired a farm in Coventry; he moved his home to the place the following spring. Some clocks are known that were made in Coventry; one known example is marked "Andover."

In about 1805, Burnap retired from active clock manufacturing, though he may have made a clock now and then on special order. He moved into a new home and turned the attic into a workshop. He perhaps felt that his jewelry and repairing business was sufficient to supplement his farming activities, and support him in his later years.

An accident in about 1826 resulted in a broken hip and as a consequence he was lame the last years of his life. He died in 1838. The *Connecticut Observer* of October 27 carried the following death notice:

> At Andover, Sept. 26, after a short and severe illness, Daniel Burnap Esq. aged 78. Though at an advanced period of life, he died in the midst of usefulness: — a kind husband and father, a highly valued and respected citizen, and an exemplary christian. To his seasonable liberality a small congregation are deeply indebted for their present prosperity.

On his death, Burnap left his chime clock and pocket watch to his fourteen-year-old son. The clock is now on exhibit at the Wadsworth Athenaeum in Hartford. Parts of an unfinished musical, or chime, clock were found among the tools he left.

Burnap's apprentices were many and included Flavel Bingham, Abiel Bliss, Ela Burnap, Lewis Curtis, Daniel Kellogg, Thomas Lyman, Nathaniel Olmstead, Levi Pitkin, Harvey Sadd, and the notable Eli Terry.

**64.** Dial of musical tall clock by Daniel Burnap, East Windsor, CT, made *c.* 1790. This example plays six different tunes. (*Edward Ingraham Library*)

**65.** Movement of Burnap musical chime clock. Note cluster of eleven bells and pinned barrel that actuates hammers to produce the tunes.

## THE CHENEYS

Wood clocks were not unique to Connecticut in the eighteenth century, but the East Hartford area is the earliest section to which production of the crude thirty-hour wood movement can be traced. Some parts of Massachusetts, New Hampshire, and Maine had limited production of this primitive style of clock movement, but only after 1750 and in many cases after the Revolution.

Benjamin Cheney, Jr., (1725–1815) was probably the first maker of these wood-movement clocks in quantity, though it is possible others made them in small numbers before Cheney started business in East Hartford in about 1745. Cheney and his associates produced the clock until about 1800, but their product remained crude in comparison to the wood tall clock movement made by Terry and others after 1800.

For its time, Cheney's wood clock was an economically feasible alternative to the brass-movement clock. Though no figures survive as to the cost of a Cheney clock when first purchased, the one that stood in Moses Butler's tavern on Main Street in Hartford was inventoried as being worth fifteen dollars in 1801. Brass-movement clocks, including the case, then sold for about forty dollars.

Cheney's early training is uncertain, though it is now believed that Seth Youngs of Hartford was his master. From all the evidence, Cheney took the initiative in developing a wood-movement clock that could be produced from cheaper materials and would require less work. Though crude in construction, his clocks did keep time.

Early wood clocks had brass dials and were as handsome as the brass-movement clocks of the day. The dials did not reveal that Cheney clocks had wood movements, but the cases often did. Because of the depth needed for the large wood movements, the cases had deep hoods that often made them appear disproportionate and top-heavy.

Cheney's wood clocks were made by the old method of finishing one clock at a time. Wheels were planed and teeth sawed by hand. Escape wheels were cut of thin steel and balanced by an inserted lead plug. Examination of some of these clocks causes one to wonder how they were able to run.

But the Cheney style filled the need for a less-expensive clock and its success attracted others into manufacture of the product. Many of the clocks produced later in the century have painted dials or paper ones glued onto wood dial plates; many of them are unsigned. As time went on, some makers added refinements. It would be fallacious, however, to say that all crude examples are early. One with a paper dial dated 1789, made by Dr. Thomas Sadd of East Windsor, Connecticut, is the most primitive this author has seen. The teeth on the wheels of the movement show hardly any uniformity in either size or shape. One would hope the doctor cut with greater skill and care into his patients than he did into his clock wheels.

Cheney trained several sons—Asahel, Elisha, Martin, and Russell—as well as other apprentices. John Fitch, pioneer inventor of the steamboat, was apprenticed to Cheney and recorded the following about him:

> My master was a pretty good sort of man, but possessed with a great many oddities and considerably deformed with the rickets in his youth, especially his head which was near double the size of common proportions and was a man of considerable genious . . . Benjamin Cheney followed nothing in the shop but wooden clocks and small brass work, and my indentures was ambigously exprest that he was to learn me clockwork and brass foundering. Before this time I had found my mistake and that he was not obliged to learn me anything but Wooden Clocks which he paid no attention to but kept me almost the whole of the time that I was in the shop at trifling pottering brass work, and was when I left him almost totally ignorant of clockwork.

During the Revolution, Benjamin Cheney made nails and tacks and, later, screws for guns being made by Simeon North of Berlin, Connecticut. In later years he went to Berlin and lived with his son, Elisha. He became extremely feeble, both physically and mentally, and had to use two canes prior to his death at the age of ninety.

His son Elisha (1770–1847) had moved to Berlin about 1793 and was producing brass and wood clocks. By 1800, he had gone into partnership with his brother-in-law, Simeon North, in the manufacture of pistols. In 1801, he purchased another shop and is said to have turned out wood clocks in quantity, though these must have been unmarked and are not readily identifiable today. Together with his son Olcott (1796–1860), Elisha produced some shelf clocks. He left Connecticut about 1835, first settling in Lima, New York, and afterward in Roscoe, Illinois, where he died at seventy-eight.

His son Olcott made wood shelf clocks in Berlin and Middletown for several years after 1830. A bond is extant in which he contracted with Henry A. Miller to furnish in monthly installments a thousand dollars' worth of clockfaces "equal in quality and workmanship to Jerome and Darrow clockfaces."

Timothy Cheney (1731–95), Benjamin's brother, was also a maker, producing brass and wood clocks; he was in the watch-repairing business, as well. John Fitch, who had been apprenticed to Benjamin, worked for Timothy, and wrote of his work:

**66.** Cheney-style wood tall clock movement and dial made in eastern Connecticut *c.* 1750. Huge movement measures 10 by 12 inches. *(American Clock & Watch Museum)*

Timothy Cheney followed making brass and wooden clocks and repaired watches, and agreed to take me for one year and learn me the three branches. I was set to work at small brass work with the exception of being shortly put to clock work and going out once in a while to work on his place and at his shop which he was building that summer, tending on masons, carpenters, &c. I was not put to one single clock, neither wood nor brass, during that time. It is true I did begin one wooden one, but never had time to finish it.

As to watch work, I never saw one put together during my apprenticeship, and when I attempted to stand by him to see him put one together, I was always ordered to my work, and what was the most singular of all, it was but seldom that I could get to see his tools for watch work, as he had a drawer where he was always particularly careful to lock them up. He never told me the different parts of a watch, and to this day I am ignorant of the names of many parts.

Fitch does not portray the Cheneys as able instructors, but only one side of the story has been told. Besides Benjamin's four sons, a nephew, Daniel White Griswold (1767–1844), was apprenticed to them. He made several wood-movement examples with engraved sheet-brass dials tacked to a wood dial plate, a method similar to that used by Eli Terry on his early wood movements after the Cheney style.

# EXPANSION IN THE COLONIES

## DELAWARE

After 1740, tall clocks were handcrafted in Delaware, particularly in Wilmington. Some tall clocks were made in the state until the mid-nineteenth century, but never in great quantity. Once manufacturing became prevalent in New England, the craft ceased and clock manufacturing was never again attempted in the state.

Settled by the Swedes in 1638, Delaware was taken over by the Dutch in 1655. Nine years later, British forces took the colony, and there was an influx of settlers from nearby British colonies.

Some clocks were undoubtedly in the colony during Swedish and Dutch possession, but it is not known if there were any clockmakers who worked there during the period. When makers did appear, most settled in Wilmington, the most populous town. William Furniss, one of the earliest Delaware makers, was working in the 1740s, and one known clock made in New Castle County is marked "S. Evans & Wm. Furniss." There is no further information about Evans.

Benjamin Chandlee, formerly of Philadelphia and Nottingham, Maryland, had settled in Wilmington by 1741 and was probably the master of some of the earliest Delaware makers.

George Crow, brother of William Crow of nearby Salem, New Jersey, was an early maker in Wilmington. He was at work by 1754 and continued to work there until his death, shortly after 1770. His son George, Jr., carried on the business until his death in 1802. Another son, Thomas Crow, worked in Wilmington until 1808, when he moved to West Chester, Pennsylvania. About 1810 he returned to Wilmington and worked there until his death in 1824.

Jonas Alrichs (1759–1802) of Wilmington was probably an apprentice to Thomas Crow. When Alrichs retired from business in 1797, he put the following notice in the *Delaware Gazette:*

> NOTICE—I take this method of returning my sincere thanks to the public for the encouragement I have received in the Clock and Watchmaking Business. As I have this day resigned the same, I request all those who have any demands against me to present them for settlement; and those who are indebted to discharge the same.
>
> JONAS ALRICHS
>
> Wilmington, April 6, 1797

Jacob Alrichs (1775–1857), nephew and apprentice to Jonas, worked with his uncle until the latter's retirement. He advertised for an apprentice on April 15, 1797, and stated also that he "has received in addition to the stock already on hand, eight-day clocks of the first quality; silver watches from London, Liverpool, and Dublin, such as can be warranted, watch main springs,

glasses, dials, gilt and steel chains, keys, seals, &c, &c." In 1816, he started a machine shop with Samuel McClary and moved his clock business to another location in Wilmington. McClary had also been apprenticed to Thomas Crow and had conducted a clockmaking business from 1803 to 1816.

Ziba Ferris, Jr., (1786–1875) was trained by his brother Benjamin, a clock- and watchmaker of Philadelphia. By 1808, Ziba had opened a shop at Fourth and Market Streets in Wilmington, where he made tall clocks. He had several apprentices, including his son Ziba Ferris III, Charles Canby, Joseph Haslet, Thomas J. Megear, and William F. Rudolph.

Ferris' first—perhaps best known—apprentice was Charles Canby (1792–1883). Canby, a native of Philadelphia, bought out the Jacob Alrichs store at Third and Market Streets in Wilmington, where he worked until his retirement in 1852.

After the 1840s, when manufacturing replaced handcrafting methods, Canby must have busied himself with repair work rather than clock construction. Few makers worked outside the town of Wilmington, but Duncan Beard of Appoquinimink Hundred noted that he was a clockmaker when purchasing land in 1767. Tall clocks made by him are known, and he apparently continued in the profession for the duration of his life. His will, dated June 29, 1797, began, "I Duncan Beard, CLOCK MAKER, of Appoquinimink Hundred . . ." Beard was in partnership with Christopher Weaver for a time. After the partnership was dissolved, Weaver ran a business in Georgetown, Delaware.

## MARYLAND

Because colonial Maryland had strong connections with Pennyslvania, the Philadelphia school had great influence on Maryland clockmaking. After 1712, when Benjamin Chandlee, who had apprenticed in Philadelphia, moved his family to Nottingham, Maryland began more than a century and a quarter of clockmaking activity. During the eighteenth century the craft was centered primarily in the towns of Annapolis and Baltimore.

After the Revolution, Hagerstown became a focal point of growth; as migrants from Pennsylvania and the mid-Atlantic area moved down the Shenandoah valley toward the southern states, they passed through the town and many settled there.

Many people believe that Benjamin Banneker (1731–1806) was Maryland's first clockmaker. Banneker—who was one quarter white and three quarters Negro—was certainly an important astronomer and mathematician, but not actually a professional clockmaker. He did some repair work and constructed one striking clock about 1753 for his own use. Of his own design, the clock employed wooden gears and was apparently used until it was destroyed by the fire that consumed Banneker's home while his funeral was in progress in October, 1806.

At Annapolis, several men conducted small businesses, but the first clockmaker of much note was William Faris. He was born August 17, 1728, in London, son of a clock- and watchmaker who died in prison because of his Quaker beliefs. His widowed mother left England with him shortly afterward, and they settled in Philadelphia. Here young Faris was raised and eventually trained as a clockmaker, watch repairman, and silversmith.

Faris advertised in the *Maryland Gazette* on March 17, 1757:

> William Faris, watch maker from Philadelphia, at his shop near the Church, next door to Mr. Wallace's, in Church-Street, Annapolis, cleans and repairs all sorts of watches and clocks, as well and neat as can be done in any Part of America; And takes the same Prices for his Work as are taken in Philadelphia. He also makes Clocks, either to Repeat or not, or to go either Eight Days or Thirty, as the Purchaser shall fancy, as good as can be made in London, and at reasonable prices. And all Gentlemen who shall be pleased to employ him, may depend on having their Work done with all possible Dispatch, by Their Humble Servant, William Faris.

In 1763, Faris advertised that he had employed an apprenticed silversmith from Philadelphia and thus was able to supply silver work at reasonable rates. In 1770, he added chair making to his business, and in 1792, he announced that he had secured competent workmen and was preparing to make frames for oil portraits as well as looking glasses.

In 1791, a rumor was spread that Faris had died. The rumor had been started as a consequence of a poem written by his daughter's friend, Charlotte Hesselius, who was the nineteen-year-old daughter of John Hesselius, a portrait painter. Faris first thought the rumor had been started by a business rival, Abraham Claude, who had been working in Annapolis since 1773. Apparently upset by the rumor, though he may have been more interested in the opportunity for publicity, Faris published the following notice:

> To the PUBLIC
> WHEREAS certain evil-disposed Persons have knowingly, wickedly, and maliciously, counterfeited the Subscriber's last Will and Testament, which was introductive of an erroneous Propagation, in several Counties of this State, that he departed this life some Time in June last; and, as further Indication of their malicious Disposition, they published, or caused to be published, a Funeral Sermon (possessed of very injurious Contents) to be delivered over his Body; both of which Circumstances, combined together, tend to very pernicious Consequences to the Subscriber's Trade and Manner of obtaining a Livelihood, by the Desertion of a considerable Degree of Custom which would otherwise have resorted to him—to detect Falsehood, disappoint Malice, and prevent further injury to himself, he hereby certifies to the Public, that such Propagations are not true, and hopes that no Person will pay the least Degree of Attention whatever to them, as they were only circulated to impair and injure the Subscriber's Trade; and the Public may rest assured, that he now remains in good Health, and full of Vigour of Life, in West Street, Annapolis, opposite Mr. Abraham Claud's, where he means to persevere in the Business of WATCH and CLOCK MAKING, in all its various Arts and Branches, and solicits once more the Patronage of a generous Public.
> WILLIAM FARIS

Annapolis, July 24, 1791

Faris was an interesting character for other reasons. His diary, which begins on January 4, 1792, contains some seven hundred pages of comments on events in the lives of the people around him—some quite spicy. With his candid records of some of the most prominent families of Annapolis and Baltimore, he might well be dubbed the town gossip.

Faris had a Negro apprentice whom he spoke of in his diary as "negro Charles." In the *Maryland Journal*, November 9, 1778, he advertised:

> To be sold, a very likely young negro fellow, by trade a silversmith, jeweler, and lapidary; there are few if any better workmen in America; any person inclined to purchase the said negro may know further by applying to the subscriber living in Annapolis.
> WILLIAM FARIS

**68.** Painted dial from preceding Jacob Alrichs clock. Jacob continued the business when his uncle and master, Jonas Alrichs, retired in April, 1797.

**69.** Dial and hood of magnificently cased tall clock by Rudolph Spangler, *c.* 1775. Made at York, PA, or Hagerstown, MD. *(Edward Ingraham Library)*

**70.** Movement, dial, and pendulum bob of eight-day musical chime clock by William Faris, clockmaker and silversmith of Annapolis, MD. *(Edward Ingraham Library)*

**71.** Complete and cased musical clock by William Faris. Engraved brass dial was painted over and decorated after painted dials became fashionable.

71

Faris' apprentices included three of his four sons. William III (b. 1762) established a business at Norfolk, Virginia, in 1790, but a few years thereafter went to Havana, Cuba. In 1797 he relocated at Edenton, North Carolina, and conducted a business there until after 1800.

Charles Faris (1764–1800) worked as a watchmaker and silversmith, but died at thirty-six from yellow fever. Hyrum Faris (1769–1800) also worked in the trade after 1793. Hyrum and his father had serious disagreements and the younger Faris left home in 1800 and died during a voyage to Amsterdam.

Faris himself died at Annapolis on August 5, 1804, at seventy-six. His inventory of clock and watchmaking tools was extensive.

William McParlin, who became a noted silversmith in Annapolis after 1800, had originally been apprenticed to Charles Faris, but on the latter's death, he completed his training under the father, William.

Other clockmakers in Maryland include John Powell, John Finley, William Thompson, Patrick Sinnott, John Burrage, Jacob Moehler, and David Evans, who was a nephew of David Rittenhouse.

## VIRGINIA

The Virginia colony, which was settled in 1607, had by 1700 about eight thousand persons living in the tidewater region. By 1754, there were two hundred and eighty-four thousand, and by 1800 over a million. But despite its sizable population and great social activity, Virginia did not have comparable activity in clockmaking. The lack of local artisans must have been due to the close social and economic ties the colony had to England before the Revolution. Clocks were apparently imported from England in sufficient numbers to supply those of the gentry who desired time-keeping devices.

Samuel Rockwell (1722–73) from Providence, Rhode Island, is the first maker known in the area, having established himself at Hampton by 1752. During October of that year he advertised in *The Virginia Gazette* at Williamsburg:

> SAMUEL ROCKWELL MAKES, cleans and mends all Sorts of Clocks and Watches, in the neatest Manner, and at a reasonable Rate, in Hampton, Virginia, who has at present two good Clocks to sell, at Mr. Finnie's in Williamsburg.

Rockwell remained in Virginia only a few years, later going to Philadelphia; he returned to his native Middletown, Connecticut, about 1760.

There was some handcrafting of clocks in the larger centers of Fredericksburg, Williamsburg, and Richmond even before 1800, but in no way did it equal the cabinetmaking and other arts that thrived in the area. After 1825, clockmaking was practically nonexistent in the state, which probably accounts for the fact that in that year, Thomas Jefferson commissioned Simon Willard of Boston to construct a clock for the rotunda of the University of Virginia. Undoubtedly, Jefferson would have chosen a local maker had he been able to locate one capable of performing the task.

Fredericksburg, now in Spottsylvania County, was the home of Thomas Walker, who made clocks from about 1760 to 1780, and John Weidemeyer, who worked as a clockmaker from about 1790 to 1820. Walker's tall clocks and a few bracket clocks are among the most sophisticated examples made in the south during that period. Nearby, in Stafford County, Edward West was making tall clocks, but by 1788 he had moved to the Kentucky territory of Virginia, which later became Fayette County, Kentucky.

Williamsburg, James City County, was the early capital of the colony and a center of political and social activity before and during the Revolution. Robert Egan and James Craig were working there about 1770 and James Galt conducted business there about 1800.

Richmond, in Henrico County, had at least three clockmakers by 1820: William Cowan, George Downing, and John Fasbender. Except what can be gleaned from their advertising notices, little is known of these men. South of Richmond at Petersburg, Thomas F. Adams from Baltimore worked from about 1804 until 1809, when he moved to Edenton, North Carolina. William Faris III (b. December 5, 1762), a third-generation clockmaker from Annapolis, Maryland, settled in Norfolk, Virginia, in 1789 or 1790. He remained there less than five years, then worked for a while in Havana, Cuba, and finally moved to Edenton, North Carolina.

Caleb Bentley, a Pennsylvanian, settled in Leesburg, Loudoun County, near the Potomac river, at the turn of the nineteenth century. His brother, Eli Bentley, was an active clockmaker in Chester County, Pennsylvania, and in Taneytown, Maryland.

At the north end of the Shenandoah valley are the towns of Stevensburg (now Stevens City) and Winchester, Virginia. Goldsmith Chandlee, oldest son of Benjamin Chandlee, Jr., set up a business in the area in 1775. He purchased a lot on the corner of Piccadilly and Cameron Streets in Winchester and built a brass foundry and shop in which he made brass clocks, surveyors' instruments, sundials, and other metal items. He had a business in Winchester until his death in 1821.

Twenty miles northeast, between Winchester, Virginia, and Hagerstown, Maryland, lies the town of Shepherdstown, West Virginia. (The town was in Berkeley County, Virginia, until West Virginia was formed in 1861.) John Woltz and Jacob Craft are known to have worked here.

John Woltz was undoubtedly a close relative and trainee of George Woltz, who produced tall clocks in Hagerstown from about 1770 to 1813. Jacob Craft (1765–1825), a native of the Marburg region of southeastern Germany, came to Shepherdstown about 1790. He produced several handsome tall clocks before retiring in 1815.

## NORTH CAROLINA

North Carolina grew remarkably in the latter part of the eighteenth century, but it remained more or less rural and did not develop the type of social centers that attracted clockmakers in numbers. Though some examples are known, North Carolina clocks are scarce, as are records of those few men who ventured into the trade in that state.

In New Bern, a Swiss settlement, Marcel Boloquet is believed to have been making clocks before the Revolution. A man named De St. Leger advertised a clockmaking business there in 1790, as did Nathan Tisdale some five years later. William Tisdale was working in New Bern after 1816.

William Faris III, son and apprentice of William Faris of Annapolis, Maryland, settled in Edenton in 1797. In 1800, William wrote his father that he had a shop with forty or fifty watches in the window.

A William Hillard advertised in Fayetteville in 1805, and made note that he had an apprentice, William Dye. A George W. Hillard also advertised there, but not until after 1823.

During the 1830s some clocks carried labels stating that they were made in North Carolina. Occasionally labels such as Reeves & Huson of Fayetteville and L. M. Churchill & Company of the now extinct town of Hamburg are found. However, Connecticut clocks were being brought to the area in great numbers. The influx of these manufactured clocks undoubtedly ended the small amount of handcrafting carried on in the state.

## SOUTH CAROLINA

Charleston, South Carolina, settled in 1683 by a group of Episcopal dissenters who came from the county of Somerset, in England, grew to become one of the great cultural centers of eighteenth-century America. Clockmakers began to work in Charleston after 1720, and some handcrafted tall clocks were made there during the balance of the century, though their numbers were never great. Because Charleston was an important southern port, it is probable that most of the clocks in the colony at that time were imported. After 1800,

**72.** Magnificent engraved dial of center sweep seconds clock by Samuel Rockwell, probably made at Hampton, VA, where Rockwell advertised in 1752. (*Author's collection*)

clocks were brought into South Carolina from New England, and apparently the small amount of domestic clockmaking being done there soon ceased.

The earliest clockmaker on record was James Batterson, who worked in Charleston during the 1720s and had previously worked in Philadelphia, Boston, and New York.

South Carolina records are scant, and the names of many local clockmakers would have been lost had it not been for their newspaper advertising. Among the names that come down to us and the years they advertised: Delonguemaire (about 1720), Joseph Massey (1722–36), John Harris (1729–39), James Hillard (1730–49), Thomas Goodman (1733–38), and Peter Mowrove (1735–39). Since examples of their work have not survived, it is not known if these men made clocks or just repaired and marketed clocks and watches, though the latter was undoubtedly true in many cases.

Tall clocks by William Lee (1747–1803; working by 1768) and by Patrick Magann, who advertised as being "from Ireland" and had shops at several Charleston locations in the 1790s, are still in existence. Though possibly a marketed English-made item, a bracket clock exists bearing the name of John James Himeley, a Huguenot, who advertised in Charleston newspapers from 1786 to 1809 as a clockmaker and watchmaker.

After 1800, the handcrafted tall clock waned in popularity, though several concerns were in business in the larger towns in the state. It is probable that many of these were only repairmen and that others were southern distributors for the Connecticut wood clocks.

## GEORGIA

Clocks were handcrafted in all the original thirteen colonies with the possible exception of Georgia. Augustine Neisser may have made some clocks in the colony before he moved to Pennsylvania (c. 1740), but none has yet been discovered. Eighteenth-century Georgia was primarily a frontier, and the majority of inhabitants were engaged in "planting." Undoubtedly the small demand for timekeepers was satisfied by Charleston-made clocks or English imports.

English colonization of Georgia began in 1733; a few years later Swiss, Italians, Germans, Scottish Highlanders, Salzbergers, and Moravians began to arrive. Most of the Moravians, unable to convert the Indians to their faith, relocated in Pennsylvania. Among these was Augustine Neisser (b. 1717 in Sehlen, Moravia), who settled in Georgia in 1736. He moved to Germantown, Pennsylvania, a few years later and conducted a clockmaking business until his death in 1780. If Neisser was conducting his business during the

years he was in Georgia, examples do not seem to have survived.

In 1788, Georgia became the fourth state to enter the Union. But even Augusta and Savannah did not attract clockmakers, and clocks must have been extremely scarce in the region before 1800. Ten years later, Joel Catlin of Augusta, Nathan Cornwell of Darien, and the firm of Clapp & Company of Augusta were noted as makers, but most probably were peddling the northern-made wood clocks.

After 1830, with the increase of wood tall clock production in Connecticut, as well as Virginia, the Carolinas, and Tennessee, where manufacturing was also limited, northern salesmen scoured these southern states and the citizens became annoyed because of the amount of money being taken away by out-of-state businesses. Some of the states levied taxes on peddlers in an attempt to discourage their activities, but the northern firms often set up assembly plants within the states to avoid them. Though the components of the clocks were manufactured in New England, they could thereby claim the clocks were made in the south, and circumvent the tariffs.

One such wood clock distributor who located in the south in the 1830s was Asaph Hall (1800–42) of Goshen, Connecticut. He conducted extensive sales in Georgia and eastern Alabama, and when the state levied the tax, he organized an assembly plant in Clinton, Jones County, Georgia. Some clocks are in existence with a label claiming Clinton, Georgia, as the place of manufacture. Hall continued to sell wood shelf clocks and a few brass-movement ones in Georgia until his death in Clinton, on September 8, 1842.

After 1835 the firms of Case, Dyer, Wadsworth & Company of Augusta (later Dyer, Wadsworth & Company) were marketing clocks made by Birge & Mallory of Bristol, Seth Thomas of Plymouth Hollow, and other Connecticut firms. Labels on their clocks claim Augusta as the place of manufacture, which was most likely not true, since the northern-made parts were only assembled in that town.

## RHODE ISLAND

Although the smallest colony had early and important clockmaking activity during the handcrafting period, it did not develop into a manufacturing center after 1800. With few exceptions, clockmaking there was centered in the towns of Newport, Providence, and Westerly.

There was little clockmaking in Newport after 1750, but many fine cases were constructed there between 1750 and 1800. John Goddard (1723–85) and John Townsend (b. 1733) were noted local cabinetmakers and produced, as did their predecessors, many sophisticated clock cases. Some of these cases had imported English movements installed in them, but many of the Providence clockmakers also utilized their cases. Another firm, Palmer & Coe of Newport, produced some clock cases in Boston styles about 1800.

William Claggett was one of the most skillful horological craftsmen in New England in the first half of the eighteenth century. Some of his clocks have musical attachments and others have unusual additions, such as dials indicating high and low tides. Claggett also made musical instruments, and in 1736 set up a large organ in Christ Church, Newport.

He settled in Newport in 1716, having worked a few years previously in Boston. Born about 1696, Claggett was probably an Englishman, though some accounts say he was born in Wales. He was undoubtedly trained before his arrival at Boston prior to 1714.

In 1745, Claggett constructed a machine to produce electricity. In December, 1746, one newspaper reported that he had "succeeded so far in the Electrical Experiments, as to set fire to Spirits of Wine." Lengthy newspaper accounts not only gave evidence of the unusual abilities of the man, but affirmed that he was still active in his clockmaking business.

Claggett died at Newport on October 18, 1749, at the age of fifty-four, and was buried in the First Baptist churchyard.

Claggett had at least two apprentices, his son Thomas and his son-in-law James Wady. Thomas Claggett produced some tall clocks, and at least two dwarf tall clocks, or grandmother clocks, are extant. James Wady worked in Newport in the 1750s. Isaac Anthony seems to have been the only other man working there at that time.

Near the end of the eighteenth century, Benjamin Dudley and David Williams worked in Newport, but little is known of either of these men. The name of Williams, who also worked at Providence, is often found on clocks, though it is possible he was a merchant rather than a maker.

Though Providence was settled three years before Newport, in 1636, there appears to have been little clockmaking activity there until about 1740. Samuel Rockwell worked there awhile, but in 1752 moved to Hampton, Virginia. In 1770, Edward Spaulding (1732–85) worked there, as did his son, Edward, Jr. Spaulding was a prolific maker and often utilized fine Newport cases. Caleb Wheaton (1757–1827), a Quaker, began his work in Providence about 1785 and produced superb clocks, some also housed in Newport cases. Calvin and Godfrey Wheaton, undoubtedly relatives, also worked there about the same time.

Other important Providence clockmakers include two apprentices of Thomas Harland, Seril and Nehemiah Dodge. Makers also include Ezra Dodge, Saunders Pitman, John Carins, David Vintan, Ezekiel Burr, William Burr, Steven Williams, and Walter H. Durfee.

The town of Westerly, on the extreme southwestern border of the state, was the home of the Stillman family, who were producing tall clocks from about 1786 until after 1815. William Stillman (b. 1767) conducted a clockmaking business from 1786 to 1809. He moved to Burlington, Connecticut, in 1789, but returned to Westerly in 1792. His brother Willet Stillman (1777–1826) worked in Westerly from 1795 to 1798, but in that year moved to Whitesboro, New York, where he went into the ministry.

William Stillman was granted a patent on March 16, 1801, for a veneering plow, a machine "for cutting grooves in various forms and figures in Cabinetware to be filled with various colored wood for ornaments in said ware, and does it with much greater precision and dispatch than anything heretofore known: likewise for cutting the furrows in Cooper's ware and sundry other uses." Undoubtedly this device also could have been used for clock cases.

Paul Stillman (1782–1810) and his brother Barton were cousins of William and Willet. They carried on business in Westerly after the turn of the nineteenth century.

## NEW HAMPSHIRE

Both wood and brass clocks were made in New Hampshire during the handcrafting period, though brass was the more common. A number of inventive artisans made small numbers of clocks in peculiar styles of their own design; to cover each of these would require a book in itself. But the pioneering spirit of the early settlers shows in their work. Tall clocks were produced here as well as Massachusetts-style shelf clocks and banjo wall clocks. One design, a simple but handsome wall clock that became known as the "New Hampshire mirror clock," was developed here and made in considerable numbers after 1810.

New Hampshire was settled in the 1620s, but it was the mid-1700s before substantial growth took place. Clockmakers in the area before the Revolution were centered in the southeastern towns of Kensington, Portsmouth, and Chester.

The Purington family of Kensington are the first documented makers in New Hampshire. There is some evidence that Elisha Purington, Sr., a blacksmith and gunsmith, was the first of this family to make clocks. Two of his sons, Jonathan (1732–1816) and Elisha, Jr., (b. 1736), were actively making clocks after 1750. At twenty-two, Elisha, Jr., sold his shop to Nathaniel Healey, a blacksmith, and apparently did not continue the business, though his brother Jonathan was active for many years. Jonathan had a son, James (b. 1759),

who followed the business for some years in Kensington, but in 1816 moved to Marietta, Ohio. The Puringtons were Quakers, and one account claims their training was with Boston's Quaker clockmaker, Benjamin Bagnall.

Caleb Shaw (1717–91), who lived near the Purington shop, produced some tall clocks. One, dated 1749, is the oldest New Hampshire clock known. Jeremiah Fellows (1749–1837) ran a blacksmith and clock shop in Kensington after 1788 and was followed in business by his son, James.

In about 1760, Thomas Jackson (1727–1806), an English-trained clockmaker, was active in Portsmouth, New Hampshire, and in neighboring Kittery, Maine. Jackson apparently remained in this area only a few years and moved south, finally settling in Preston, Connecticut, where he conducted business in the latter part of the century.

Inland a few miles, in the town of Chester, Isaac Blaisdell (1738–91) was working after 1762. He produced the unusual posted-style-movement tall clock that had been a product of his father, David Blaisdell, in Amesbury, Massachusetts. Isaac produced these in the thirty-hour variety for the most part, though he did make a limited number of eight-day examples. His son Richard (1762–90) produced a small number of clocks during his short career. Isaac's younger brother, Nicholas Blaisdell, lived in Newmarket, New Hampshire, from about 1764 to 1774, producing clocks there before moving on to Maine.

For over fifty years after the Revolution, brass tall clocks were produced in several parts of the state. Abner Jones worked in the town of Weare. (He is not the same Abner Jones who lived in East Bloomfield, New York, and produced an unusually large-style shelf clock of unique design.) Stephen Hassam, or Hasham (1764–1861), worked in Charlestown, New Hampshire, after 1787. His clocks were signed and numbered; clock number 50 has a brass dial with a painted lunette portion on which is an animated figure of a lady in a swing. Actuated by the escapement, the lady swings as the clock runs.

Clocks with similarly actuated rocking ships were commonly produced in Rochester, New Hampshire. Edward S. Moulton commenced business there in 1807 and James C. Cole (1791–1867) finished his apprenticeship with Moulton about 1812. Both men often produced clocks with the rocking ship. Elisha Smith, Jr., of Sanbornton, was another to adopt this feature on some of his tall clocks.

Benjamin Clark Gilman began making tall clocks in the town of Exeter about 1790. Jedediah Baldwin, an apprentice of Thomas Harland of Norwich, Connecticut, came to Hanover, New Hampshire, from Northampton, Massachusetts, in 1794 and carried on business until 1810, when

73. Maple-cased eight-day tall clock made c. 1795 near Westerly, RI, and attributed to the Stillman family of clockmakers. (Courtesy, Mrs. Amos G. Avery)

**74**

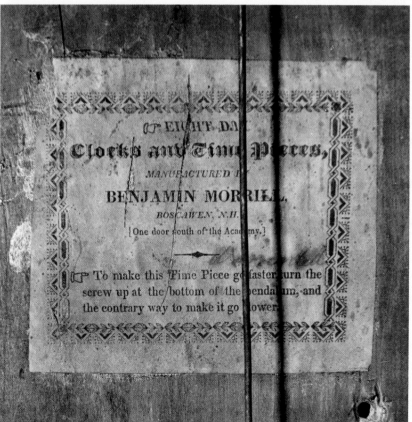

**75**

**74.** Eight-day timepiece movement developed by Benjamin Morrill of Boscawen, NH, for his New Hampshire-style mirror clocks. Note sparing use of brass for economy. **75.** Printed paper label from back of Benjamin Morrill mirror clock, *c.* 1820. *(Edward Ingraham Library)*

he sold out to John Robie and moved to upstate New York.

New Hampshire also had a number of wood clock makers. One of the earliest to produce wood movements was Jesse Emory (1759–1838) of Weare. Emory might have received instruction from Abner Jones of that town, but it is doubtful. Jones apparently produced only brass clocks and Emory only wood ones. Emory was certainly an ingenious artisan and his are probably the finest designed and -made wood-movement clocks in America. His plates and wheels were of maple, of unusually large size and thickness, and very finely finished. Some of his movements had wood covers fitted tightly around the plates to protect the inner movement from dust.

Robinson Perkins (1766–1837) worked in Jaffrey after 1790, producing wood clocks somewhat similar to those being made in Ashby, Massachusetts. He moved to the neighboring town of Fitzwilliam in 1810, and continued his business. One dial, numbered 148, shows that some of his wood clocks were more complicated than the usual ones. Besides the regular time-keeping dials, the clock had dials for the day of the week and of the month, and for the stage of the moon.

Timothy Gridley carried on the manufacture of wood tall clocks in the Connecticut pattern in Sanbornton for a few years after 1808. He sold the

**77.** Abel Hutchins (1763–1853) was trained by Simon Willard and in 1788 went to Concord, NH, where he made clocks for 30 years thereafter. *(Edward Ingraham Library)*

**76.** Animated dial from tall clock by Stephen Hasham of Charlestown, NH, made *c.* 1790. Note swinging lady in painted portion of dial. *(Edward Ingraham Library)*

business to Simeon Cate (1790–1835), who continued it, as well as manufacturing chairs and hats.

Another unusual style of clock, incorporating both brass and wood gears in the movement, was made in the town of Hollis. Abijah Gould (1777–after 1841) worked after 1800, making an unusual eight-day movement with wood plates and wood motion gears, but with brass gears and steel arbors and pinions between the plates. Another variation of this movement had only a wood great wheel and second wheel, metal having been used for the remaining wheels and pinions of the train. Several of these clocks carry Gould's name; a greater number are unmarked. One example is known with the name of Samuel Foster, who worked in Amherst, New Hampshire, until about 1810, when he bought a shop in Concord that had been run by John Robie.

About 1850, a craftsman named Harvey Ball (1818–1902) was working in Westmoreland, New Hampshire. Among his products was a large banjo-style wall clock, nearly fifty inches high, which looked similar to those being produced at the time by Howard & Davis of Boston, except that the movement was wood.

The capital, Concord, had clockmaking activity after 1775, when Ephraim Potter began to make wood clocks there.

**78.** Animated dial clock by E. S. Moulton, Rochester, NH, c. 1810. Ship in lunette of dial rocks as pendulum swings. *(Courtesy, Amos G. Avery)*

**79.** Posted-style one-day pull-up wind movement from tall clock by Richard Blaisdell, Chester, NH, *c.* 1785. **80.** Complete Richard Blaisdell clock. *(Courtesy, C. S. Parsons)*

**81.** New Hampshire-style mirror clock made by Joseph Chadwick, Boscawen, NH, c. 1820. *(Courtesy, Amos G. Avery)*

**82.** Unmarked New Hampshire mirror clock with only one wheel in striking train. *(Courtesy, Amos G. Avery)*

**83.** Massachusetts-style shelf clock made by Levi Hutchins, Concord, NH, c. 1815. *(Edward Ingraham Library)*

In 1788, Levi Hutchins (1761–1855) and his brother Abel (1763–1853) came to Concord from Roxbury, Massachusetts, where they had been apprenticed to Simon Willard. The handwritten indenture by which Gordon Hutchins bound his son Abel to Willard on December 6, 1777, is extant. In his autobiography, Levi Hutchins stated that he served three years apprenticeship under Willard and then went to Abington, Connecticut, where he served eight months to acquire some knowledge of watch repairing.

L. & A. Hutchins carried on business as a partnership until 1807. Levi wrote of the business in Concord:

My brother and I were successful in our business transactions and mutually enjoyed many other blessings. We carried on clockmaking together about twenty-one years. Our names may now be seen on the faces of many timekeepers, standing in the corners of sitting rooms in houses situated in all the New England States; and probably there are eight-day clocks, or timepieces of our manufacture, in all the original thirteen States of the Union. Two eight-day clocks we made to order and sent to the West Indies.

After the dissolution of the partnership, both men continued business on their own until retiring about 1819.

Timothy Chandler (1760–1848) also began business before 1800 in Concord and in that year built a factory in the town. The factory burned down in 1809—at a loss of over five thousand dollars, a very large sum for that time—but it was later rebuilt with assistance from the townspeople. Chandler made many tall clocks with brass and, later, painted dials. His clocks are often identified by the impression "T. Chandler" in the wooden seat board for the brass movement. Timothy took his apprentice and son, Abiel (1807–81), into the firm, renaming it T. Chandler & Son, but retired shortly afterward, in 1829. Abiel continued the business until about 1846, producing primarily mirror clocks and banjo clocks.

## THE NEW HAMPSHIRE MIRROR CLOCK

The New Hampshire-style mirror clock was possibly a development of Benjamin Morrill and Joseph Chadwick of Boscawen. The style was undoubtedly developed to offer an attractive and useful clock with a looking glass, but at a lower cost than the clocks selling in Boston. Morrill (1794–1857) worked from about 1816 to 1845, producing mainly the eight-day mirror timepiece. One of the earliest of these has tin steel plates, rather than brass, and a movement attached to the case by two long screws passing through the entire movement

into the back, a method often used by Simon Willard to attach movements in his banjo clocks. Joseph Chadwick carried on a similar business from about 1810 until 1831.

Another quantity producer of the mirror clock was James Collins of Goffstown, who began working about 1830. Collins also produced a striking version of the mirror clock, though they are less commonly found than is the ordinary mirror timepiece.

During the second quarter of the nineteenth century, many other craftsmen were at work in the state. Willard-style clocks were being made by E. H. Nutter of Dover and Leonard W. Noyes of Nashua, among others. The mirror-style clock gained in popularity, and many unusual and inventive designs were made. Many of these, unfortunately, do not carry the maker's name.

But as 1850 neared, it was evident that native clockmaking could not compete with Connecticut manufacturing, and most production of handcrafted clocks ceased.

**84.** Die-stamped movement seat board identifying clock made by Timothy Chandler, Concord, NH. **85.** Pine-cased clock attributed to Abijah Gould of Hollis, NH. Movement has wood plates and motion train, but brass time and strike trains. Case reminiscent of Boston fashion, but of country simplicity. *(Author's collection)* **86.** Eight-day brass-movement clock by Gurdon Huntington, Walpole, NH, dated 1791. Huntington moved to New Hampshire from eastern Connecticut and case shows influence from that area. *(Courtesy, Charles S. Parsons)* **87.** Striking mirror clock by Abiel Chandler, Concord, NH, c. 1830. *(Edward F. LaFond)*

# HANDCRAFTING IN THE FRONTIER STATES

## OHIO

Clockmaking came to Ohio close on the heels of the first influx of settlers in 1790. The state proved an appealing frontier and, especially after 1803—when Ohio gained statehood—attracted clockmakers as well as other artisans from the East. However, early handcrafters generally farmed or pursued other businesses as well. There was little demand at that time for expensive clocks. Ohio timepieces were probably first produced on special order and in limited quantity.

Among Connecticut migrants was Comfort Starr Mygatt (1763–1823), of Danbury, who settled in Canfield, Mahoning County, in the summer of 1807. Thomas Lyman, an apprentice of Daniel Burnap, came from Windsor, Connecticut, and settled in the southern part of the state at Marietta, Washington County, about 1791. Both men made brass-movement tall clocks while in Connecticut, but if examples made by them in Ohio exist, they are indeed rare.

A native Swiss, Jacob Hostetter, settled in Columbiana County in Lisbon in 1806 and produced tall clocks. Richard Jackson worked in Jefferson County, on the mideastern border of the state. He settled in the area just after 1800 and continued to work there until his death, sometime after 1840. An unusual tall clock is extant, marked inside the hood, "Made by R. Jackson, Made 1828." This superb clock has a movement of unique design and runs thirty days per winding. Though little is known of Jackson, the clock definitely reflects Pennsylvania workmanship.

Settlers in the northeastern extremity of the state, known as the Western Reserve, were for the

**88.** Thirty-day tall clock movement by Richard Jackson, East Springfield, OH, made in 1828. Note skeletonized plate and large lantern pinions. (*Author's collection*)

**89.** One-day wood-movement clock by Luman Watson, Cincinnati, OH, c. 1835. (*American Clock & Watch Museum*)

**90.** Rare one-day wood-movement shelf clock made by
Luman Watson, Cincinnati, OH, *c.* 1830. Weights pass
through sheet-metal columns. *(Courtesy, Edward F. LaFond)*

most part migrants from New England. The central part of Ohio did not attract many clockmakers, but there was considerable activity around Cincinnati. The first clockmaker in that town was reportedly a Daniel Symmes, but little record remains of his work. In 1806, Philip Price advertised in local newspapers that he had dissolved a partnership with Harmon Long and would continue his jewelry and clock and watchmaking business. In July, 1806, Joseph Hough, who came to the area from Fayette County, Pennsylvania, finally settled north a few miles in Butler County.

Gamaliel Bailey, who had previously been in Mt. Holly, New Jersey, and in Philadelphia, settled in Cincinnati after 1830, but his business was

**91.** Thirty-day tall clock, 8½ ft. tall, by Richard Jackson, East Springfield, OH, 1828. Fourteen-inch dial of Philadelphia manufacture. (*Author's collection*)

probably only that of repair. Joseph Budd, also from Mt. Holly, came to the area in the early 1830s and settled in Hamilton, in Butler County. Samuel and Robert Best were working in Cincinnati after 1800 on Front Street; tall clocks known to be their work are extant.

Jacob Jameson, a Lancaster County, Pennsylvania, maker settled in Springfield, Clark County, before December, 1830, at which time he advertised that he was making eight-day brass clocks and timepieces. Oliver Roberts, also from Lancaster County, settled in Eaton in Preble County, and continued his business. Thomas Best worked in nearby Warren County from about 1808 to 1826, and Humphrey Griffith, a Welshman, moved to Warren County from Pennsylvania in 1819, but migrated westward into Indiana a few years later.

Though the state did draw these makers of the brass tall clock, the demand for their products was not great. After the wood-movement tall clock became popular in Connecticut, several Ohio firms ventured into this field. Most noted of these were Ansell Merrell and the firm of Hart & Truesdale in Trumbull County, and Luman Watson and the firm of Read & Watson in Hamilton County.

Luman Watson (1790–1841) of Cincinnati must be admired for his ability to realize the need and potential for a less-expensive clock. By 1815, he had begun to manufacture wood tall clocks, and for twenty-five years he supplied the western frontier with both these and the Connecticut-style wood shelf clocks.

Watson had come to Ohio from Connecticut about 1810, and first went into partnership with Ezra, Abner, and Amasa Read in the firm of Read & Watson. In 1815, the firm brought Ephraim Downs from Connecticut to assist them in making movements. Downs had been an employee of Lemuel Harrison & Company in Waterbury and, after a fire destroyed its factory in the winter of 1814, he had worked for Clark, Cook & Company of Waterbury. In his accounting records under the date April 26, 1815, Downs entered: "Today Commenced Work for Read & Watson." About 1817, Watson gained control of the business; Downs continued to work for him until 1821.

In 1819, Watson advertised wood clocks. At that time he employed fourteen workmen, who used machinery driven by horsepower to produce thirty thousand dollars' worth of clocks a year. By 1826, his factory had eighteen workmen, but they produced only twenty thousand dollars' worth of clocks annually, "of which fifteen thousand dollars' worth was exported." Nearing 1830, Watson phased out the production of tall clocks and made shelf models, some of the Connecticut style and some of his own design. In 1829, he advertised the sale of "improved mantle clocks," and in 1836, he described his "clock factory, which is quite an extensive concern, making annually 2,500 clocks, and operated by waterpower."

Watson's success, along with that of the Connecticut manufacturers, enticed other Ohio men to venture into the clock business in the 1830s and 1840s, but the majority of them merely purchased Connecticut clocks, attached locally printed labels, and marketed them as Ohio-made clocks.

## INDIANA

Indiana, admitted to the Union in 1816 as the nineteenth state, was a territory settled somewhat late to have seen extensive handcrafting methods in clockmaking. But the state did have an interesting craftsman by the name of Humphrey Griffith.

Griffith was not a native American. He was born December 23, 1791, at Dolgelly, Merionethshire, Wales. Having served a normal apprenticeship as a clock- and watchmaker at Shrewsbury in the west English county of Gloucester, Griffith emigrated to America in the spring of 1818. He first settled in Huntington, Pennsylvania, but about a year later moved to Lebanon, Ohio, and continued his trade there for a short time.

Prior to 1825, Griffith had settled in Indianapolis. There he continued to make brass-movement tall clocks until his retirement in 1834, at the age of forty-five. It is thought that his retirement was forced by the severe decline of his business, because of the influx of the inexpensive Connecticut clock, rather than to poor health, for he lived to the age of seventy-nine.

The sale of Connecticut clocks must have begun to hurt his business as early as 1828, for the following newspaper advertisement, dated October 2 of that year, expresses his displeasure with them:

> BRASS CLOCKS. The subscriber Wishes to inform his former customers, and the public in general that he still continues to make BRASS CLOCKS, of every description required, and repair Repeating, Horizontal, Duplex and Plain Watches, on as low terms as any other competent Workman in his line, at his former stand opposite Mr. Henderson's Tavern; but Wooden Clocks or Wooden Watches, he would rather buy to burn than repair them, if other firewood was not so plenty in this new country.
>
> H. GRIFFITH

## KENTUCKY

Kentucky, the fifteenth state, was for many years considered a part of Augusta County, Virginia, but in 1776 became known as Kentucky County, Virginia. By 1792, when the state was formed, many settlers, especially from the southern states, migrated there. Many stayed only a few years, then moved on to midwestern frontiers, but the population grew large enough in some towns for clockmakers to establish businesses. The total

number of Kentucky-made clocks must have been small, however, for the state was too rural for the most part, and settled too late, to stimulate much activity in handcrafting clocks.

The town of Lexington had several makers, the first noted one being Edward West (1757–1827) from Virginia. West advertised in the *Lexington Gazette* on August 9, 1788, that "watchmaking and clockmaking will be done in the neatest and shortest manner; also has watch crystals for sale." He later advertised as a silversmith and gunsmith. George Smart advertised in the same paper on January 27, 1794, as a clockmaker and watchmaker from Britain "at the back of the jail" who had "a neat assortment of thirteen-inch plain double moon and seconds from the center, eight-day and thirty-hour Clocks; likewise a few Gold and Silver watches, which will be sold upon reasonable terms."

Henry Hyman of Lexington advertised in the *Kentucky Herald* on January 21, 1799, that he had come from London and had served an apprenticeship in England as a goldsmith, silversmith, clockmaker, and watchmaker. In 1808 Asa Blanchard began to advertise as a silversmith and continued to do so until his death in 1832. Though he did not claim to be a maker, a tall clock with his name on it is extant. Its similarity to New Jersey-made clocks suggests the possibility of its being purchased from the East and marketed by Blanchard.

Two brothers, B. B. and T. K. Marsh, who claimed Philadelphia training, worked in Paris, Kentucky, for several years. A number of unmarked clocks also exist that are believed to have been made and cased in Kentucky.

## VERMONT

Although there was considerable clockmaking activity in the New England states, there were not a great many makers at work in Vermont (before statehood, a part of New Hampshire). After 1791, makers moved west, but settlement was slower than in nearby states. Some tall clocks and Willard-style wall clocks were produced in Vermont, however, perhaps as late as 1850.

Three sons of Benjamin Cheney of East Hartford, Connecticut, settled in the state after 1800. Martin advertised in Windsor in 1801 and his brother, Russell, advertised in Woodstock in 1806 as "from East Hartford, Connecticut." A third brother, Asahel, first settled in Northfield, Massachusetts, but moved to Royalton about 1808 and then to Rochester about 1816. These men had been trained in both wood and brass clock making, though they were engaged primarily in the latter while in Vermont.

John Peabody advertised as a Woodstock clockmaker in 1808 and Jacob Kimball was working in Montpelier about 1810. After a brief period in Rindge, New Hampshire, Nathan Hale (1771–1849) settled in the town of Chelsea in 1797 and produced tall, shelf, and wall clocks in Willard styles. Edward Ells (1773–1832), a native of Preston, Connecticut, settled in Middlebury, Vermont, before 1810 and established a silversmithing and clockmaking business. Ells later moved to Medina, New York, where he died.

Lemuel Curtis (b. 1790) moved to Concord from Massachusetts in 1811 and, between that date and 1816, developed a highly gilded version of the banjo-style case. The case was undoubtedly influenced by the fancy mirrors of the day, and has become known as the "girandole" clock.

In 1816, Curtis went into partnership with

Joseph Nye Dunning (1793–1841) as the firm of Curtis & Dunning. Prior to October, 1821, the firm moved to Burlington, Vermont. In 1827, they advertised for sale timepieces "with mahogany or gilt cases $23. to $35. each and Warranted to keep time." They dissolved the partnership about 1833.

Dunning continued in business alone until his death at the age of forty-six. Curtis continued his business until at least 1844; his activities after that date are unknown.

Joseph Dyar (1795–1850), who had apprenticed under Lemuel Curtis, followed Curtis & Dunning to Vermont, settling in Middlebury about 1822. On August 29 of that year he advertised his new establishment, where he manufac-

**92.** Eight-day lyre-style wall clock made by Samuel Abbott, Montpelier, VT, dated 1810. A pleasant variation of the banjo-style case. (*American Clock & Watch Museum*)

**93.** Eight-day brass timepiece movement by Samuel Abbott. Note skeletonized plates for economy and unusually thin anchor. (*Edward Ingraham Library*)

**94.** Banjo clock made by Curtis & Dunning, Burlington, VT,
c. 1820. Unusual hands are peculiar to Lemuel Curtis' clocks.
*(Courtesy, Frederick R. Downs, Jr.)*

tured eight-day timepieces and sold watches and jewelry. The *Middlebury Register* of February 26, 1850, carried the following tragic story:

> Fatal Accident — On Friday evening last, Mr. Joseph Dyar (of this place) was returning from his store just as the Boston train of cars was leaving the station for Burlington. A span of horses (attached to a lumber sleigh) which had been hitched to a post near Mr. Sheldon's store, took fright at the noise of the cars and of the steam whistle, broke away and ran violently up the street. Mr. Dyar had taken to the middle of the road, the sidewalks being icy, and not seeing his danger, was thrown down by one of the horses, one runner passing over his head, and dragging him a short distance before he was extricated. He was taken up senseless and remained so most all of the time before he died about 24 hours after. Mr. Dyar was one of our most respected citizens and leaves a family to mourn his sudden bereavement. His age was 55.

## MAINE

Maine is the largest and most rural of the New England states, although it was settled very early in its southern part and along the Atlantic coast. Clockmakers began moving into the state from southern New England about the time of the Revolution and brought with them varied styles of clocks. Besides tall clocks, Massachusetts-type wall and shelf clocks were made, as were wood clocks. Because of the remoteness of the state, some of the makers departed from standard practices and made movements of unusual designs, utilized iron plates rather than brass, and adopted more primitive case styles. Some production continued as late as 1850, but the manufacturing of clocks was not carried on there as it was in neighboring states.

Nathaniel Hamlen (1741–1834) first worked in the town of Oxford, Maine, and an example—a wood tall clock movement marked "No. 7"—survives. It is huge. The plates are ten by eleven inches, and are four and a half inches apart. Teeth on the wheels were cut by hand with a saw. The pattern on the movement resembles those made by John Bailey of Massachusetts and the Cheney family of Connecticut. There are also records of Hamlen in Augusta, where he settled before 1780. Besides tall clocks, examples of his dwarf, or grandmother, clocks survive.

Benjamin Snow was conducting business in Augusta before 1783. His clocks have brass gears, but are characterized by the use of iron plates rather than brass ones. This feature was also used by Paul Rogers of Berwick. Samuel Ranlet (1780–1867) was a native of Gilmanton, New Hampshire. He settled in Augusta about 1800 and possibly was apprenticed to Snow. In 1809, he moved to Monmouth and set up business, making tall clocks

**96.** Wood tall clock movement by Nathaniel Hamlen, Oxford, ME, *c.* 1770. Plates are 11 inches wide and wheel teeth are hand sawn. *(American Clock & Watch Museum)*

and banjo clocks, both using iron plates.

About 1804, Frederick Wingate (1782–1864) moved to Augusta from Haverhill, Massachusetts, where he had recently been trained. He made tall clocks as well as the New Hampshire-style mirror clock. Many of his cases utilized burled maple, a wood not often used. Benjamin Swan (1792–1867) also settled in Augusta from Haverhill and was apprenticed to Wingate. He established his business in Augusta and later in Hallowell. Paine Wingate (1767–1833), Frederick's elder brother, moved to Augusta about 1811 and carried on clockmaking there for about six years, after which he returned to Haverhill, Massachusetts.

Paul Rogers worked in the southern town of Berwick about the time of the Revolution. He often used iron plates for his clocks' movements, as did his son and apprentice, Abner Rogers (b. 1777). Reuben Brackett (1791–1867), a Shaker, learned the clockmaking trade in Berwick, apparently from either Rogers or his son. Prior to 1820, Brackett moved to Vassalboro, Maine, and about 1827, to Unity. After 1830, he moved to Massachusetts, Ohio, and later to Denmark, Iowa, where he died. Reuben's brother, Oliver Brackett (1800–69), conducted a small clockmaking business at Vassalboro for a few years.

Nicholas Blaisdell (1743–c. 1800), son of David Blaisdell of Amesbury, Massachusetts, settled at Falmouth (now Portland), Maine, after 1774, having worked previously at Newmarket, New Hampshire. Nicholas had received clockmaking training from his father and continued to produce the unusual thirty-hour posted-style tall clock movement associated with his family.

Lebbeus Bailey (1763–1827), son of John Bailey of Hanover, Massachusetts, moved to Maine in 1791, settling just north of Portland in North Yarmouth, where he continued clockmaking. The history of North Yarmouth recorded that "here too was the foundry of Lebbeus Bailey who previous to 1824 manufactured tall old-fashioned clocks. In his foundry were cast not only the metal movements of these clocks but sleigh bells, and in fact every kind of metal work of which his customers had need." Tall clocks and some shelf models are known, usually marked "L. Bailey, N. Yarmouth." Calvin Bailey, Lebbeus' brother, moved to Bath, Maine, in 1828, but probably did not make many clocks. He died seven years later.

Other important Maine clockmakers were Nathan Adams (1755–1825) and Daniel Noyes Dole (1775–1841) of Wiscasset, Enoch Burnham (before 1800) of Paris and Portland, Jonathan Bemis (about 1800) of Paris, Phineas Parkhurst Quimby (1802–66) and his brother William Quimby (1793–1879) of Belfast, Abiel B. Eastman (1788–1822) of Belfast, Robert Eastman (about 1805) and James Carey (1790–1865) of Belfast and Brunswick.

**97.** Primitive tall clock attributed to David Blaisdell, Amesbury, MA, *c.* 1750. Rocking ship in dial lunette a restoration. *(Courtesy, Edward F. LaFond)* **98.** Unsigned gilt presentation-style banjo made in Boston, MA, area *c.* 1825. *(American Clock & Watch Museum)*

**100**

**101**

**99.** Dial to primitive one-day wood-movement clock by Nathaniel Hamlen, Oxford, ME, *c.* 1770. Note iron hands and primitive decoration on dial. Numbered "7." *(American Clock & Watch Museum)* **100.** Primitive banjo with dial removed, probably of Maine origin. Note movement with iron plates and brass gears as often used by Benjamin Snow, Paul Rogers, and other Maine artisans. **101.** Maine banjo with dial and panels replaced. Note unusual wood side arms. *(Courtesy, Hershel B. Burt)*

*Part III:*
*The Age of*
*Manufacturing:*
*1800–1970*

*T*hough fine clocks had been made in America for a century, the handcrafting methods allowed neither for quantity nor for low-cost production. A clockmaker and his apprentices constructed the clocks one or two at a time, laboriously finishing and fitting the movement components to each clock.

By standardizing movement components, clocks could be produced in "batches"; finishing and assembling could be accomplished more simply and at greater speed. Undoubtedly Harland and Burnap realized this potential and attempted standardization to some degree.

Soon after 1800, Eli Terry began to harness waterpower to drive crude machinery, and thereby was able to make wood components by the hundreds. In the 150 years that followed, his successors increased their production to hundreds of thousands of components. Through volume production the expense of making clocks was reduced to the point where a manufactured clock cost only a fraction of a handcrafted item.

*Preceding pages:* **Two of Ingraham's steeple-case shelf clocks.**

# THE WOOD TALL CLOCK

Eli Terry (1772–1852) was undoubtedly the "father" of the clock manufacturing industry. Beginning his clockmaking career of more than sixty years in 1793, Terry developed methods that transformed American clockmaking from handcrafting to manufacturing. He developed and manufactured wood tall clocks, wood shelf clocks, and brass clocks of various designs. He also made contributions in the fields of tower clocks and precision clocks. Several of his sons and fellow workers carried on this manufacturing, which became the nucleus of the American clock manufacturing industry.

Terry was born in East Windsor, Connecticut, on April 13, 1772. He probably started training under Daniel Burnap in 1786, learned to make brass-movement tall clocks, and probably finished his training near his twenty-first birthday. One month after that event, Burnap's accounts show a charge of one pound four shillings to Terry for the engraving of a clock dial.

Terry also received additional training "in East Hartford by a Mr. Cheeney," Eli's son Henry recorded. Whether Terry received this training intermittently during the time he was training under Burnap or after he completed his apprenticeship is not known. The "Mr. Cheeney" was probably either Benjamin Cheney or his brother Timothy, who began producing wood clocks in East Hartford prior to 1750.

Terry realized that remaining in East Windsor would mean competing with his famous master, so he wisely decided to settle in an area with greater potential for a beginning artisan. By that time he had most likely realized the potential for a less-expensive clock. So in 1793 he settled in a section of west-central Connecticut known as Northbury, a wilderness that was then part of Watertown. In May of 1795, the area became known as Plymouth.

During the first few years of business in the area, Terry produced tall clocks in limited numbers in both wood and brass styles. His son wrote that uncased wood clocks sold for four pounds (those having engraved brass dials bringing nearly double that amount) and brass-movement clocks for ten pounds to fifteen pounds. During the remainder of the century, Terry produced his clock by the old-fashioned methods, using a foot-treadle lathe for turning and a hand-cranked clockmaker's engine to cut wood or brass teeth.

Terry's earliest wood-movement examples are similar to those made by the Cheneys, having large teeth, wheels, and plates. It is probable that most of these had unsigned painted dials or paper dials glued to wood dial plates and have gone unidentified or have been classified as Cheney-

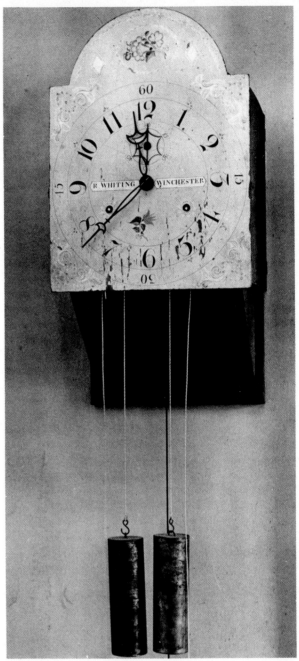

**102.** Eli Terry's "Ireland" factory, birthplace of the American clock manufacturing industry. Here Terry developed production techniques and produced 4,000 wood tall clock movements between 1806 and 1809. This factory was later used by Silas Hoadley until 1849. *(Edward Ingraham Library)* **103.** Wood tall clock movements, such as this one by Riley Whiting, Winchester, CT, *c.* 1820, were meant to be cased. Some owners, unable to afford a case, hung them as wag-on-wall clocks. *(Edward Ingraham Library)*

type clocks. Since examples with brass dials were more costly, fewer were made. However, some do exist, and this early style can be identified.

Henry Terry described his father's procedures at the time:

> So limited was the demand for clocks at this time, and so inadequate his means for making them, that after finishing three or four he was obliged to go out with them on horseback, and put them up, where they had been previously engaged or sold. His usual way was to put one forward of the saddle on which he rode, one behind, and one on each side in his portmanteau.

In about 1797, Heman Clark began to work for Terry, learning to make both brass and wood clocks. Clark was probably the only apprentice Terry trained to work with brass, and the master himself ceased making brass tall clocks shortly after 1800.

Terry was an ingenious mechanic. On November 17, 1797, he was granted a patent for an "equation clock"—a clock having two dials, one showing the apparent time (the time indicated by the sun) and the other showing the mean (or true) time. The difference between these two times is known as the equation of time. A clock of this design was constructed for the city of New Haven in 1826, but the public was so confused as to which time, mean or apparent, was correct that one of the dials had to be removed.

At the turn of the nineteenth century, Terry was producing a thirty-hour wood tall clock movement with a paper dial glued onto a wood plate. These movements had teeth that had been cut on a hand engine. After 1803 he developed a faster method, utilizing water power and cutting teeth with saws.

In about 1805, Terry went into partnership with his former apprentice, Heman Clark, in the firm Terry & Clark. In December of 1807, Terry sold his original shop to Clark.

In about 1806, Terry adopted the use of painted and decorated wood dials, which were gaining popularity. On July 22 of that year he purchased a gristmill located in the southern part of Plymouth at a place called Ireland, and converted it into a clock factory.

Terry was approached in 1807 by Edward and Levi G. Porter, two brothers from Waterbury, with a proposition. They wanted him to produce four thousand wood grandfather clock movements for them in three years. Terry was to supply the movement, dial, hands, weights, and pendulum, but not the case. Eli's son Henry recorded: "Three years elapsed while these clocks were being made. A great part of the first year was spent in fitting up the machinery, the next in the manufacture of one thousand clocks, and the third year in completing the remaining three thousand." To assist him in

**104.** Tall clock by Joseph Ives, Bristol, CT, made *c.* 1814. Painted pine case and eight-day wood movement with rolling pinions. *(American Clock & Watch Museum)*

the project, Terry hired two joiners, Seth Thomas and Silas Hoadley.

It was during this time that Eli Terry made his greatest contribution to clockmaking: adapting the craft to true mass production. Though his predecessors, Harland and Burnap, had made strides toward standardization of movements and had achieved greater production than their local contemporaries, neither had produced clocks in outstanding quantities. By using wood for major clock components and utilizing a waterwheel to drive machinery, Terry was able to produce serviceable clocks in great quantity. The waterpower was converted through a series of belts and pulleys to drive wood-turning devices, drills, saws, and other machinery for producing wood parts. Since the clock parts that they made were of standard size and shape, they were interchangeable in movements. Wheel banks could also be lined up for cutting, so that a dozen or more wheels could be cut in the time it previously took to cut one.

Having completed the Porter contract by 1809, Terry sold his Ireland factory to his assistants, Thomas and Hoadley, for six thousand dollars on July 7, 1810. The firm continued in business for three years and on December 4, 1813, Thomas sold Hoadley "all such right, estate, title & demand whatsoever, as I now have or ought to have in or to the Clock shop, Tools and Utensils . . ." Hoadley continued in business at the Ireland factory, producing thirty-hour and eight-day tall clocks until after 1820, and later becoming involved in shelf-clock production. He retired in 1849.

Five days after selling to Hoadley, Seth Thomas purchased a shop in Plymouth Hollow that had been built by Heman Clark in 1809. Clark had been producing wood tall clocks there, and Thomas continued this production until becoming involved with Terry's shelf clock toward the end of the decade.

Other groups of men were also involved in the development and manufacture of the wood-movement grandfather clock, notably in the nearby towns of Waterbury, Bristol, and Winsted.

The Waterbury, Connecticut, wood tall clock manufacturers probably trace their training to Timothy Barnes, Jr., of Litchfield, Connecticut. Barnes was born on April 8, 1749, in Branford, and was possibly an apprentice of Macock Ward of Wallingford. Barnes produced both brass and wood tall clocks, some of the latter having printed paper dials identical to those used by Gideon Roberts of Bristol.

Besides clockmaking, Barnes conducted a silversmith business in Litchfield, beginning about 1770 and continuing for more than forty years. Among his apprentices were his nephews Lemuel, James, and Wooster Harrison, sons of his

**105.** Pine-cased clock, 7½ ft. tall, made by Eli Terry, Plymouth, CT, c. 1802. One-day wood movement with printed paper dial. (*American Clock & Watch Museum*)

**106.** Eight-day brass-movement tall clock with engraved dial by Eli Terry, Plymouth, CT, c. 1800. Completing apprenticeship under Daniel Burnap in 1793, Terry made some brass tall clocks until shortly after 1800, when he began concentrating exclusively on the wood-movement clock. (*Courtesy, Amos G. Avery*)

sister Lois and Lemuel Harrison, Sr. Barnes died in Litchfield on October 11, 1825, at the age of seventy-six.

Wooster Harrison, youngest of the three nephews, was born in Litchfield on June 18, 1772, and finished his training about 1793. In 1795, he moved to Trumbull, Connecticut, and in 1800 to Newfield, where he made brass clocks and employed a watch repairman. Wooster is not known to have engaged in the production of wood clocks as his brothers did.

James Harrison was born on July 23, 1767, in Litchfield. Some of his accounting records were apparently in existence in 1858, as Henry Bronson, in his *History of Waterbury*, noted that Harrison's first clock was sold to Major Morris on January 1, 1791, for £3 12s. 9d. and the second to Rev. Mark Leavenworth (grandfather of the clockmaker of the same name) on February 2, 1791, for four pounds. The third was sold for the same amount to Capt. Samuel Judd on February 19, 1791. Daniel Burnap of East Windsor was selling brass clocks during the same year for ten pounds, with an additional five pounds for a case, so it is apparent the first clocks sold by Harrison were wood, probably not cased.

At Southington, Connecticut, on February 9, 1795, Harrison advertised:

> James Harrison, Respectfully informs his friends and the Public at Large, that he carries on the business of Clock Making, which are made of brass, steel, and wood (the principal part however is of wood) in the neatest manner and warranted. Gentlemen who will please to favor him with their custom may be supplied on short notice and cheap for cash.

Later in 1795, he moved to Waterbury and continued in the wood clock business. In about 1800, he relocated in a small shop on the south side of North Main Street on Little Brook, and installed a waterwheel for power. On April 15, 1802, he leased the shop for seven years.

On Saturday, December 29, 1804, Candace Roberts, daughter of Gideon Roberts of Bristol, made the following entry in her diary:

> Arose early, waited very anxiously until about 9 o'clock when it began to snow, expected to carry my Sister home, but just as I was getting into the sleigh a gentle man came in & my Father introduced him to me as a Mr. Harrison from Waterbury; he wanted me to go & paint clock-faces for him. I consented with some reluctance but knowing it was for the best contented myself with the idea that I might find Friends if I deserved them.

Harrison continued in business until about 1806, when the firm of James Harrison & Company was taken over by Edward Porter and Anson Sperry. Harrison later moved to Boston, where, in 1814, he was granted a patent for "the time part of the common wood clocks." He returned to Waterbury before 1840 and worked in a shop on Grand Street belonging to his nephew, James Harrison (1791–1865); here he made metal frames and other small articles. A few years later he moved to New York, where he died a bachelor on October 13, 1845, at the age of seventy-eight.

Though most of James Harrison's clocks are not marked, many are recognizable because he used tiny wood threads on the ends of plate posts and arbors. Arbors were screwed to the wheels and glued, but the threads were so cut that if the glue released with age, the wheels would become unscrewed, and the clock would stop. Threaded arbors are believed also to have been used on some clocks by William Leavenworth, Lemuel Harrison, and probably others.

Lemuel Harrison, elder brother of James, was born on November 17, 1765, in Litchfield. Little is known of the first forty years of his life; however, he stated in 1818 that in his youth he "by his industry and economy decently supported a large family, and was clear from any pecuniary embarrassments."

On August 14, 1805, Lemuel purchased a gristmill located on the east side of the Mad river in Waterbury. He operated it until September 21, 1808, when he deeded it to Abel Porter and others; it was used then as a gristmill and for the manufacture of buttons. For the next few years Lemuel apparently engaged in farming. The 1810 tax listing for his homestead does not indicate that he had yet ventured into the clock business and, in fact, he owned only one wood-wheeled clock, worth seven dollars.

On about January 1, 1811, Lemuel went into partnership with Daniel Clark, Zenas Cook (1773–1851), and William Porter of Waterbury—in the firm Lemuel Harrison & Company—for the purpose of manufacturing wood movements for tall clocks. The firm occupied a small shop on Great Brook, now near the corner of Canal and Meadow Streets in Waterbury.

In mid-1811 Ephraim Downs moved from Plymouth, Connecticut, to work for the firm, assembling and finishing wood tall clock movements. His account books show that from June 17, 1811, until October 30, 1814, he finished 9,162 clocks for Lemuel Harrison. Of these, 81 percent had day-of-the-month calendar features.

Three days after Downs's last entry, the clock shop was destroyed by a fire, of which Harrison later said: "The shop and establishment of said firm was consumed by fire, and the property of said firm consisting of said shop, machinery, tools, notes, and book, and a variety of other property to the amount of ten thousand dollars was entirely destroyed by fire."

Because of the fire, Lemuel became financially insolvent and petitioned the Connecticut General

**107.** Cased wood tall clock by Riley Whiting, Winchester, CT, made c. 1825. Producing this style until nearly 1830, Whiting was one of the last to abandon manufacture of the wood tall clock. (*American Clock & Watch Museum*)

Assembly to declare him bankrupt. The petition was granted in 1818. Among the seventy persons listed as creditors in the petition were the following clockmakers: William K. Lamson, then a resident of New Haven; Heman Clark of Plymouth; Mark Leavenworth of Waterbury; and Ephraim Downs, who by that time was residing in Cincinnati, Ohio.

Lemuel was nearly fifty-five years old at the conclusion of the bankruptcy proceedings and did not again venture into clock manufacturing. He died in Waterbury on November 25, 1857, at the age of ninety-two.

What remained of his clockmaking business passed into the hands of his creditors and was purchased in about 1820 by David Pritchard (1775–1838). Pritchard was a cabinetmaker and made cases, purchasing movements from both Silas Hoadley of Plymouth and Norris North of Torrington.

In about 1810, William King Lamson and Anson Sperry of Waterbury had become associated with Mark Leavenworth in the firm Lamson, Sperry & Company. The firm continued in business until about 1817, and on May 5 of that year the accounts of the "late firm of Lamson, Sperry & Company" were settled. One undated tall clock label survives that reads: "Clocks, made and sold by Lamson & Sperry, Waterbury."

Soon after the firm was dissolved Lamson moved to New Haven, and in about 1820 left Connecticut and settled in Berwick, Pennsylvania, where he ran a mercantile business. He later moved to Columbus, Ohio, where he died on September 8, 1832.

Anson Sperry was interested in the clock business as early as 1806, when, in partnership with Edward Porter, he purchased the ailing business of James Harrison & Company. On August 22, 1814, he was granted a patent for a "machine for pointing wire for Clocks." After the dissolution of Lamson, Sperry & Company, Anson moved to Camden, New York, and then to Farmington, Michigan, where he died on August 28, 1856.

Two members of the Leavenworth family of Waterbury were also interested in the wood clock business. William, son of the Reverend Mark Leavenworth, was born on February 23, 1759. He appears to have been a carpenter by trade, and in about 1800 established a sawmill and gristmill on the west side of the Mad river. Either in this or a nearby building he carried on a turning shop and after the War of 1812 made wood tall clocks.

Leavenworth also conducted a large mercantile business, which dealt extensively in domestic products, and ran a distillery. He was appointed the first postmaster of Waterbury in 1803 and remained prominent in the public affairs of the

**108.** One-day wood tall clock made by Thomas & Hoadley, Plymouth, CT, *c.* 1812. Painted case grained to simulate expensive wood. (*American Clock & Watch Museum*)

**109.** Eight-day wood tall clock by Silas Hoadley, Plymouth, CT, c. 1825. Wound by pull cord, dial has false painted key winding holes. *(Courtesy, Frank H. Murphy)*

town. "Colonel" Leavenworth, as he was known, built one of the most beautiful homes in Waterbury at the time. It was mentioned by the clock-dial painter Candace Roberts in her diary under the date December 29, 1804: "As we were about three miles from our destined port, about 8 o'clock set forth with full speed and soon arrived at Captain Levingsworths [sic] a beautiful place indeed . . ."

Leavenworth failed in business before 1818 and moved to Albany, New York, where he engaged in enterprises similar to those he had founded in Waterbury. He continued making tall clocks in Albany, part of the time in partnership with his only son, William Leavenworth, Jr. (1786–1829). He apparently retired from the clock business sometime after 1823, as in May of that year Riley Whiting of Winchester, Connecticut, challenged a patent claim Leavenworth was said to have on wood clocks. No patent granted to Leavenworth has been found, though he may have purchased the right to the patent on wood clocks granted to James Harrison in 1814. He remained in Albany after his retirement and died during a visit to Bridgeport, Connecticut, on November 24, 1836, at the age of seventy-seven.

Mark Leavenworth, William's nephew, was born on August 31, 1774, in New Haven, Connecticut, and spent several years in his youth working for Jesse Hopkins, a Waterbury silversmith, making knee and shoe buckles. In about 1795, he began to manufacture axes and steelyards, as well as ramrods, bands, and bayonets for small guns. By 1800, his business had grown to such a degree that he was able to employ several workers and take occasional trips to South Carolina and Georgia to sell his wares.

As mentioned, Mark was in partnership with William Lamson and Anson Sperry of Waterbury in 1810. From existing account books, it is evident that he was well-established in his own clock business prior to July of 1814.

When Eli Terry's wood shelf clock began to increase in popularity, Leavenworth realized its potential marketing possibilities, especially in the southern states. In about 1822, he began to eliminate tall clock production. Under the date of September 27, 1822, his accounts mention "to eighteen large & fifteen small clocks."

To circumvent the possibility of infringement on Terry's patent, he developed a distinctively different shelf clock movement arrangement. His venture was successful and he remained a prolific manufacturer for about twenty years. Though close examination shows the Leavenworth movements were more crudely made and finished than those of Terry, they were nevertheless serviceable and a marketing success. He sold some uncased movements to various firms—including Wads-

110

110. Highly decorated one-day wood movement attributed to James Harrison, Waterbury, CT, c. 1805. Arbors have tiny wood threads and are screwed to wheels, as are posts to plates. *(Courtesy, Frank H. Murphy)* 111. Tiny wood threads on arbors allow them to be screwed to wheels. This feature was used by James and Lemuel Harrison, William Leavenworth, and others. 112. Eli Terry (1772–1852), "father" of the American clock manufacturing industry. Terry's manufacturing career spanned more than 40 years. 113. Silas Hoadley (1786–1870) began working with Terry about 1807. In partnership with Seth Thomas, Hoadley purchased Terry's factory in 1810. *(E. Ingraham Library)*

worths, Lounsbury & Turners of Litchfield—and to clockmaking notables such as Chauncey Jerome, Mark Lane, David Pritchard, James Harrison, and Norris North.

Leavenworth was the largest wood-movement manufacturer in New Haven County in the 1820s and early 1830s. His accounts show that from May, 1822, to February, 1825, he sold 3,265 clocks, all of which probably were housed in pillar and scroll cases. In about 1825, his son, Benjamin Franklin Leavenworth (1803–50), joined him in the firm Mark Leavenworth & Son. By 1829, he had taken in his son-in-law, Green Kendrick (1798–1873), and the firm became known as Mark Leavenworth & Company.

In May of 1834, the partnership was dissolved and production of the Leavenworth-design movement was ceased. For a short time he marketed a few clocks with Terry-style movements, which were undoubtedly purchased. The last entry in Leavenworth's clockmaking accounts is dated July 2, 1834.

After retirement from clockmaking, Leavenworth continued with his brass button business until his death in Waterbury on September 5, 1849, at the age of seventy-five.

Wood clock producers in the northern Connecticut town of Winchester originally came from Waterbury. Samuel (b. November 25, 1776) and Luther Hoadley (b. March 30, 1781) moved from the Waterbury area in 1803 and settled in the town of Winchester. In 1804, Samuel was admitted into the town of Winsted and soon after, together with his younger brother, acquired land, a dam, and water rights on the Still river, where they built a gristmill. The two men had undoubtedly been taught the principles of making wood clocks by James Harrison of Waterbury, as their clocks closely resemble his pattern.

In February of 1806, their younger sister Urania (1788–1855) was married to a Winchester native, Riley Whiting (b. January 16, 1785). In about 1807, the Hoadley brothers and Whiting started a clock business under the name Samuel Hoadley & Company. About three years later they began casting clock bells by a "closely guarded secret process" and in 1812, the company erected an addition on the west wing of the clock factory and began one of the earliest operations for drawing wire through hardened forms to obtain a desired diameter.

Both Hoadleys served in the War of 1812. Samuel was appointed major of the Thirty-seventh Connecticut Infantry Regiment in March of 1813, and lieutenant-colonel of the Thirty-first Infantry in October of 1814. Luther, an appointed captain, was killed at Groton, Connecticut, on September 8, 1813.

Upon his return home, Samuel continued the

clock business with his brother-in-law as Hoadley & Whiting. Some accounting records exist for this firm from 1815 to 1818. In 1819, Whiting purchased all interests in the business and continued it under his own name. Samuel Hoadley remained in Winsted until about 1825, when he moved to Columbia, Ohio. He died in Ohio on September 30, 1858, at the age of eighty-one.

Riley Whiting continued to manufacture wood tall clocks, or grandfather clocks, after November, 1819. Most clocks by him that exist are easy to identify, as he always had his name boldly painted on the decorated dial. (Unfortunately, it was common practice for most early makers of wood tall clocks to enclose a separate printed identification and instruction sheet for the clock in its packing box. Since the labels were not permanently attached to the clocks' cases, many of these clocks are unidentifiable as to maker.)

For the next decade, Whiting carried on extensive business, judging from the number of his wood tall clocks that survive. Silas Hoadley of Plymouth would seem to have been his only competition, as most makers ceased production of the

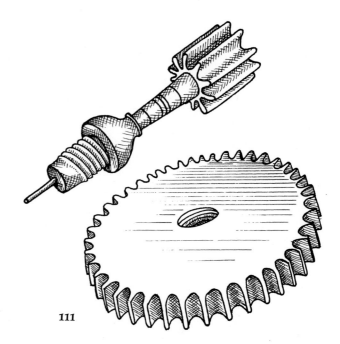

111

112

113

111

**114.** Outside-escapement pillar and scroll clock developed by Eli Terry, Plymouth, CT, *c.* 1818. Handsome example with striped maple case trim and cast pewter hands. *(Courtesy, Amos G. Avery)* **115.** Another visible escapement clock by Eli Terry. Note that weight has fallen through hole in case bottom. *(American Clock & Watch Museum)*

114

115

116

117

**116.** Pillar and scroll made by Seth Thomas, Plymouth, CT, *c.* 1820, with pendulum hanging right of center. **117.** Eli Terry's earliest shelf clock design in simple box case with dial painted on reverse of door glass. Labeled examples were sold by Seth Thomas from *c.* 1815 to 1818. *(Both, American Clock & Watch Museum)*

tall clock by the early 1820s in order to produce the shelf clock. In 1823, Whiting became concerned with the patent claims of William Leavenworth, and wrote the following to William's nephew:

Winchester 7th May 1823

Mr. Mark Leavenworth
Sir—I am full of faith that Wm Leavenworths Patent on Wooden Clocks can be laid asside as he made no improvement—I will give you thirty dollars—if you will get it done or I will endeavor to do it if you will give me that sum (if I do it) I wrote you some time since that I had a quantity of Cherry on hand—but have had no answer from you—suppose you are supplied.
My family are tolerably well

Yours
Riley Whiting

It would appear that the patent claims were "laid aside," as no more mention was made of this supposed patent.

Toward the end of the 1830s, Riley Whiting did adopt the shelf-clock styles and phased out the old-fashioned tall clocks. He made very few pillar and scroll models, but did become a prolific producer of stenciled and carved-column shelf styles.

In the summer of 1835, Riley made a business journey to the midwest and, while visiting with a daughter in Jacksonville, Illinois, became ill and died on August 5, 1835. The *Annals of Winchester* stated that "he was a man of quiet, unassuming manners and feeble constitution, who more than most men, minded his own business and prosecuted it with the same perseverance in adverse, as in prosperous circumstances; and though twice compelled to assign his property, yet in both instances succeeded in paying off his debts, and left a handsome estate at his death. . . . He was a man highly esteemed. He represented the town in the legislature in the years 1818 and 1832."

It is probable that the factory was used to produce wood shelf clocks with Whiting's labels for the next six years, as it was not until October 29, 1841, that his widow, then Mrs. Erasmus Darwin Calloway, sold the factory to Lucius Clarke, William Lewis Gilbert, and others.

Six miles east of Plymouth, Connecticut, at Bristol, several makers of wood clocks began working at the turn of the nineteenth century. Gideon Roberts was the first of these and was making tall clocks at a shop on Fall Mountain in the southern part of the town before 1800. Roberts, along with several sons, produced wood tall clocks in some quantity for fifteen or more years, though he utilized more antiquated methods of manufacturing than did Terry. Other shops were established there about 1810 by Dr. Titus Merriman, Joseph Ives, Chauncey Boardman, and oth-

ers. Most of these men had abandoned the manufacture of wood tall clocks before 1820, though Chauncey Boardman carried it on until about 1825.

Tall clock production was not as extensive in Bristol as in Plymouth, but the manufacturing that did exist paved the way for the establishment of many firms in the third and fourth decades of the century. By the mid-1840s Bristol had become a world leader in clock production, a position it held into the twentieth century.

Gideon Roberts, born on March 5, 1749, in the part of Wallingford, Connecticut, now known as Meriden, came to the Bristol area in 1758. His father, Elias Roberts, had purchased a blacksmith shop on Wolcott Street in June of that year. Gideon's mother, Susannah Ives, was a great-aunt to Joseph, Chauncey, Amasa, and Shaylor Ives, who later became prominent in Bristol clockmaking. The family moved to the Wyoming Valley of Pennsylvania in 1770, where the father, Elias Roberts, was killed in the Wyoming Valley Massacre on July 3, 1778. Gideon returned to Bristol in 1782.

In 1798, Gideon purchased a home on Fall Mountain, where he lived the remainder of his life. It is likely that he became involved in the clockmaking business at this time.

Most of the identified Gideon Roberts clocks have paper dials glued on a wood dial plate, and are numbered. Number 37 is the lowest number now known; the highest is 643. It is probable that his later clocks had unsigned, painted dials. The Roberts style of movement can be differentiated from the Terry and Waterbury styles because Roberts spaced his movement plates more than three inches apart, farther than those of the others. His movements were well finished, the wheels being cut with a clockmaker's engine. He produced many thirty-hour wood tall clocks, but did not, apparently, venture into the production of brass clocks.

In his autobiography, Chauncey Jerome wrote that "Gideon Roberts got up a few clock movements in the old way. He was an excellent mechanic and made a good article. He would finish three or four at a time and then take them to New York State to sell. I have seen him many times, when I was a small boy, pass my father's house on horseback with a clock on each side of his saddle and a third lashed on behind the saddle with the dials in plain sight." Since Jerome was born in 1793, it was probably 1800 when he saw Roberts traveling to peddle movements.

By 1810, Roberts' clock business had grown so much that he was able to establish an agency in Richmond, Virginia, to distribute clocks. In a letter dated February 11, 1813, written to his sons Elias and Hopkins in Richmond, Gideon stated, "I have the parts of eighty clocks which I mean to put

Made By
Gideon Roberts
Bristol
Nº

118

together by May 1 and I have been collecting lumber for a thousand more this winter."

Gideon Roberts did not live to see the winter mentioned in his February letter. He died of typhoid fever on June 20, 1813. His estate inventory listed a wheel-cutting machine, two lathes, several tools, and a set of small tools for putting together clocks. The estate was appraised at $11,-501.02, which was a tremendous sum for that day.

Gideon's eldest son, Elias Roberts (1779–1841), was also very active in the clock business. By 1805 he had a separate establishment and was in partnership with Sextus S. Newell (1782–1818) and Daniel Miller in the firm Elias Roberts & Company. The clocks of this firm were similar to those produced by Gideon, but unsigned painted wood dials were used. Many of these were painted by Candace Roberts (1785–1806), his sister. As early as November 15, 1805, she recorded in her diary that she was painting clockfaces for her brother. The firm was dissolved by 1818.

Other early makers of wood tall clocks in Bristol included John Rich, Levi Lewis, Gideon Roberts, Jr., Ebenezer and Solomon Griggs, Dr. Titus Merriman, Merriman & Dunbar, Barnes & Waterman, Chauncey Boardman, Seth Richards & Son, and several firms represented by members of the Ives family.

119

118. Dial of one-day wood tall clock by Gideon Roberts, Bristol, CT, made *c.* 1800. Roberts often used printed paper dials that were hand colored and glued to wood dial plates. Painting wood dial plates became common practice *c.* 1805 in Connecticut. *(Edward Ingraham Library)* **119.** Riley Whiting (1785–1835), wood clock manufacturer at Winchester, CT, from *c.* 1807 to 1835. First in partnership with his brothers-in-law, Samuel and Luther Hoadley, Whiting purchased the entire business in 1819 and continued alone. He was one of the biggest producers of wood clocks after 1820. *(Edward Ingraham Library)* **120.** Eight-day brass-movement shelf clock by George Marsh & Company, Bristol, CT, *c.* 1832. Movement, developed by Joseph Ives, had riveted straps of brass to serve as plates, and rolling pinions. Weights fall through center of hollow columns. *(Courtesy, Edward F. LaFond)*

## PEDDLING THE EXPANDING PRODUCTION

Clock production began to increase rapidly after 1805, and the industry felt a growing need for a way to market and distribute them. Retail stores could sell them in small quantities, but that was not enough.

Gideon Roberts is said to have made trips on horseback to neighboring states before 1800 to peddle clock movements that he had made during seasons of the year not suitable for travel. Eli Terry did the same in his early years, but after he began to manufacture in quantity, he sold clocks wholesale to peddlers, or to middlemen who distributed through peddlers. The industry was indebted to the peddlers, for it probably would not have grown as prosperous as it did in the first decades of the nineteenth century had it not been for quantity distribution.

Mr. G. W. Featherstonbaugh, an English scientist who traveled through America in the early 1840s, during a visit to Arkansas wrote: "As to the Yankee clocks peddler . . . in Kentucky, Indiana, Illinois, Missouri, and here in every dell of Arkansas and in every cabin where there was not a chair to sit on there was sure to be a Connecticut clock."

Peddlers seldom sold the clocks for cash. Money was scarce and the people with whom they were dealing were not often wealthy. Mules, horses, furs, chickens, and numerous other commodities or wares that in turn could be sold were often taken in trade. Shrewd peddlers devised a system. They would set a clock running in the home of a potential, but wary, buyer and leave it for a length of time "on trial." Upon their return for "collection" they would either collect payment or the clock. It is most difficult to give up a luxury once enjoyed, so the peddler was usually assured of a sale.

Some of the trials and problems of the early manufacturers and their peddlers are apparent from letters written by the peddlers themselves. The following was written from South Carolina during the time of the War of 1812, when money was particularly scarce. The problems of the peddler, Benjamin W. Miller, had been compounded by a fire that had recently destroyed the shop of his supplier, Lemuel Harrison & Company of Waterbury, Connecticut. The company, in serious financial difficulty, had requested payment for clocks they had let their peddlers have on credit. Miller replied:

Spartanburgh January 20th 1815
Gentleman: Yours bearing date Dec 31 came to hand last evening & its contents have been duly noted. The loss you have sustained by fire is truly serious & is no more than I anticipated when I wrote you last. I recd your Springs. If you have recd my last Letter which continues the draft and

it meets your Approbation please to inform me as quick as this may reach you if you have not done it and if Checks cannot be procured in future. if you will except of a Draft I will do my best to send on $1000 in the month of March next. I can get New York Paper or could get when in Augusta last if that will answer your purpose better than Drafts and I can get it. I will send that on if you will run the risque of sending it on. If you except any of the above proposals I think I may venture to so you may have sent in March from 500 to 1000 Dolls and if you should not if Peace or an Armistice takes place I may make a Shipment of Cotton Indego Furr & Feathers. You wish to know my present situation & future prospects & with pleasure I will inform you but am sorry I cannot give you a better account. Have between 1 & 200 Dollars on hand. have lately expended for goods in Augusta & elsewhere from 1 to 200 Dolls.

Have about 50 Clocks on hand. Capt Pooles Horse is so cripled as to be unable to travail but extra's excepted he will continue for us, expect he will go to collecting here shortly. he then extra's excepted will bring the Va. buisness to a close & I hope to sell & bring our buisness to a close in this state if the Capt. continues with me in the Spring if he discontinues I cannot untill in the summer. Am wanting a number of parts of a Clock to replace damagd parts shall try to get them made here as the Mails are so dillatory if you sent them they would not arrive in season. I want the Receit for our one Horse Waggon which is in Va if you ever recd it & if Burnt to send an authenticated certificate of its fate and want it immediately sent as the Capt when he goes to Va will want to get it the waggon Am ready now to start out with a load of Clocks. am going collecting and selling.

Wish you to write on the receit of this how high the different kinds of Furr sells to the North if you possess that knowledge. I think sirs that you will have something left after the Bills are paid off & my wages paid if we do not have to lose to much in collection. I fear the Va notes will not be so well paid as So. Ca. Notes. Clock buisness is very dull here in consiquence of others having bad Clocks to sell and some of ours not doing so well. I suppose not less then 2000 are in the state to sell now.

I will thank you to send me all information which may be necessary for me with regard to things I have named which I wish to carry to the Northerd how the times are in particular and what prospects thare are of the termination of our present unhappy Warr. Have nothing more in particular to write. My health is very good at present — Please to excuse these scrables as they are made in great haste. Have some distance to ride to Night to put this in mail before it is closed
With due consideration I am &c
Benj. W. Miller

Mssrs L. H. & Co

Another extant letter, written to Mark Leavenworth of Waterbury, Connecticut, in 1824, during the marketing of pillar and scroll shelf clocks, showed problems had changed little in twelve years. The peddler noted money was scarce, but though he claimed clocks were hard to sell, he asked for a hundred more on eight months credit. The pillar and scroll was then selling in Tennessee for as low as eight dollars, out of which the peddler paid the manufacturer three twenty-five.

Resentment grew in some of the southern states because of the peddling of clocks. Tennessee residents entered a petition in 1829 to hinder the practice. It stated: "Speculators from the North are sweeping the country of what little money remains, and we feel ourselves supported by truth and reason in asserting that $100,000 is carried out of the State annually." A law was subsequently passed on January 5, 1830, taxing the trader twenty-five dollars plus seventy-five cents in fees for an annual license to peddle, with a penalty of a hundred-dollar fine for noncompliance.

In his autobiography, clock manufacturer Chauncey Jerome wrote:

> The southern people were greatly opposed to the Yankee pedlars coming into their states, especially the clock pedlars, and the licences were so high by their Legislatures that it amounted to almost a prohibition. Their laws were that any goods made in their own States could be sold without licence. Therefore clocks to be profitable must be made in those states. Chauncey and Noble Jerome started a factory in Richmond, Va., making the cases and parts at Bristol, Connecticut, and packing them with the dials, glass &c. We shipped them to Richmond and took along workmen to put them together. The people were highly pleased with the idea of having clocks all made in their State. The old planters would tell the pedlars they meant to go to Richmond and see the wonderful machinery there must be to produce such articles and would no doubt have thought the tools we had there were sufficient to make a clock. We carried on this kind of business for two or three years and did very well at it, though it was unpleasant. Every one knew it was all a humbug trying to stop the pedlars from coming to their State. We removed from Richmond to Hamburg, S. C. and manufactured in the same way. This was in 1835 and '36.

It is not known just when this type of clock peddling ceased. It declined considerably after 1840; some, however, continued to exist throughout the Civil War years.

## ELI TERRY'S SHELF CLOCK

After the sale of his shop to Thomas & Hoadley in 1810, Eli Terry went into semiretirement but did not cease work. In December of 1812, he began to acquire more land near the Naugatuck river; among his purchases were a gristmill, a sawmill, and a carding shop. It was at this place, often called "Terry's Mill," that he developed the wood-movement shelf clock. He undoubtedly also devel-

**121.** Unusually proportioned clock, probably intended as a shelf clock, but often called a Connecticut "banjo." Examples attributed to Eli Terry, Jr., Henry Terry, and firm of E. Terry & Sons. Some collectors consider these to be fakes made in modern times from old parts. Though probably true in some cases, there is evidence that some of these were made c. 1830. (*Courtesy, Connecticut State Library*)

**122.** E. Terry's eight-day shelf clock with mahogany-plate movement, made about 1832. *(Courtesy, Amos G. Avery)*

**123.** E. Terry's ingenious crown-wheel alarm mechanism from clock at right. *(American Clock & Watch Museum)*

**124.** Simple box-style case with one-day wood movement and alarm, made by E. Terry & Sons, c. 1830.

oped better machinery and methods to allow for even greater quantity production than he had accomplished with the tall clock. The three-mandrel sawing method for wood wheels, which had been invented by Asa Hopkins of Northfield, Connecticut, before 1814, was almost certainly adopted by him at this time.

By this time, Eli Terry recognized that future growth of the clock business would depend on something other than the old-fashioned tall clock. Uncased, the clocks were not especially attractive. The parts, unprotected, ultimately needed to be cased, which created an additional expense for an already wary buyer. The peddlers who sold them, for their part, found it difficult to transport large cases. Realizing these drawbacks, Terry developed a shelf clock. It was smaller, placed in a handsome case before being sold, and easily transported. Buyers liked it; it was good looking and unusual, self-contained and thus free from additional expense, and could easily be moved from one room to another.

In 1814, Terry applied for a patent to protect his invention; it was granted on June 12, 1816. Several clock manufacturers in the area, realizing the potential of the clock, wanted to produce a similar product, but feared legal action by Terry if they did so. Seth Thomas, however, obtained license from Terry to manufacture wood shelf clocks. Norris North, Mark Leavenworth, Joseph Ives, Silas Hoadley, and Chauncey Boardman all developed different designs in order to capture a portion of the market without paying Terry a fee or risking a law suit for patent infringement.

Though Terry had also developed a brass shelf clock, he apparently felt that the wood clock had greater potential and did not himself engage in the manufacture of his brass clock. However, his apprentice Heman Clark procured the rights, and by about 1818 had gone into production, developing the clock into an eight-day model. Though he manufactured these clocks for several years at Plymouth and Salem Bridge, Clark had a hard time competing with the more cheaply produced wood shelf clock. He also was in competition with Joseph Ives of Bristol and Silas B. Terry of Plymouth, who were makers of brass clocks.

Terry's wood shelf clock was first marketed in a simple box-style case. It was without decoration except for the dial, which was painted on the reverse of a piece of glass in the door.

An agreement was reached on October 2, 1818, by which Seth Thomas could produce Terry's shelf clock; he was to pay Terry a royalty of fifty cents for each clock made. Under the agreement Thomas subsequently manufactured about five thousand clock movements.

After Terry allowed Thomas to make the clock, he decided to design an improved model. After perfecting the new model, he abandoned the earlier style, but allowed Thomas to continue making it.

After 1818, Terry was producing his improved clock with the escapement visible on the front of the dial. This model, commonly called the "outside escapement," was especially attractive because the motion of the clock's running was visible. A few were housed in the box-style case, but most of them were encased in a pillar and scroll case.

Development of the Connecticut pillar and scroll case has been a controversial matter for many years, but evidence seems to substantiate that Terry originated the style and refined it. The design was undoubtedly inspired by the pillars and scrolled tops on many tall clock hoods. Though probably in error somewhat as to dates, Chauncey Jerome recorded the following in his history:

> I went to work for Mr. Terry, making the Patent Shelf Clock in the winter of 1816. Mr. Thomas had been making them for about two years, doing nearly all of the labor on the case by hand. Mr. Terry in the meantime being a great mechanic had made many improvements in the way of making the cases. Under his directions I worked a long time at putting up machinery and benches. We had a circular saw, the first one in the town, which was considered a great curiosity. In the course of the winter he drew another plan of the Pillar Scroll Top Case with great improvements over the one which Thomas was then making.

By 1819, Terry was also making a variation of his new model with the escapement hidden behind the dial. It was more difficult to assemble and because it did not have the appeal of the visible-escapement model, it was made in smaller quantity. Samuel Terry, Eli's younger brother, who had come from Windsor to assemble movements for him in 1818, mentioned in his accounting records that "with swing wheel under the face is extra work. . . ." Terry continued to manufacture this particular style until about 1822.

Still not fully satisfied with his shelf clock, Terry developed another model by 1822 in which he incorporated five wheels in the time-keeping side and five in the striking side. (His earlier models had four wheels on each side.) The new-style movement had the escapement hidden under the dial and was housed in a case that was about one and a half inches taller than the previous models. Terry applied for a patent on the new model, which was granted on July 5, 1826.

Terry offered the use of his improvements to Seth Thomas in about 1822, but the latter declined. They did enter into an agreement on February 23, 1822, in which Terry accepted one thousand dollars in lieu of the fifty-cent royalty that had been a part of the 1818 agreement. Though the 1822 agreement did not give Thomas the right to make the new design, he almost immediately began to do so. His motives for this action are unclear, but Terry later stated that Seth Thomas made over twelve thousand of the new-style movements between February of 1822 and April of 1827.

Because of Thomas' actions, Terry initiated a

**125.** Variant on the pillar and scroll case design by Eli Terry, Plymouth, CT, *c.* 1819. Case with striped maple trim, probably produced special order. Note Masonic scrollwork symbols and keyhole escutcheon. This model, introduced shortly after the outside escapement, has the escape wheel hidden behind the dial and is commonly called the "inside-outside" escapement model. *(E. Ingraham Library)*

**126.** Miniature pillar and scroll clock made by Ethel North at Torrington, CT, *c.* 1825. It stands 29 inches tall. One-day wood horizontal movement designed by his brother, Norris North. *(Courtesy, Amos G. Avery)* **127.** Miniature half-column design by Eli Terry, Jr., Plymouth, CT, *c.* 1830. Painted and stenciled case. *(American Clock & Watch Museum)* **128.** Unique pillar and scroll with calendar by E. Terry & Sons, Plymouth, CT, *c.* 1825. *(Amos G. Avery)*

court suit in 1827 in an attempt to protect his patent rights. Though Thomas was temporarily stopped from producing the clocks, the disagreement was later settled and Terry voluntarily dropped the charges in April of 1829. It is probable that by then he realized his patents were not legally enforceable.

Terry was also active in the 1820s setting his sons up in clockmaking businesses. In 1823, he formed the firm Eli Terry & Sons with his sons Eli, Jr., (1799–1841) and Henry (1801–77). The firm apparently continued until 1833, when Eli retired from active clock manufacturing.

Before 1830, four other Terry firms had been formed. Eli and his brother Samuel were in partnership in Plymouth from 1824 to 1827, marketing pillar and scroll clocks. Eli, Jr., made clocks under his own name and later in company with Milo Blakeslee of Plymouth. This firm existed until the younger Terry died of consumption in 1841. Speaking of Eli, Jr., Chauncey Jerome wrote: "He was a good businessman and made money very fast. He was taken sick when about forty years old, leaving an estate of about $75,000."

In about 1830, Henry Terry began making clocks under his own name. In 1836, he retired from clockmaking and began a wool business.

Silas Burnham Terry (1807–76), the youngest son of Eli, also went into the clockmaking business. Having little interest in wood clocks, he began, after 1831, the manufacture of the more expensive brass shelf clocks.

According to Henry Terry, his father "had no connections with his sons in business after the year 1833. He did not make clocks by the hundred, nor even by the dozen, for many years before his death, and still he never abandoned his workshop. . . . No year elapsed up to the time of his last sickness without some new design in clockwork, specimens of which are now abundant."

During those later years, Eli Terry worked quite a good deal with his son Silas, experimenting with brass clocks. Among his later improvements was the application of the balance wheel to clock movements, for which he was granted a patent on August 9, 1845. This, as well as other of his inventive ideas, was used by Silas Terry.

Eli Terry died on February 24, 1852. Three days later the following notice was carried in the *Waterbury American*:

(DEATHS) In Terryville on the 24th inst., Eli Terry, Esq., aged about 80. Mr. Terry some 25 years ago was one of the most extensive clock manufacturers in the United States — a man of great mechanical genius, and the inventor of the mantle clock, so called, in contradistinction of the old-fashioned case clock. His sons founded the village of Terryville, where for many years Mr. T. has pursued a retired life. He was a highly respected and valued citizen, and an exemplary christian.

## CIRCUMVENTING THE PATENT

Once Terry's patents had been tested and found unenforceable, the threat of court suit was alleviated, and by 1830 the number of firms interested in clock production was growing rapidly. Prior to this, however, several men were actively engaged in shelf clock production. They had developed different movement designs, thereby circumventing Terry's patent specifications. Among these adventurous designers were Norris North, Joseph Ives, Chauncey Boardman, Silas Hoadley, and Mark Leavenworth.

Norris North (1788–1875), a native of Goshen, Connecticut, was the first to design a shelf clock movement that was different from Terry's. His earliest clocks were developed at his shop in Waterbury, on Spruce creek, just a few miles from the "Ireland" shop that Terry had sold to Thomas & Hoadley in 1810. North's earliest clock had long, rectangular plates that ran the entire width of the case. The movement undoubtedly was developed from the one-day tall clock movement; the earliest examples were wound by a pull cord as were the tall clocks.

As was the case with Terry, North's first shelf clocks were not marketed under his own name. Two brothers, Frederick Sanford (b. 1790) and Ephraim Sanford (1785–1845) marketed the clocks after 1818. The labels read "T. & E. Sanfords, Goshen, Conn."; the "T" was most likely a printing error. The Sanfords may have made the cases for these clocks—known examples are scrolled-top cases made of burled and striped maple. They are longer than the Terry-style cases and have no feet. The pillars on the Sanford clock cases were square and reeded rather than turned. It is doubt-ful that this style was made for more than two or three years.

In about 1820, North improved upon his original model and introduced a design that was similar but key-wound. It was marketed under the name Norris North & Company, Waterbury, Connecticut, and sold in pillar and scroll cases as well as flat-topped cases with reeded columns.

In 1823, North moved from Waterbury to Torrington, Connecticut, where he set up a shop on land belonging to his father, Dr. Joseph North. On November 17, 1824, Norris sold the shop to his brother, Ethel (1800–73), and the firm of Norris North & Company was dissolved. Ethel North continued clockmaking in this shop until about 1830, when he gave up the business and moved to Bristol. After 1850, he and his family moved to Hastings, Minnesota, where he died in 1873.

Norris North set up another shop in Torrington in 1824, where he developed a five-arbor movement. The first of these had extremely small wheels and proved unsatisfactory. He then developed a similar movement of slightly larger size; it proved successful and was made in the Torrington area for nearly twenty years thereafter. The Torrington-style movement, as it has been called, was an admirable piece of horological engineering, but was not as successful as Terry's design.

Norris North continued to produce movements in his style until 1831, housing them in popular case designs of the day. However, his financial situation deteriorated to such a point that in March of 1831, he was forced to sell out to his biggest creditor, Erastus Hodges (1781–1847) of Torrington. Hodges was not a clockmaker, but a successful Torrington merchant. He set up his son Edwin (1810–84) in the business. The younger Hodges managed the firm from 1831 until 1842,

127

128

**129.** "Torrington"-style-movement shelf clock by Norris North, *c.* 1827; 24 inches tall. *(Courtesy, Amos G. Avery)*

**130.** Experimental pillar and scroll by Joseph Ives powered by wagon spring. *(Courtesy, Connecticut State Library)*

**131.** One-day pull-up movement (from illus. 132) with cord drums turned smaller to achieve shorter weight fall.

during which time he sold complete clocks and uncased movements to Rodney Brace (1790–1862) and other casemakers.

Rodney Brace, a native of Torrington, went to North Bridgewater, Massachusetts, in the latter part of 1831, and until 1835 made cases and purchased movements from Hodges. Other than those with the label of Norris North, Torrington-style clocks are most commonly found with Rodney Brace's label.

After selling his business in 1831, North remained in Torrington for only about two years, during which he sold some clock hardware and occasionally clocks with purchased movements of the Terry and Leavenworth designs.

In 1834, North went to Oswego, New York, and set up another clockmaking business. It proved unsuccessful and very few clocks were made. The following year he settled in Mexico, New York, and in 1867 moved to Roscoe, Illinois. In 1870 he went to Alice, Grundy County, Iowa, to live with a daughter, and died there on February 6, 1875.

Joseph Ives of Bristol developed a shelf-model clock movement to compete with Terry's. Ives's movement required a case several inches taller than Terry's and he also utilized rolling pinions in his movements. Though some of the movements were housed in large pillar and scroll cases, most were in three-foot-high cases with reeded columns and scrolled tops.

Ives became more interested in the making of brass clocks by 1818, and left the production of the wood shelf clocks to two Bristol firms, Ives & Lewis, and Merriman, Birge, & Company. Ives & Lewis was a partnership between Joseph's brother Chauncey and Sheldon Lewis; it was formed on March 18, 1818, and continued until 1823 or 1824. Titus Merriman and John Birge were in business by 1822 and possibly earlier, though their firm seems to have had a shorter existence than the former.

Another Bristol maker who became interested in the shelf clock was Chauncey Boardman (1789–1857). Boardman had begun to make tall clocks in Bristol in 1811. His clockmaking activities spanned forty years, during which he produced wood tall clocks and wood and brass shelf clocks and supplied thousands of uncased movements to the trade. In 1822 or 1823, he was approached by Chauncey Jerome, who had recently established a small shop in Bristol for the making of clock cases. Jerome needed movements for his cases and contracted with Boardman for them. Jerome recorded in his autobiography:

The clocks of Terry and Thomas sold first rate, and it was quite difficult to buy any of the movements, as no others were making the Patent Clock at that time. I was determined to have some movements to case, and went to Chauncey Boardman, who had formerly made the old-fashioned hang-up movements, and told him I wanted him to make me two hundred of his kind with such alterations as I should suggest. He said he would make them for me. I had them altered and made so as to take a case about four feet long, which I made out of pine, richly stained and varnished. This made a good clock for time and suited farmers first rate.

The movement Boardman made for Jerome was basically a tall clock movement with the winding drums turned down smaller so that the weights would not fall so far in a day's running. The movement has often been mistaken for the overhead-striking shelf clock movement, commonly called the "groaner." Though no definite proof exists as to who designed the "groaner" movement, it is thought that Jerome approached Boardman about two years later—when again in need of a shelf clock movement—and that Boardman developed the overhead-strike design.

Boardman apparently phased out of tall clock production about 1825 and continued producing the overhead-striking shelf clock movement. Because of its unusual design, it did not infringe on Terry's patent claims. Boardman supplied the movements to several Bristol firms and also to Jonathan Frost and Daniel Pratt, Jr., in Reading, Massachusetts. After the threat concerning Terry's patent had lessened, Boardman also began to produce the Terry-design movement.

In 1832, Boardman went into partnership with his son-in-law, Joseph A. Wells. Until its dissolution in 1843, the firm was a large producer of wood movements. Many of their clocks and movements were supplied to Daniel Pratt, Jr., of Reading, Massachusetts, and to Hiram Hunt of Bangor, Maine, as well as to a number of other smaller concerns. Boardman & Wells also bought wood parts from Elisha Manross (1792–1856), who ran a wood-turning and clockmaking shop in Forestville, Connecticut.

In regard to Boardman's business, Joseph L. Hawley, speaking at Bristol's Centennial Celebration on June 17, 1885, recounted:

One of my early recollections is going to the Boardman & Wells' clock factory on the Hartford turnpike, where I took my first lesson in clockmaking. I watched the piles of thin boards of cherry, touched by swift saws, falling as clock wheels in boxes below. Then I found that the clocks were not made by one man, but by as many sets of men and women as there were pieces; and then they were assembled. . . .

In 1837, Boardman purchased a shop that had been established about 1834 by the firm of Barnes, Bartholomew & Company for the manufacture of brass clocks. When Eli Bartholomew sold his interests in that company about 1836, the firm became known as Philip Barnes & Company. Boardman became interested in the manufacture of brass clocks and, along with Joseph A. Wells, was granted a patent on January 1, 1847, for fusee

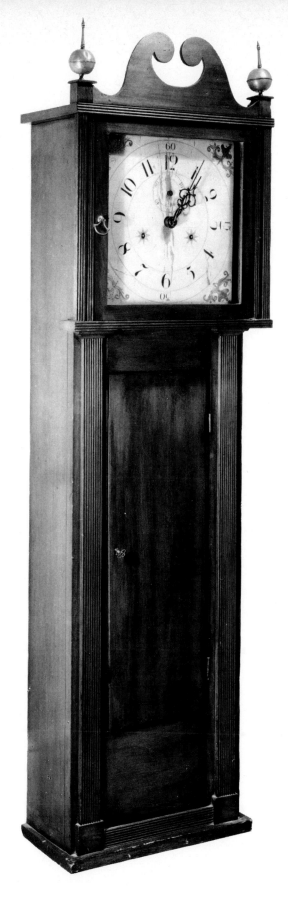

**132.** Dwarf clock, about 4 ft. tall, made c. 1824. Movement made by Chauncey Boardman, cased and sold by Chauncey Jerome, Bristol, CT. *(Courtesy, Edward F. LaFond)*

**133**

**134**

133. "Torrington" or horizontal wood movement developed by circumventing Terry's patents. *(Edward Ingraham Library)* 134. Eight-day brass-movement clock by Heman Clark, Plymouth, CT, c. 1820 *(Courtesy, Amos G. Avery)* 135. Fusee-spring-driven steeple clock with balance-wheel escapement attributed to Silas B. Terry, c. 1845. *(American Clock & Watch Museum)* 136. Unusually shaped "wall acorn" clock made c. 1850 by J. C. Brown's Forestville Mfg. Co., Bristol, CT. *(Courtesy, Mrs. Virginia A. LaFond)* 137. One-day fusee-spring-driven balance-wheel-escapement steeple clock by Silas B. Terry, Terryville, CT, c. 1845. *(Am. Clock & Watch Museum)*

attachments to clocks. Boardman finally sold the Barnes shop to the firm of Brewster & Ingrahams in 1849. He continued in business at his other shop in the Stafford district, Bristol, until 1850, when he went bankrupt.

Silas Hoadley of Plymouth was not as eager to abandon the manufacture of the tall clock as other makers were, but he did adopt a shelf clock arrangement about 1825 or perhaps a little later. Hoadley arranged his shelf clock movement in an inverted design, wherein his gear trains ran opposite to those of Terry. Hoadley's winding drums and bell were at the top of his movement, his escapement was at the bottom—again in opposition to Terry's.

Hoadley's style is often called the "upside down" arrangement, though Hoadley called them "Franklin" clocks. He often used case labels with Benjamin Franklin's likeness and the motto, "Time Is Money." Hoadley's shelf clock production was apparently small until after 1830, the approximate time he stopped making tall clocks.

By 1830, Terry's patent was no longer a threat and Hoadley produced the Terry-style movement and his own Franklin style in about equal numbers. He also produced the latter style in an alarm model and, after 1830, developed another style of alarm timepiece, which he produced in some quantity. By 1836, Hoadley was producing about two thousand wood clocks a year.

After 1840, Hoadley began to decrease his production of clocks and market some one-day brass clocks in ogee cases. It is doubtful that he retooled for brass-movement manufacture at such a late date in his career—it is more probable that he purchased the brass movements. Hoadley retired from business about 1849 and rented his shops for the making of knives and shears. He died at Plymouth on December 28, 1870, at the age of eighty-four.

## THE BRASS SHELF CLOCK

Though most of the Connecticut clock industry was engaged in the production of wood shelf clocks between 1820 and 1840, there were a few men who were convinced of the superiority of brass movements for clocks. Asa Munger manufactured brass-movement shelf clocks for several years in New York State, as did Heman Clark, Joseph Ives, and Silas B. Terry in Connecticut.

Though brass clocks were produced in substantial quantities by all these men, their clocks were considerably more expensive to make than the wood clocks and had to be sold for a much higher sum. Prices for brass clocks ranged from about fifteen to thirty-three dollars or more,

135

whereas most wood shelf clocks sold for less than ten dollars.

Because of the competition between manufacturers of the wood clock, not one of them was completely successful. However, their efforts to produce brass clocks at less cost laid the foundation for the development and introduction of Jerome's cheaper brass clock.

Heman Clark, apprentice to Eli Terry, was taught the principles of making both brass and wood clocks, though he probably made only wood clocks in quantity until 1816 or later. He had purchased a shop in Plymouth from Terry on December 30, 1807, but apparently set up an additional shop at Plymouth Hollow a few years later, which he sold to Seth Thomas on December 9, 1813.

In September of 1809, Clark sued Samuel Hoadley, Luther Hoadley, and Riley Whiting, "dealers in company under the firm of Samuel Hoadley and Company," for default on a note. In September of 1812, he sued the firm of Lemuel Harrison & Company of Waterbury; they owed him fifty dollars for "wheel stuff for 1,000 clocks."

Clark apparently obtained the right to produce Terry's one-day brass clock movement after 1816. An example of his clock is known, which is housed in a pillar and scroll case, the latter sug-

137

136

**138.** Domed candlestand clock with balance-wheel escapement by Terryville Mfg. Co., Terryville, CT, *c.* 1854. Milk glass base. **139.** Huge Empire clock, 42 inches tall, by Forestville Mfg. Co., Bristol, CT, made *c.* 1845. Etched glass tablets. *(Both, American Clock & Watch Museum)*

**138**

gesting production about 1818. No doubt Clark realized that his clock was no competition for the wood clock. He redesigned the movement so it would run eight days, and thereby increased its appeal. Though some of these eight-day movements were sold in pillar and scroll cases, most were housed in flat-topped cases with four pillars, possibly designed by Clark.

Until about 1822, Clark produced brass clocks at a factory in Plymouth. During these years his financial situation deteriorated, and in 1818 he was forced to mortgage his land and factory to Myles Morse, Sr., of Plymouth. Apparently Clark settled a portion of his debt with clocks, as the Morse name can sometimes be seen on the dial of a Clark clock.

Clark sold the Plymouth factory about 1823 and moved to Salem Bridge, where his brother Sylvester had set up a factory. He apparently worked as a movement maker for his brother, for his name is not known to have appeared on clocks dating after that period.

Heman Clark lived at Salem Bridge until his brother sold the factory in 1835, and then moved to his native town, West Haven, where he died on January 23, 1838, at the age of fifty-five.

Heman's son, George, did not continue the business. His three brothers—Jehiel, Virtue, and Sylvester—were, however, in the business of clockmaking. Jehiel (*c.* 1781–1854), who was two years older than Heman, left Connecticut as a young man and settled in Cazenovia, New York, where he made tower clocks.

Virtue (b. *c.* 1799) went into partnership with Garner Curtiss about 1824 and in April of that year Curtiss & Clark contracted with Sylvester Clark to do all the turning of iron and steel and make screws for 200 clocks. These are believed to have been for small shelf clocks, designed by Heman Clark, that had imported springs instead of weights for motive power. These little clocks are among the earliest spring-powered clocks produced in any quantity in America.

Sylvester Clark (1801–81) established a shop at Salem Bridge about 1822 for the manufacture of brass movements designed by Heman. The business continued until 1835, when it was sold to Richard Ward. Sylvester later moved to Milford, Connecticut, where he spent the remainder of his life. His clocks are especially noted for their well-made cases. One of them—with the label of Israel Harrison, a cabinetmaker in New Haven—is in existence.

Richard Ward (1787–1854) ran this clock shop from 1835 until the time of his death. He produced some movements of Clark's design, but later designed a variation on it, using long, narrow plates. Ward's business was taken over for a short time by his two sons, Lewis and Lauren.

139

Two other firms that produced Clark-style movements were active in the late 1830s in Salem Bridge—Spencer & Hotchkiss and Spencer, Wooster & Company. Many of their clocks were housed in two-decker Empire-style cases.

Another prolific user of the Clark movement was Lucius Brown Bradley (1800–70) of Watertown, Connecticut. He was casing movements as early as August, 1823. It is believed that he purchased his movements from Sylvester Clark's firm. In April of 1827, he sold a mechanic's shop to Clark "for the valuable sum of one dollar," probably because he was indebted for movements.

As early as October of 1824, Bradley had mortgaged his shop to two merchants, James Bishop and Merit Hemingway. James Bishop (1786–1840) was not a clockmaker, but became Bradley's partner for a number of years, giving financial aid. Bishop & Bradley probably discontinued marketing clocks with the Clark brass movement in 1827, though they continued the production of wood-movement clocks. The clock shop was still in operation in April of 1832, but was destroyed by fire soon after, "with a warehouse full of clocks ready for shipment."

Bradley remained in Watertown for the remainder of his life, but did not resume the clock business. James Bishop suffered financial reverses and moved to East Haven, where he died in 1840. Though he had once been a wealthy man, his estate was valued at only $115.75.

Judson Williams Burnham (1793–1857) marketed movements purchased from Heman Clark in 1820. Burnham was a merchant in Salisbury, Connecticut, and sold clocks both under the name J. W. Burnham and in partnership with J. Rommele of that town. It is doubtful that he made clocks, but it is interesting to note that the name of his father, Abner Burnham (1771–1818) of Sharon, Connecticut, has been seen on one brass-movement tall clock. Burnham later moved to Carbondale, Pennsylvania, where he carried on a mercantile business.

A study of the development of the brass shelf clock is incomplete without including the achievements of Joseph Ives (1782–1862) of Bristol. Ives began making wood tall clocks in 1810, but by 1817 had become interested in the development and production of brass-movement clocks. His productive career extended over a period of fifty-two years, in which he invented the wagon-spring clock—the first attempt to produce a cheaper spring-motivated clock in America—and manufactured brass shelf clocks and wall clocks, eight-day brass shelf clocks, clocks with tin—rather than brass—plates and wheels, and wood tall clocks and shelf clocks.

On March 18, 1818, Ives sold his clock factory to Sheldon Lewis and his brother Chauncey, who formed a partnership for the manufacture of wood-movement shelf clocks of his design. Joseph then moved to the shop of Elias Roberts of Bristol and formed a partnership, known as Joseph Ives & Company, with Elias and Titus Merriman Roberts. The firm made brass-movement wall clocks housed in cases, about four and a half feet long, that had mirrors—then called looking glasses—and scrolled tops.

Chauncey Jerome records that "in 1818, Joseph Ives invented a metal clock, making the plates of iron and the wheels of brass. The movement was very large, and required a case about five feet long. This style was made for two or three years, but not in large quantities." Jerome did not mention the fact that these large clocks had looking glasses. Perhaps he did not want to diminish his own claims to the invention of the bronzed looking-glass clock a few years later.

Ives felt that his use of the looking glass was a new invention and in August of 1817 applied for a patent for looking-glass clock cases. Ives's addition of the looking glass was not a new feature in clockmaking, though perhaps it was in the Bristol area. This fact is substantiated by a letter written to Samuel Terry of Bristol on March 11, 1830, by Aaron Willard, Jr., of Boston, in which he said: "I have, since being in business say twenty-five years, been in the habit occasionally of putting looking glasses into the fronts of my clocks and timepieces of all descriptions, and I believe it has been practiced by many others, some of whom are of longer standing in the business than myself." Nevertheless, Ives was granted the patent on March 21, 1822.

Ives used rolling pinions in his brass clocks, as he had previously done in his wood ones. Dials were obtained from the firm of Nolan & Curtis of Boston. His wall clocks sold for thirty-three dollars in 1819, and could hardly have competed with Terry's pillar and scroll shelf clocks, which sold for fourteen dollars.

The firm of Joseph Ives & Company was dissolved in July of 1819 and Thomas Barnes, Jr., William Johnson, and Wyllys Roberts leased the shop as the firm of Thomas Barnes, Jr. & Company. Joseph Ives continued to make the large wall clocks for them at least until January of 1822. One of these clocks exists with the notation "Thomas Barnes Clock Maker"; it appears to have been finger-painted inside the case while the painted inner finish was still wet.

On December 4, 1821, Ives petitioned the Hartford Superior Court to declare his bankruptcy; the petition was granted the following month. Ives's creditors numbered over fifty and his estate was apparently liquidated in their behalf.

In about 1824, Ives settled in Brooklyn, New

140. One-day wood-movement clock by E. Terry & Son, Plymouth, CT, c. 1830. Case decoration influenced by stenciled furniture styles. (Am. Clock & Watch Museum)

**141.** "Skeleton" clock under glass dome, by Silas B. Terry of Terryville, CT, *c.* 1845, with balance-wheel escapement and sweep seconds. *(Courtesy, Old Sturbridge Village)*

130

York, and there renewed his clockmaking activities. Here he perfected his spring-driven shelf clock. Instead of using coiled springs, Ives used a series of flat leafed springs attached to the bottom of the case. When the clock is wound, the ends of the flat springs are bent inward, and the force that the springs exert to return to their original shape is sufficient to run the clock.

Clement Davison of New York placed the following advertisement of Ives's clock in the *Connecticut Courant* of June 29, 1830:

TO TRAVELLING CLOCK DEALERS.
IVES' PATENT LEVER-SPRING CLOCKS.

The above CLOCKS are made upon a new principle, and are found to perform well. The Springs are not tempered, and can never break or be affected by the changes of weather, and are of sufficient strength to make the Clock run eight days, or longer if required. They can be sold much lower than any other brass clock of equal appearance and durability; they strike the hours, and are easily kept in order. The cases are made of mahogany, with metal doors, and are of various and elegant patterns. From their lightness (not exceeding 14 lbs.) they are well calculated for the country market; and not having pullies and weights, are easily set up by those not acquainted with the business.

C. DAVISON
No. 42 Fulton-street, near Pearl, New-York

During his stay in New York, Ives also developed a new method of supporting the movement's wheels. Rather than using solid plates, he used strips of brass riveted together. It was an attempt to modify the amount of brass used and thereby reduce the cost. The method was continued by Ives and other firms, as was the use of roller pinions, until 1868.

In 1828, Joseph's brother Chauncey and their nephew Lawson C. Ives started a clock shop in Bristol, where they produced some wood shelf clocks, but concentrated their production on eight-day brass-movement clocks. The lever spring was sometimes used, but most of their clocks were driven by weights. Elias Ingraham, who worked for C. & L. C. Ives for about three years, developed a three-decker Empire case for their movements.

Joseph Ives was granted two patents on April 12, 1833, one for the rolling pinions he had been using for years and the other for an improvement in count wheels for striking clocks. Movements that used these features were produced by the firm of C. & L. C. Ives until it was dissolved in 1837. The movements were marketed by John Birge; Birge & Ives; Birge, Case & Company; Birge, Mallory & Company; Birge & Fuller; Birge, Peck & Company; Birge & Gilbert; C. & N. Jerome; and S. C. Spring.

In 1839, Joseph Ives moved to Plainville, then a part of the town of Farmington, Connecticut, to continue clockmaking. The area was expected to grow as a social and industrial center. The Farmington canal had been completed in 1829 and goods could be readily shipped to New Haven.

Ives was loaned a great deal of money to go back into business, but financial troubles plagued him from the onset. He started by manufacturing an ogee-cased clock with a newly designed movement, in an attempt to share some of the success being enjoyed by Jerome and his associates. Ives's clock was a better product than their brass clock, but it was more expensive to produce and was therefore not successful.

In 1841, William Hills, Jared Goodrich, and Porteous R. Ives, Joseph's son, started the firm of Hills, Goodrich & Company. They assumed part of the financial burden of Ives's clock business, and the clocks were sold under their name. Ives's final financial failure occurred in May of 1842, but he was allowed to remain with the firm, finishing clocks, until August of 1843.

**142.** "Venetian" style clock by N. L. Brewster, Bristol, CT, c. 1860, with Joseph Ives's tin-plate, tin-wheel clock movement. (*American Clock & Watch Museum*)

On February 24, 1845, Ives was granted a patent for the leafed-spring design of motive power for clocks that he had developed about twenty years earlier. The right to use his patent was obtained by one of his creditors, John Birge, and the firm of Birge & Fuller sold a large number of clocks in Gothic-style cases with the wagon-spring power plant, as it is commonly called.

In 1850, the firm of Atkins, Whiting & Company was formed to manufacture clocks using Ives's designs. The partners in the firm—Irenus Atkins, George Rollin Atkins, and Adna Whiting—had made an agreement with Ives on June 1 of that year, obtaining the right to use his patents. The firm produced wall and shelf clocks—usually with thirty-day movements, using Ives's "wagon spring" to power them. In 1855, the firm was dissolved and a firm called the Atkins Clock Manufacturing Company was formed. Ives was dissatisfied with the new firm and wrote to the partners on June 23, 1856:

> I forbid you and each of you to use or allow to be used, my Patent Elliptical Spring referred to in said contracts in the manufacture or sale of any clocks or in any manner . . . particularly by a certain Company styled the Atkins Clock Mfg. Co.

The firm failed the following year and a successor, the Atkins Clock Company, was formed in 1859. This firm produced clocks for the next twenty years but did not use Ives's designs.

Toward the end of his life, Joseph Ives was granted a patent for a movement he felt was the answer to cost reduction in manufacturing. The movement had plates and wheels made of tin rather than brass, with brass bushings used at points of pivot. Rolling pinions and an unusual multiple rolling-pinion escapement also were used, as the clock would not run with conventional pinions.

Ives produced his tin-plate movements for about seven or eight years; they were sold by Noah L. Brewster, E. & A. Ingrahams, and Elias Ingraham & Company of Bristol. Production of them ceased on his death, April 18, 1862, at the age of seventy-nine. Today, clocks with this movement are rare.

Silas Burnham Terry (1807–76), son of Eli Terry, was an early promoter of the brass-movement shelf clock and produced many types during his forty-five-year career. He established his own clock shop in Plymouth in 1831 and began to produce weight-operated eight-day shelf clocks. Movements produced by him at this time were nicely made but relatively expensive to manufacture (though not more so than the brass shelf clocks being produced at Bristol and Salem Bridge).

143. Flat-topped shelf clock by Norris North & Company, Waterbury, CT, c. 1820. Four-arbor wood movement with escapement between plates. (Author's collection)

144. Eight-day wood clock by E. Terry & Sons, Plymouth, CT, c. 1831. (Courtesy, Connecticut State Library) 145. Norris North's early four-arbor-movement pillar and scroll made at Torrington, CT, c. 1823. (Author's collection)

**146.** Gilt-column shelf clock with Ives's rolling-pinion strap-plate movement made by S. C. Spring & Company, Bristol, CT, *c.* 1865. (*American Clock & Watch Museum*)

**147.** Three-decker Empire case by C. & L. C. Ives, Bristol, CT, *c.* 1833. Elias Ingraham designed this case style *c.* 1831. (*Courtesy, Connecticut State Library*)

As the brass clock industry developed and less-costly styles were introduced, Silas Terry adopted many of the manufacturing techniques for his own use and tried to adapt his designs to the cheaper production. He had worked with his father for several years to develop designs of new and less-expensive escapements, but most proved still too costly to produce.

After 1850, in Terryville, Silas experienced financial setbacks and several successive firms were established and dissolved. The first was S. B. Terry & Company (1852–53), followed by the Terryville Manufacturing Company (1853–55), and finally by S. B. Terry (1855–59). In 1859, he was bankrupt. He subsequently moved to Winsted, where he worked as a movement designer and engineer for William L. Gilbert. He moved to Waterbury by 1867, and there he and three sons formed the Terry Clock Company.

After Silas' death in 1876, the three sons—Cornelius Elam, Solon Mark, and Simeon Gunn—continued the business at Waterbury until the summer of 1880. In that year the operation was moved to Pittsfield, Massachusetts, where it went well until about 1885, when financial strain began to be felt. In 1888 the firm passed from the hands of the Terry family into those of their creditors. (The new firm, known as the Russell & Jones Clock Company, was in business until 1893, when it was finally disbanded.) The year marked the end of an involvement in clock manufacturing enterprises spanning over ninety years for the Terrys.

## SUPPLYING THE TRADE

Though the number of wood clock firms grew rapidly after 1830, many were not able to manufacture the entire clock. Those that could made movements for their own as well as others' products. Many firms made only cases and either purchased the movements outright or traded their products for them. Some bought complete clocks, then had labels printed and attached, claiming they were the manufacturers. Others made only components and traded them for complete clocks.

Among firms that supplied movements to the trade were Ephraim Downs and Samuel Terry of Bristol; Elisha Hotchkiss, Jr., of Burlington; Hopkins & Alfred of Harwinton; Northrop & Smith of Goshen; and some of the firms in which Chauncey Jerome had an interest.

Ephraim Downs (1787–1860) had been involved in clockmaking since December of 1811, the year he went to work for Lemuel Harrison & Company of Waterbury. According to records, he assembled 9,162 wood clocks for the firm during the three-year period he was with them. After their factory fire in 1814, Downs worked for the firm of Clark, Cook & Company in Waterbury.

In April of 1815, he moved to Cincinnati, Ohio, and was employed by Read & Watson; they were producing similar clocks for the western trade. After Read & Watson was dissolved, Downs continued to work for Luman Watson until about 1822, when he returned to Plymouth, Connecticut.

In Connecticut, Downs first worked with his brother-in-law, Silas Hoadley. In 1825, he moved to Bristol, where he purchased a home and a clock shop and partial interest in a gristmill and cider mill from George Mitchell, a prominent Bristol merchant. From 1826 to about 1828, Downs sup-

**148.** Ephraim Downs's mill, Bristol, CT, *c.* 1900. In 1825, Downs purchased this from George Mitchell, using it as a gristmill and clock shop. (*Edward Ingraham Library*)

135

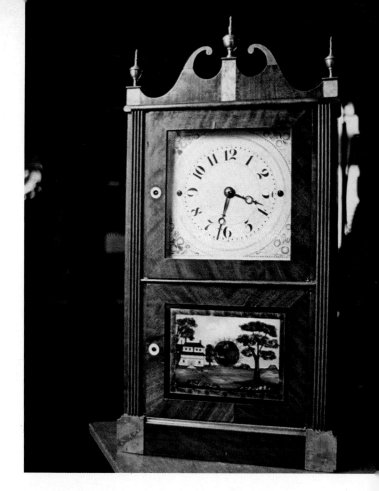

plied over three thousand wood shelf clock movements to Mitchell.

George Mitchell used his money and ingenuity to become involved in the clock business. He contracted with several suppliers of movements and cases and, from about 1825 to 1831, marketed a great number of wood clocks with his label attached.

Downs's manufacturing business continued to be successful until his retirement in May of 1844. He supplied thousands of movements to the trade. When he received cases in trade for movements, he would sell them with his own label, but clocks with his name are not common, for he was content to supply his movements to others.

Samuel Terry (1774–1853) became an important producer of wood movements in Bristol after 1829. He purchased a sawmill, clock shop, and waterwheel, as well as a residence, in the southern part of town. (His home is now occupied by the Bristol Historical Society.) The clock shop had belonged to Charles Kirk, who had conducted a small business there; Terry continued to use it until his retirement in 1835. The shop was destroyed by fire in 1841.

The years between 1829 and 1833 were busy ones for Terry; accounting records show that he was supplying hundreds of clock movements to merchants and case makers. When he was sixty years of age, in 1834, he retired from active business. His sons, Ralph Ensign (1804–92) and John Burnham (1806–70), formed a partnership known as R. & J. B. Terry, and for two years sold a number of eight-day brass-movement clocks housed in three-decker Empire cases.

Elisha Hotchkiss, Jr., (1789–1882) of Bristol and Burlington, Connecticut, another prolific manufacturer of wood shelf clocks, went into business about 1830. Hotchkiss may have been peddling wood tall clocks in the southern states as early as 1819; his family Bible records that his second daughter was born in North Carolina. His older brother, Alva (b. 1785), established a business about 1825 in New York, where he sold clocks supplied to him from Connecticut.

Elisha apparently began to market clocks with his own label about 1830. At that time he lived in Bristol and was buying movements from Ephraim Downs. In June of 1830, he purchased land and half interest in a mill in the neighboring town of Burlington. There he began to manufacture clocks. He cased many of the clocks with his own label and sold a number of uncased movements.

Hotchkiss became heavily indebted in 1833 and during the years that followed was forced to mortgage his home, gristmill, sawmill, and clock factory, including his "lathes, engines for cutting

cog wheels, circular saw with all the machinery and gearing in said mills and clock manufactory." He survived the financial crisis, and by 1837 had formed a partnership with his son-in-law, Edward Fields. Hotchkiss & Fields ventured into the manufacture of brass clocks, and in 1845 were producing wood and brass movements. But financial problems constantly plagued them and, in June of 1844 and later in July of 1845, they were forced to mortgage their shops, tools, and fixtures. Fields sold his interests to Hotchkiss in July of 1846, and in February of 1847, Hotchkiss was forced to turn over the business to his creditors. He moved to Hartford and died there on May 9, 1882, at the age of ninety-five.

Edward Hopkins (1797–1876) and Augustus Alfred (1806–64) went into partnership to manufacture clock movements about 1830 in Harwinton, Connecticut. They produced an exceptionally well-made movement in one-day and eight-day styles; some had alarms. Many of their movements had what were termed "ivory" bushings—so called, but the bushing material was actually animal bone.

An account book shows that from January, 1834, until 1842, the firm sold 3,397 clocks for $17,018.96 and another 849 uncased movements for $1,134.50. A one-day movement sold for $1.25—or $2.25 if it had an alarm. Eight-day movements were $2.00 each, $3.00 with an alarm.

Hopkins & Alfred had a contract with Thomas

**150.** Miniature shelf clock, 22½ inches tall, made by Curtiss & Clark, Plymouth, CT, *c.* 1825. Probably the earliest clock powered by coiled springs manufactured in America. **151.** Label from Curtiss & Clark clock claiming that the springs were "imported from Geneva." (*Thomas E. Grimshaw*)

Moses of nearby Wolcottville, Connecticut, for their cases. One undated contract was contained in their accounts:

Moses agrees to make 1200 cases and furnish stock & deliver to the shop for 90 cts. each, and take 50 eight day movements 50 common alarms 500 common (movements) in payment & out of the 1200 to make eight day cases enough to case all the movements we now have on hand excepting the 50 sd. Moses is to have.

| We are to call eight day movements | 2.00 |
| common movements | 1.25 |
| common alarms | 2.25 |
| cases at 90 cts. each | |
| alarms 1 dollar extra | |

The sd. cases he is to make in good style & whatever the balance is after on either hand to be paid in movements or cases enough to balance & the stock we let him have is to be paid for in cash at the prices agreed.

HOPKINS & ALFRED
THOS. MOSES

By 1839, business was poor because of keen competition and a local recession, and Hopkins and Alfred went back into farming, closing out their clock business accounts in 1842.

Herman Northrop (1801–90) and Benjamin F. Smith (1803–65) formed a partnership about 1833 and purchased the tools and machinery of Henry Hart of Goshen, Connecticut, when the latter gave up the clock business and moved to Farmington, Illinois. Northrop & Smith produced one-day wood movements for about three years, supplying them to concerns in the Goshen area.

Their business ceased on March 19, 1836, when the firm filed for bankruptcy. Their largest creditor was Putnam Bailey of Goshen, but bills were also owed to Asaph Hall and Alpha Hart of Goshen, all of whom were in the clock business. George Welch & Son of Bristol, who had a foundry and cast clock bells and weights, was also among their creditors.

152

# THE GREAT EXPANSION

Once it was common knowledge that Eli Terry's patents were not enforceable, many men ventured into the wood clock business. Since movements could be purchased from various manufacturers, most of the firms that went into business at this time made only cases or, in some instances, acted as middlemen and bought and sold clocks completed by others.

Large businesses after 1830 (including those just discussed) were conducted in Bristol by Atkins & Downs, R. & I. Atkins, Jeromes & Darrow, and E. & G. W. Bartholomew; at Plymouth by M. & E. Blakeslee and Henry C. Smith; at Farmington by George Marsh, by Williams, Orton, Prestons & Company, and by Seymour, Williams & Porter; at Goshen by Henry Hart and Putnam Bailey; at Colebrook River by Elijah Bills; at Winsted by Riley Whiting; at Watertown by Bishop & Bradley; and at Berlin and Middletown by Olcott Cheney. There were more than a hundred other smaller firms, many of them short-lived.

Connecticut wood movements and clocks found their way to the markets of Massachusetts, Vermont, New Hampshire, Maine, New York, and Ohio, and in rare instances to those of New Jersey, Pennsylvania, the southern states, and even Canada.

Of the out-of-state labels, those of Daniel Pratt, Jr., (1797–1871) of Reading, Massachusetts, are most commonly found. Pratt formed a partnership with Jonathan Frost in 1832; they purchased movements from Boardman & Wells of Bristol, which were then cased at their shops in Reading. The partnership was dissolved in 1835, and Pratt continued alone. His wood clocks were marketed as far afield as India—his accounts show that many shipments of wood clocks arrived there and were sold at auction. Pratt was successful in marketing the wood clocks, even after the demand for such clocks had fallen in Connecticut. He purchased remaining stocks of the movement and, perhaps until as late as 1850, continued to sell a few wood clocks.

Chauncey Jerome (1793–1868) began his clockmaking career as a case maker, and for the next forty years the industry was influenced by his case designs. Typically, competitive designs were introduced in an effort to share his success. Not only did his "bronzed looking-glass" clock design replace the pillar and scroll in importance, but Jerome was one of the first to use the ogee shelf clock case, which became extremely successful.

Jerome was a carpenter by trade, and in the winter of 1816 went to work for Eli Terry as a clock case maker. He stayed with Terry only a short time before starting his own business, buying clock

**152.** Samuel Terry (1774–1853) was a prolific producer of wood movements and supplied many case makers in western Connecticut. (*Edward Ingraham Library*) **153.** Reeded-pilaster and scrolled-top clock by Jerome, Darrow & Co., Bristol, CT, *c.* 1825. Overhead-striking, one-day wood movement probably designed by Chauncey Boardman. (*Courtesy, Edward F. LaFond*)

**154.** Striped maple and mahogany Empire-case clock by Sylvester Clark, Salem Bridge, CT, *c.* 1830. Eight-day brass movement. *(Author's collection)*

**155.** Pillar and scroll by Lucius B. Bradley, Watertown, CT, *c.* 1825. Case shows no evidence of having had finials. *(Connecticut State Library)*

**156.** Wall clock, 47 inches tall, made by Joseph Ives, Bristol, CT, *c.* 1820. Brass-plate, iron-wheel movement. *(Connecticut State Library)*

movements and parts and constructing cases for them. In May of 1821, he sold his home in Plymouth to Eli Terry for seven hundred dollars, taking a hundred wood clock movements in trade. Jerome recorded:

> I went over to Bristol to see a man by the name of George Mitchell, who owned a large two-story house, with a barn and seventeen acres of good land in the southern part of the town, which he said he would sell and take his pay in clocks. I asked him how many of the Terry Patent Clocks he would sell it for; he said two hundred and fourteen. I told him I would give it, and closed the bargain at once. I finished up the hundred parts which I had got from Mr. Terry, exchanged cases with him for more, obtained some credit, and in this way made out the quantity for Mitchell.

The deed to this land and home from Mitchell was signed July 12, 1821.

Jerome's account of the exchange is a good example of the bartering that went on in much of the industry. It also demonstrates the way in which men who had no formal clockmaking training often established themselves in the business.

In 1822, Jerome built a small shop in Bristol, "for the making of cases only, as all of the others made the movements." Jerome was buying movements from many sources, a fact that is substantiated by the following entry in the accounting records of Mark Leavenworth of Waterbury:

> July 2, 1822—To 50 Clocks for Jerome without cases M[iddle] size.

In about 1823, Jerome went to Chauncey Boardman of Bristol, who was engaged in the manufacture of wood tall clock movements, and asked Boardman to make 200 of his movements with modifications. Since his cases were about four feet long, he required that the weight fall that made the clock run for one day be short enough to be contained within the case. Few of these have survived, but those that have are sometimes called Connecticut grandmother clocks.

Jerome stated in his autobiography that in the fall of 1824, "I formed a company with my brother, Noble Jerome, and Elijah Darrow, for the manufacturing of clocks, and began making a movement that required a case about six or eight inches longer than the Terry Patent." Jerome's memory may have been in error, as the Bristol land records indicate that this firm may have been formed in August of 1823. The firm, known as Jerome, Darrow & Company, consisted of Chauncey and Noble Jerome, Elijah Darrow, and Chauncey Matthews; it continued in business until Darrow and Matthews sold their interests on October 2, 1826. Clocks produced by the firm were housed in scrolled-top cases with reeded columns, similar in appearance to cases used by Merriman, Birge & Company and Ives & Lewis of Bristol. The movements used by Jerome, Darrow & Company are believed to have been designed by Chauncey Boardman and may have been purchased from him, though Jerome's account stated they "began making a movement" about that time. This over-

**157.** Mirror clock made by Joseph Ives, Bristol, CT, *c.* 1820. Eight-day short-pendulum movement with iron plates and wheels. Case made as integral part of Empire desk. *(Courtesy, Richard J. Ziebell)* **158.** Early banjo clock attributed to Simon Willard, Roxbury, MA, *c.* 1810. *(Courtesy, Edward W. Mink, Sr.)* **159.** Joseph Ives mirror clock in gilt gesso frame, made *č.* 1820 in Bristol, CT. *(American Clock & Watch Museum)*

head-striking movement has been called the "groaner" movement because of the noise caused by the meshing of the wheels in the striking train.

In about 1827, Jerome had an interest in a firm known as Jerome, Thompson & Company, producing clocks similar to those of the preceding firm. On October 6, 1828, Elijah Darrow again entered into partnership with the Jerome brothers, as Jeromes & Darrow, though the firm may have been in existence a year or more before Darrow purchased a portion of the shop. The new firm continued production of the reeded scrolled-top clock and soon after began production of a new style that changed the case-making practices of most of the wood clock industry. Jerome stated:

> The writer invented a new case, somewhat larger than the Scroll Top, which was called the Bronze Looking-Glass Clock. This was the richest looking and best clock that had ever been made, for the price. They could be got up for one dollar less than the Scroll Top, yet sold for two dollars more.

Jerome was somewhat boastful here, but he had introduced a case design patterned after stenciled furniture, which became increasingly popular in the area after 1825. He claimed that this clock was developed in 1825, but again his memory was apparently in error; there is evidence that the style was actually introduced in 1827 or 1828.

Jerome's brother Noble (1800–61) developed a new style of movement for use in the bronze looking-glass clock; it was used only a short time, for it proved unsuccessful. The movement was difficult

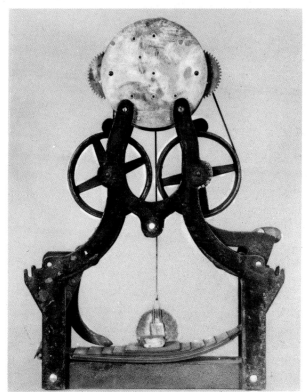

161

160. Empire-case clock, 40½ inches tall, with whistle pipe organ, made by Kirk & Todd, Wolcott, CT, c. 1850. (True pipes are hidden.) Clock actuates organ once per day, at noon. (*American Clock & Watch Museum*) 161. Joseph Ives's wagon-spring power plant. When clock is wound, leafed spring is bent as shown on right side of movement. Power exerted by spring returning to original position drives clock. (*Edward Ingraham Library*) 162. Eight-day brass-movement shelf clock with rack and snail striking mechanism, made c. 1835 by C. & N. Jerome, Bristol, CT. (*Edward F. LaFond*)

162

to keep running and the positions of the escapement, count wheel, and other movement parts must have made it a nightmare to work on. The cases were tall, very thin, and the heavy sash made a case dangerously unbalanced when the door was open. If not attached to the wall, the case might easily tip off the shelf.

Complaints from customers obviously forced them to abandon the use of Noble Jerome's "thin" movement. The case was then adjusted to use the overhead-striking movement. Once Terry's patent threat ended, his movement style was also used.

Jeromes & Darrow continued to produce clocks in their stenciled cases and also in carved-column cases, which had been introduced in Bristol by George Mitchell about 1828. Elias Ingraham, a cabinetmaker, had come to Bristol in the spring of 1828 to work for Mitchell and had produced a case with carved columns and animal-paw feet. Ingraham recollected in 1884 that when he came to Bristol, "Chauncey Jerome and Elijah Darrow were in company, making wooden clocks. Their factory stood on the west side of Main Street, north of the bridge. It has been burned since. They were at that time getting up the bronzed, looking-glass clock, which proved to be a great success, as it was very popular."

Elijah Darrow (1800–57) was an ornamental painter who produced clock dials and painted glasses. His name was dropped from the firm in 1833 and the concern thereafter became known as C. & N. Jerome. Darrow did not sell all of his interests to the Jerome brothers until July 14, 1837, when he did so for three thousand dollars.

Manufacture of wood clocks was continued by C. & N. Jerome and the firm also became interested in the eight-day brass shelf clock and marketed a number of examples of two-decker Empire cases. The brass movements for these clocks were bought from other makers in Bristol.

By 1835, the firm of C. & N. Jerome had established a plant in Richmond, Virginia, where

163

164

**163.** Unusually large pillar and scroll, over 3 ft. tall, by Joseph Ives, Bristol, CT, c. 1820. (*Connecticut State Library*) **164.** Early eight-day wagon-spring-powered clock by Joseph Ives, made c. 1825 in Brooklyn, NY. **165.** Eight-day wagon-spring-powered clock by C. & L. C. Ives, Bristol, CT. Case made by Elias Ingraham, c. 1833. **166.** Thirty-day wagon-spring-powered clock by Atkins, Whiting & Co., Bristol, CT, made c. 1853. (*164, 165, 166, Am. Clock & Watch Museum*)

they assembled Bristol-made clock parts. They later moved the plant to Hamburg, South Carolina.

By 1837, the financial situation of C. & N. Jerome was deteriorating. On April 8, 1837, they sold one of their Bristol factories, known as the "Red Clock factory," to the firm of Jerome, Thompson, Peck & Company, who manufactured and vended carriages. The deed noted them "reserving to ourselves the use of the aforesaid Clock Factory long enough to finish the Clocks which we now have making." During May and July of 1837, the Jeromes obtained mortgages amounting to twenty-three thousand dollars. Their financial situation was indeed gloomy.

This was the situation Chauncey Jerome faced as he traveled to the southern states to collect money and clocks owed to his firm. But by coming upon the idea of a cheap brass clock, Jerome not only brought his firm out of financial difficulties but also gave the clockmaking industry a much needed stimulant.

## THE DARKNESS AND A NEW DAWN

During the year 1837, a financial recession hit the country, and the Connecticut clock industry was seriously affected. The industry was weakened during the third decade of the nineteenth century by the tremendous number of promoters who had entered the field and the keen competition among them.

Accounting records of Ephraim Downs of Bristol clearly show the effects of this competition: the wholesale prices of wood clocks were forced down from nine dollars each in 1830 to four dollars by 1837. The profit margin was so low that many firms were having serious financial problems, and some smaller companies went bankrupt.

The following letter, apparently written by Philip Barnes—then living in Massachusetts—to his brother-in-law Renssalaer Upson, says much about the financial problems of the day.

167

168

**167.** Early model of Chauncey Jerome's cheap brass shelf clock, probably manufactured by C. & N. Jerome, Bristol, CT, *c.* 1839. *(Courtesy, Samuel W. Jennings)* **168.** Small ogee-case clock with one-day brass, spring-driven movement and label of Chauncey Jerome, Austin, IL, made *c.* 1866. This was Jerome's last involvement with the clockmaking industry. *(American Clock & Watch Museum)*

Great Barrington
26 Jan'y, 1838

Friend Upson—

As I wrote you when at Bristol what I thought interesting to you at the time, I have but little to say to you at present, and first, — as I wrote you that any bank paper was good here, I must say that times in this respect have changed, and somewhat sooner than I had expected. Some of the heaviest of the banks in this state have failed, and many others are expected daily to follow. Of the banks that have failed thus far, they are almost all of the pet government banks. These banks that have had the deposits are somehow much worse off than those without them, but a general rush among the banks is looked for. A great many will stand, and a great many will fail, and no betting can tell which. Only I should have more fear of the pets than others. Money is ten times as scarce as last year. Not one dollar can be got from any bank in the country and the specie change is all locked up in the petty offices—about 600 locked up in Bristol P. office, not a dollar yet called for. Now, while Government is seizing and locking up all the specie, and perhaps nothing to circulate, I can not see how times are ever to be any better. I have this moment seen a man from Alliance. Most of the safety fund banks there are offering to pay specie, but not a dollar of their money can be found. The rascality of the Commonwealth Bank in Boston is unprecedented. This was the first bank selected by Gen'l Jackson in the nation, after which you will recollect, he retreated suddenly back to Washington. When on his eastern tour at this bank, he issued his famous order for the removal of the deposits, and this bank is owned and conducted mostly by officers of the gen'l Government.

I can not give you any idea of what money will be good in the spring, but would advise you to keep clear of all pets—specie is worth little or nothing. There is none circulating and nothing to get it with. I think but had best have all clocks that the peddlers can sell before there times are out. I do not know what else we can do with the brass clocks. They will sell for nothing at home—I can purchase the best of wood clocks in Bristol at $3.00. That appears the common price.

· I hope that you will get something from that western business this winter, for on that hangs our destiny—thousands upon thousands have been sent there and nothing returned. I think there will be ten failures the ensuing spring to one last spring—not in New York. They have had their worst. But it will sweep the country like a tornado, banks and everything else. May God deliver us from this administration—huzza for Henry Clay wherever you go. He is the only man in my candid opinion that can save the country from utter destruction.

Yours truly,
P. Barnes

Unfortunately, the fate of the firm P. Barnes & Company had been sealed and the company became defunct soon after this letter was written.

**169.** Chauncey Jerome (1793–1868) built America's largest
clock manufacturing concern by 1850, but lost all through
financial reverses in 1855. (*Am. Clock & Watch Museum*)

**170.** Eight-day ogee clock by Hills, Goodrich & Co., Plainville, CT, *c.* 1842. (*Connecticut State Library*) **171.** One-day wagon-spring "double steeple" by Birge & Fuller, Bristol, CT, *c.* 1845. **172.** One-day "hour glass" with wagon spring by Joseph Ives, Plainville, CT, *c.* 1840. (*Am. Clock & Watch Museum*)

Other companies found themselves in a similar situation. It is possible to envision the entire industry ceasing to function had it not been for Chauncey Jerome and his introduction of the cheap brass-movement clock.

Brass clocks were not new in America at this time—the first clocks made in the colonies had had brass movements. But the development of a brass clock that could be made and sold so cheaply that most Americans could afford one *was* something new. Several firms in the second and third decades of the nineteenth century had attempted to make less expensive brass clocks in the form of wall and shelf models, but they had all failed to produce a brass-movement clock that could compete in price with a wood clock.

In the fall of 1837, Chauncey Jerome, then associated with his brother in the firm C. & N. Jerome, set out for Virginia and South Carolina to collect on notes and pick up some scattered clocks. Jerome recorded that while in Richmond and contemplating his serious financial condition, he came upon the idea of the cheap brass clock. He stated, "I was looking at the wood clock on the table and it came into my mind instantly that there could be a cheap one-day brass clock that would take the place of the wood clock. I at once began to figure on it; the case would cost no more, the dials, glasses, and weights and other fixtures would be the same, and the size could be reduced."

Whether Jerome deserves all of the credit he claimed for the development of the cheap clock

has been a subject for debate for some years. It must be admitted, however, that Chauncey Jerome was a successful promoter and in most cases a good businessman, and the industry is indebted to him for the introduction of the new style at a time when it was in dire need of revitalization.

Jerome did not have the ability to make a movement for the proposed clock, but his brother, Noble, was a trained movement maker and designed a mechanism for which he was granted a patent on June 27, 1839. Early examples of this clock were sold by the firms of C. & N. Jerome; Jeromes & Company; Jerome, Grant, Gilbert & Company; and others. Most of these were housed in simple ogee cases, which had become popular about that time. They were relatively plain, but handsome and inexpensive to produce. By 1840, the ogee had become one of the most important case styles and was produced in tremendous quantity for more than fifty years thereafter.

Hiram Camp, Chauncey Jerome's nephew, recorded that "Mr. Jerome had hired a large satinet factory with a new set of tools for movements, and had let out a job of making 40,000 one-day brass movements to his brother Noble, and a man by the name of Zelotas Grant, Jerome to furnish everything, they to do the work for which they were to receive $1.40 each. . . . This went on for a time, but it became evident that the work on the same movements at the old shop did not cost half as much."

By 1840, other companies, realizing the potential of the cheap brass clock, sought to produce it. It became apparent that the industry was

**173.** "London" model eight-day spring-driven clock by Atkins Clock Co., Bristol, CT, *c.* 1870. **174.** Presentation "London" model with thirty-day fusee-spring movement by Atkins Clock Manufacturing Company, Bristol, *c.* 1856. (*American Clock & Watch Museum*)

not going to collapse, and several new promoters became interested and new companies were formed. Even Seth Thomas, who always had been reluctant to adopt new methods, sent his nephew to Jerome in 1840 to learn how to make the new movement.

Jerome wanted to capture British business as well as American. In June of 1842, he prepared a shipment of clocks for England, contracting with a young Bristol man, Epaphroditus Peck (1812–57), to travel with his son, Chauncey Jerome, Jr., (1821–53), to sell the clocks. Jerome agreed to pay Peck's traveling expenses plus seventy-five dollars a month, but "if said Peck does not meet with good success in the business, he, the said Peck, shall pay his own expenses home." Jerome stated that "as soon as it was known by the neighboring clockmakers, they laughed at me, and ridiculed the idea of sending clocks to England where labor was so cheap."

The clocks were invoiced at a value of a dollar and a half apiece and 20 percent duty had to be paid on their arrival. They retailed in England for twenty dollars each. The Revenue Laws of England at the time were such that the owner of goods being imported could declare the value of his goods, but the government had the right to purchase them for the declared value plus 10 percent. When Jerome made his first shipment, he recorded:

> I had always told my young men over there to put a fair price on the clocks, which they did; but the officers thought they put them altogether too low, so they made up their minds that they would take a lot, and seized one ship-load, thinking we would put the prices of the next cargo at higher rates. They paid the cash for this cargo, which made a good sale for us. A few days after, another invoice arrived which our folks entered at the same prices as before; but they were again taken by the officers paying us cash and ten per cent in additions, which was very satisfactory to us. On the arrival of their third lot, they began to think they had better let the Yankees sell their own goods and passed them through unmolested, and came to the conclusion that we could make clocks much better and cheaper than their own people.

Jerome was not making better clocks than the

English makers, but he certainly was making them cheaper, and they won general acceptance. For the next twenty years, the clockmaking industry in England declined to near extinction, and though it would be foolish to believe the imported clock was the only factor causing the decline, it certainly was a contributing one.

Jerome's success led other firms into the exporting of clocks. Among them were Sperry & Shaw of New York and several Bristol firms, including E. C. Brewster, Brewster & Ingrahams, and Birge, Peck & Company. After 1850, the number of exporters increased and clocks were being sent to many foreign countries. In 1865, over nine hundred thousand dollars' worth were exported to over thirty countries.

During the winter of 1844, Chauncey Jerome went to the port town of New Haven, Connecticut, and established a factory for making clock cases and boxing finished clocks to be shipped. The movements were made in Bristol, then sent to New Haven to be cased. On April 23, 1845, a fire destroyed one of Jerome's Bristol factories. Hiram Camp, Jerome's nephew and foreman, recorded in his memoirs:

> They (the shops) were built in the winter, standing on pillars considerably up from the ground, with a quantity of pine shavings under them, which with the leaves of the fall previous left things much exposed to fire, which took place in April, 1845.— Supposedly to be the work of some boys playing with matches. There was no chance to put the fire out, as when first discovered the fire appeared to be under the whole shop at once, we had at this time large quantities of movements and parts in process, the movements mostly were in the 2nd story piled on the benches. The windows were opened and the movements pitched out on to the ground enough to fill an Office building that stood outside that was sixteen feet square, the tools to some extent were got out, but all presses, and dies, went through the fire. . . . The lathes that were saved and the benches were pulled up with the lathes on them. This fire was a great loss, probably not less than $75,000.

Soon after the disaster, Jerome moved all his operations to New Haven.

In 1850, the Jerome Company formed a firm known as the Jerome Manufacturing Company. Benedict & Burnham, brass manufacturers of Waterbury, became interested in the new company as an additional market for their brass. They invested thirty-five thousand dollars; Jerome put up an equal amount. But later, they became dissatisfied and sold their share to Jerome.

In 1855, the Jerome Manufacturing Company became financially entangled with Theodore Terry (1808–81) and his partner, the great showman Phineas Taylor Barnum (1810–91).

Theodore Terry had been conducting a clock business in Ansonia in conjunction with the Ansonia Clock Company and when that factory burned in 1854 he was left with nothing but damaged clocks and parts. Despite P. T. Barnum's financial backing, the cost of reestablishing the business was prohibitive. The two men merged their interests with the Jerome Manufacturing Company, but the combined financial burdens were too great and they went bankrupt in November of 1855.

**176**

**175.** One-day weight-driven brass-movement clock by Chauncey Jerome, Bristol, CT, c. 1845. (*American Clock & Watch Museum*) **176.** Noble Jerome's 1839 patent one-day brass movement. With small modifications, thousands of these were made between c. 1840 and 1900. See illus. 167. (*Courtesy, Samuel W. Jennings*)

177

178

Hiram Camp wrote an account of how the financial problems came about:

The Jerome Manufacturing Company were struggling along, Mr. Jerome himself not being posted up as to the standing of the Company but thinking the Company was making money, engaged in building a Church on Wooster Square, New Haven. But, things began to go hard, and in their extremity the Secretary, Mr. S. B. Jerome [Chauncey's son], made an agreement with P. T. Barnum, the great showman, who had been interested in the clock business with one Theodore Terry in Bridgeport where Barnum resided. Terry had sold out to Barnum a refuse lot of almost useless stuff. The plan now was a merge—the two companies into one. Barnum said that their Company owed about $20,000 which afterwards proved to be over $70,000 which the Jerome Company had to assume after the merging of the two companies. In this trade it was provided that Barnum should endorse the Jerome paper, which he did for a time, but as the old claims against Terry & Barnum came forward, a large amount of those were paid. This amount, added to the liabilities of the Jerome Company, caused the failure of the Company in November, 1855. Barnum was still around, and made his boasts of his ability to put things through, and thus drew the wool over the eyes of those interested to quite an extent. He got everything available in his hands belonging to the Company that was possible, deceived those that were brought into trouble by the failure of the

Jerome Company, even offering and taking, long business paper to New York for discount, the proceeds of which was never returned, and one poor sufferer became deranged and drowned himself. But, after he had gotten things in his own hands as much as possible, he put his property out of his hands, and claimed that he had been ruined by the Jerome Company.

After the company failed, Jerome moved to Waterbury for about a year and made cases for Benedict & Burnham. In 1857, he moved to Ansonia, staying about two years. He returned to New Haven and became a superintendent in a concern known as the United States Clock Manufacturing Company. He moved with the company to Austin, Illinois, in 1866.

Biographer James Parton, while traveling in the Midwest, wrote: "Chauncey Jerome . . . is now at the age of seventy-three, far from his home, without property, and working for wages. I saw him, the other day, near Chicago, with his honorable gray hairs, and his still more honorable white apron, earning his living by faithful labor for others, after having had hundreds of men in factories of his own."

Chauncey Jerome later returned to New Haven, where he died on April 20, 1868, at the age of seventy-four. Besides listing his clockmaking activities, his obituary noted that he was mayor of New Haven (1854–55), a state legislator in 1834, and a presidential elector in 1852.

**179.** Eight-day weight-driven clock with rack-and-snail striking, made *c.* 1835 by C. & N. Jerome, Bristol, CT. Unusual dial with black chapter ring and gilt numerals. *(Connecticut State Library)*
**180.** Beveled case design with one-day wood movement by Daniel M. Tuthill, Saxton's River, VT, dated 1841. *(American Clock & Watch Museum)*
**181.** Eight-day brass-movement timepiece in pillar and scroll case made by John Kirk, Bristol, CT, *c.* 1830. Painted false left keyhole. *(Courtesy, Helen Watters Riga)*

## NEW HORIZONS

Introduction of the inexpensive brass clock opened new avenues for research, development, and manufacture. Springs were adapted to the mechanisms, allowing for styles that were smaller, more compact, and portable. The development of balance escapement movements paved the way for styles such as travel clocks and alarm clocks. Cal- endar clocks, precision regulators, and tower clocks were produced in great numbers after 1850.

The production of mechanical timekeepers was foremost until about 1930, when the produc- tion of electrically powered clocks began to supersede it. The electric clock and, later, the bat- tery-operated clock eventually put an end to pro- duction of the pendulum clock and seriously reduced that of the marine-movement clock.

182

**182.** "Eagle" model cast-metal-front clock by the American Clock Co., NY, NY, *c.* 1865. Eight-day brass movement enclosed in wood box behind metal front. *(Courtesy, Ellis M. Bidwell)* **183.** Cast-metal-case clock with one-day marine movement. Listed as "Tucker-bronze" model in American Clock Co. trade catalog, 1869. *(Courtesy, Mrs. Helen Watters Riga)* **184.** "Cigar box" style cottage clock by New England Clock Co., Bristol, CT, 1851. One-day brass timepiece movement, decalcomania decoration on glass. *(American Clock & Watch Museum)* **185.** Rare skeletonized calendar clock by Ithaca Calendar Clock, Ithaca, NY. Uncertain date, but probably *c.* 1875. *(Courtesy, Mrs. Rose P. Brandt)*

## SPRING-DRIVEN CLOCKS

Weights were generally used for motive power until about 1840 (though some rare examples of spring-driven clocks made before that date have survived—usually in the form of bracket clocks). After 1840, and continuing until the introduction of the electric clock in the 1930s, the spring was the most important source of motive power.

Joseph Ives was probably the first to produce a spring-driven clock in any quantity. This was his lever spring, or wagon spring, which he used after 1824. The spring consisted of a series of flat leafed springs attached to the bottom of the case; it differed totally from the usual coiled springs.

Coiled springs had been imported in the eighteenth and early nineteenth centuries, but were far too expensive to be used profitably in inexpensive clocks. Sheet steel was also imported—it was cut into strips and coiled—but the spring produced from it was also costly.

Silas B. Terry, son of Eli Terry, was first to develop a method for tempering coiled springs and thereby producing them cheaply. He received a patent in 1830 for the process, and sold it to Edward L. Dunbar of Bristol about 1847.

John Pomeroy of Bristol also experimented with the tempering of steel springs and developed another method after 1840. Springs made by the Pomeroy process had better surfaces than those developed by the Terry method.

On May 23, 1836, Joseph Shaylor Ives, nephew of Joseph Ives, was granted a patent for making coiled springs from brass. Two years later he was granted another patent for a device that could be attached to the front plate of a weight-driven clock movement to convert it to a spring-powered movement.

Brass springs were commonly used in Bristol during the 1840s and extensively used by Brewster & Ingrahams, Elisha Manross, and Terry & Andrews, among others. Brass springs were cheaper to produce than imported steel ones, because the temper could be achieved by cold working of the brass during the rolling process.

By 1845, spring-driven clocks were attaining popularity and by 1850, they were made in greater numbers than weight-driven models. Though some brass springs were probably used until the Civil War, they were rare after 1850. By then steel springs had proved to be more suitable and less expensive to produce.

186    187

**186 & 187.** One-day brass-movement timepieces by Jerome Mfg. Co., New Haven, CT, *c.* 1853. Both have unusual marine escapement designed by S. N. Botsford. *Left:* papier-mâché case with inlaid mother-of-pearl. *Right:* Thin gilt metal case. *(American Clock & Watch Museum)* **188.** "Gloria"-model swinging-ball clock by Ansonia Clock Co., Brooklyn, NY, *c.* 1910. Clock and pendulum both swing, pivoting on figurine's hand. *(American Clock & Watch Museum)* **189.** Imported three-color Majolica china case with movement by New Haven Clock Co., New Haven, CT, *c.* 1900. *(Author's collection)* **190.** "Gilt Column" model one-day weight-driven shelf clock by Seth Thomas Clock Co., Thomaston, CT, *c.* 1870. *(American Clock & Watch Museum)*

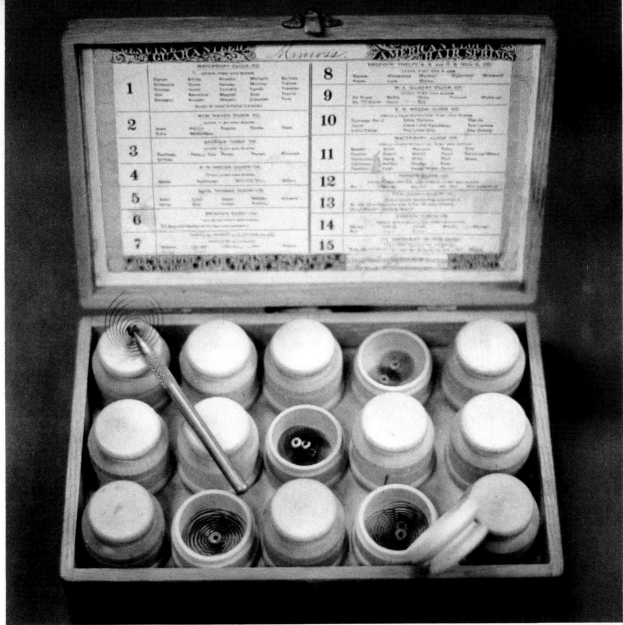

**191**

**192**

**191.** Set of marine clock hairsprings manufactured by F. N. Manross, Bristol, CT, *c.* 1890 for fourteen different clock manufacturers. Note that Ezra F. Bowman of Lancaster, PA, was an agent. (*American Clock & Watch Museum*) **192.** Globe clock made by Globe Clock Co., Milldale, CT, *c.* 1883, with Laporte Hubbell marine movement. (*American Clock & Watch Museum*) **193.** Two-dial calendar clock made by Burwell & Carter, Bristol, CT, *c.* 1860. Calendar mechanism patented by B. B. Lewis of Bristol in 1862. (*American Clock & Watch Museum*)

**194**

**195**

**194.** Eight-day weight-driven gilt-column model by Seth Thomas Clock Co., Thomaston, CT, made *c.* 1870. Originally cost $12. *(Connecticut State Library)* **195.** Regulator "No. 1, Extra" made by Seth Thomas Clock Co., Thomaston, CT, *c.* 1870, in burled walnut case. Eight-day weight-driven movement with dead-beat escapement, designed by Silas B. Terry. Original cost of clock was $27. *(Author's collection)*

## MARINE CLOCKS

Marine, or lever, clocks are those which operate with a hairspring balance. The name does not necessarily connote a ship's timepiece. Most often of small dimension, the marine clock continues to run while being carried or when on an uneven surface, which is not true of the pendulum clock.

Reliable marine clocks were developed for mass production in the 1840s and became popular in various styles. In about 1890, a clock was evolved, using the marine clock movement, that became the forerunner of today's alarm clock. The movement powered the alarm clock almost exclusively early in the twentieth century; its use was diminished eventually by the increased use of electricity and battery power.

Silas B. Terry produced several types of marine clocks, using features from a patent granted to his father in 1845, but they were not economically successful. In 1847, Charles Kirk of Bristol, Connecticut, was granted a patent for a marine-type clock with a two-pallet escapement. In describing Kirk's clock thirty years later, Rodney Barnes (1818–98) wrote in his memoirs: "Charles Kirk made one with two crown wheels. It was an unsightly thing. . . . About the year 1848, William B. Barnes got up a thirty-hour marine clock, the first that was ever made that could be called a clock."

In 1849, William Bainbridge Barnes formed a company in Bristol with Ebenezer N. Hendrick, Laporte Hubbell, Daniel Clark, and Rodney Barnes for the manufacture of these clocks. The firm was known as Hendrick, Barnes & Company and also as Hendrick, Hubbell & Company. They produced Barnes's marine clock until 1852, when they were succeeded by the firm of Hendrick, Hubbell & [Levi] Beach. Chauncey Jerome, who had previously been the largest user of their movements, bought the firm about 1854. When the Jerome Manufacturing Company failed in November of 1855, the Bristol firm found itself in a financially embarrassed position, but its creditors allowed the firm to continue. Ebenezer Hendrick committed suicide, but Hubbell and Beach survived the crisis and absolved the debts, reorganizing the business under their names in 1859.

In 1863, Hubbell and Beach went into partnership with Don J. Mozart in order to produce a calendar clock with a marine movement of a year's duration. A patent was granted on January 5, 1864, but few of the clocks were ever produced. Beach died shortly after and Mozart went to Providence, Rhode Island, where he endeavored to manufacture a watch of his own design.

Laporte Hubbell (1824–89) continued in business alone until his shop burned in 1873. He rebuilt the factory in 1874, took his son Frederick into partnership, and they continued manufacturing until 1889. Hubbell was an ingenious mechanic and supplied marine movements to the trade for about forty years. Few clocks carried his name as maker, but many contained his movements.

Among the other manufacturers of marine movements were Mathews & Jewell of Bristol, who made Samuel N. Botsford's style of movement for the Litchfield Manufacturing Company from 1851 to 1854. Noah Pomeroy (1819–96) of Bristol manufactured movements for the trade from 1849 to 1878, as did Samuel Emerson Root (1820–96) from 1851 to 1896.

## CALENDAR CLOCKS

From about 1855 until after the turn of the century, calendar clocks were very popular and the larger companies manufactured several models of them. Though many had simply days of the month surrounding the dial, many had two dials, the separate calendar mechanism being actuated by the clock. There were often further additions: the day of the week and month of the year and, in some cases, the phases of the moon and high and low tides. In most cases the mechanisms corrected for the irregular number of days in different months and for leap year.

Calendar mechanisms were considered important by colonial clockmakers; day-of-the-month indicators were carried on most eight-day clocks and on some thirty-hour ones. Calendars were used on more than half of the wood tall clocks made.

When the wood shelf clock was developed, the use of the calendar was generally abandoned, probably as an economy measure. Though a few pillar and scroll clocks had calendars, shelf clocks rarely show this feature until after 1855.

John H. H. Hawes of Ithaca, New York, was the first to be granted a patent for a separate calendar clock mechanism. His invention, patented on May 17, 1853, did not correct for leap year and apparently was never put into production. Two other Ithaca men, William H. Akins and Joseph C. Burritt, were granted a patent in 1854 for a mechanism and in 1857 for an improvement on it. Rights to both patents were purchased by Wait T. Huntington and Harvey Platts of Ithaca and turned over to James E. Mix and Eugene M. Mix, their mechanics, to produce. The Mix brothers made improvements that were patented in 1860 and 1862; in about 1863, their perfected mechanism was sold to the Seth Thomas Clock Company. The firm used the calendar mechanism until 1876, when it adopted a design developed by Randall T. Andrews, Jr., an employee.

Henry B. Horton of Ithaca, New York, patented a mechanism in 1865 and an improvement on it the following year. Soon after, he was instrumental in the formation of the Ithaca Calendar Clock Company, which produced calendar clocks exclusively until it went bankrupt in 1917. Clock movements for the Ithaca clocks were obtained from various Connecticut sources; the calendar mechanisms as well as the cases were made in Ithaca.

Benjamin Bennett Lewis (1818–90) of Bristol, Connecticut, developed a mechanism that was patented in 1862, with improvements in 1868 and 1881. Lewis' calendar was used by several Bristol firms, including Burwell & Carter (Elias Burwell and Luther F. and William W. Carter), L. F. & W. W. Carter, the E. Ingraham Company, the E. N. Welch Manufacturing Company, and Welch, Spring & Company.

One of the most complicated mechanisms was that made by Daniel Jackson Gale (1830–1901) of Sheboygan, Wisconsin, and patented in 1877. Gale sold the right to manufacture his clock to Welch, Spring & Company of Bristol, who produced several models. Because of their unusually complicated dials and gadgetry, his clocks are very popular with collectors.

Many smaller firms were formed for the manufacture of clocks with yet another new calendar design. Among the better known were the Southern Calendar Clock Company of St. Louis, Missouri, and the Prentiss Improvement Clock Company of New York. The movements for their clocks were generally purchased from Connecticut companies.

## PRECISION CLOCKS

Though much of the American clockmaking industry was occupied with producing a cheaper clock for the general public, some firms manufactured quality timekeepers on a limited basis. Precision clocks were expensive to produce, but there was a market for them—for public buildings, churches, and observatories, and for use as regulators by jewelers.

One such maker in New York State was Charles Fasoldt (1819–98). A native of Dresden, Germany, he trained there as a clockmaker and watchmaker before arriving in America in 1848. He worked in New York City for a while, then in Rome, and finally settled in Albany in 1861. With the aid of his son Otto, he manufactured watches, tower clocks, and numerous styles of regulators and smaller clocks. As an inventor of precision time-keeping devices, Fasoldt was a genius. He was granted several patents during his career and the precision engineering and features seen on many of his clocks have not been surpassed.

During the last two decades of the nineteenth century several Connecticut manufacturing firms offered fine regulators in their trade catalogs. Some were made by them, others were purchased or imported. From about 1890 to 1910 the Seth

Thomas Clock Company produced a line of fine regulators with precision mercury pendulums. In 1888, Thomas introduced a precision clock that it made specifically for astronomical observatories. Though the model was carried in the catalogs for more than twenty years, few examples were produced.

In Boston there was much activity in the production of fine quality clocks and by 1850, fine regulators were already being made there, especially by members of the prominent Willard family. One outgrowth of the efforts in that area and, in fact, the only work of the Boston clockmaking school that has been carried into modern times is that of Edward Howard.

Edward Howard (1813–1904), a native of Hingham, Massachusetts, was Boston-trained. In 1893, he wrote, "My connections with clockmaking commenced at age sixteen, in 1829, under Aaron Willard, Jr., with whom I served an apprenticeship of five years."

Though he finished his training about 1834, it was 1840 before Howard ventured alone into the business of clockmaking. In 1842, he became associated with David Porter Davis, another of Willard's apprentices, as Howard & Davis. About a year later they took on another partner, Luther S. Stephenson; the firm then became known as Stephenson, Howard & Davis. It manufactured gold balances and church, gallery, regulator, and Willard-timepiece models. Stephenson withdrew

196. Watchman's regulator made on special order for Charter Oak Life Insurance Co., Hartford, CT, 1873, by E. Howard Watch & Clock Co., Boston, MA. (Am. Clock & Watch Museum)

from the firm in 1847 and Howard and Davis continued in business together until 1857. Besides clocks and watches, Howard & Davis manufactured sewing machines, fire engines, and balances; the firm received distinguished awards for its production in these as well as other fields.

In 1857, Davis left the firm, which had been constantly plagued by financial problems, and it was reorganized as E. Howard & Company. On March 24, 1861, a joint stock company, the Howard Clock and Watch Company, was formed with one hundred and twenty thousand dollars, and continued business successfully for some years, but in 1879 experienced a serious financial setback because of the failure of a firm with which it had done extensive business. New capital was brought in and the company was reorganized on December 1, 1881, the name becoming the E. Howard Watch and Clock Company.

A few months later, the company bought out Edward Howard's personal interests and he retired from the firm. The company made clocks in Boston until 1934, when it moved to Waltham, Massachusetts. It became the present-day Howard Clock Products Company—which no longer produces clocks.

## TOWER CLOCKS

Clocks for public buildings were the first type produced, appearing in England during the latter part of the thirteenth century. During the colonial period, numerous tower clocks could be found in the American colonies, but most of these were imported from England.

It was not until after 1845 that such clocks were manufactured in quantity here. The E. Howard firm of Boston and the Seth Thomas Clock Company of Thomaston, Connecticut, led in their production and controlled the greater part of the business until after 1930. By then, however, the demand for tower clocks had diminished considerably; public clocks were not as popular as they had been at the turn of the century and the less-expensive electrically driven clock—on special order—could be adapted to suit the purpose.

Ebenezer Parmele of Guilford, Connecticut, constructed the first known domestically made public clock in that colony in 1726, but nine years earlier, Benjamin Bagnall of Boston had been contracted to construct one for that town. Other craftsmen in the eighteenth century produced tower clocks, but since they were specially

**197.** Wood tower clock movement made in 1832 by Samuel Terry and presented by him to Bristol, CT, Congregational Church. (*American Clock & Watch Museum*)

ordered, no one maker produced them in any quantity.

Some wood tower clocks were made in Connecticut by Eli Terry, his brother Samuel Terry, and also by Elisha Hotchkiss. In the latter part of the nineteenth century small concerns dotted over the country often produced tower clocks for their areas. Among these makers were Jehiel Clark, Jr., of Cazenovia, New York; Charles Fasoldt of Albany, New York; Nels Johnson of Manistee, Michigan; Mathias Schwalback of Milwaukee, Wisconsin; Joseph Barborka of Iowa City, Iowa; and Adam E. Pollhans of St. Louis, Missouri.

The Howard Company and its predecessors, Stephenson, Howard & Davis, and, later, Howard & Davis, made these clocks from about 1842 to 1934. In those years, many styles were offered: time-only, striking, and quarter-chiming models. Models could have from one to four dials. Howard's tower clocks were installed in hundreds of public buildings in America and abroad, and though many have since been replaced or dismantled, some are still in use.

Howard's biggest competitor was the Seth Thomas Clock Company. The firm purchased the business of Andrew S. Hotchkiss of New York prior to 1860 and manufactured tower clocks of his design. The company installed its last tower clock, number 3,232, in 1942.

## ELECTRIC CLOCKS

The utilization of electro-magnetic current to power clocks is perhaps not as modern as many would suspect. A reliable electro-magnetic clock was developed in Edinburgh, Scotland, by Alexander Bain and patented by him in 1845. A similar clock was patented by Mr. S. A. Kennedy of New York on December 3, 1867.

Though the electrically driven clock has become the most common domestic clock of the present day, it was not until after 1930 that it gained public acceptance in America. By the end of World War II its production had supplanted that of the pendulum clock, and since then it has almost eradicated production of the marine clock.

Henry Ellis Warren, a successful inventor and manufacturer, was the "father" of the modern American electric clock. Warren was experimenting with electric mechanisms for clocks after the turn of the century and received a patent for his invention on July 13, 1909. Before 1933 he had received thirteen horologically related patents.

In 1914, Warren organized the Warren Telechron Company in Ashland, Massachusetts, and operated it successfully for many years. It was eventually sold to the General Electric Company.

Warren's mechanism was so well protected by patents by the time electric clocks became popular

that it was difficult for a while for others in the industry to produce successful movements. But eventually many new companies were formed. Among the early ones were the Hamilton-Sangamo Corporation of Springfield, Illinois, and the Hammond Clock Company of Chicago. The Hamilton-Sangamo concern produced a very expensive electrically wound clock about 1928 and did not survive the Depression. The Hammond Company remained in business until 1936; it was owned and operated by Laurens Hammond, who also perfected the Hammond electric organ.

Many of the smaller companies that had been formed were absorbed by larger firms, and the electric clock became a staple of their production. Since electric motors were readily available from specialized companies, electric clock production was found to be more economically feasible than production of either the pendulum or marine clock and both were gradually phased out.

**198.** "Act of Parliament" model electrically wound clock made by Sangamo Electric Co., Springfield, IL, c. 1927. Retail cost: $290. *(American Clock & Watch Museum)*

**199.** "Adams" model sold by General Electric Co., Bridgeport, CT, 1941, for $375. Movement built by Herschede Hall Clock Co. (*American Clock & Watch Museum*)

**200.** Electrically wound master clock by Standard Electric Time Co., Springfield, MA. Originally installed in Winsted, CT, school, 1890. (*American Clock & Watch Museum*)

## THE GIANTS OF THE BRASS CLOCK INDUSTRY

After 1850, small clockmaking companies began to expand and develop into firms. Seven of these firms grew into industrial giants and controlled the bulk of clock manufacturing for the next hundred years. The giants were Ansonia Clock Company (1850–1929), New Haven Clock Company (1853–1959), Seth Thomas Clock Company (1853–present), Waterbury Clock Company (1857–1944), E. Ingraham Company (1857–1967), William L. Gilbert Clock Company (1866–1964), E. N. Welch Manufacturing Company (1864–1903) and its successor, the Sessions Clock Company (1903–68). Affected by the depression, the trials of World War II, and the inflation, rising labor costs, and other economic trials they precipitated, the great concerns one by one suffered economic ruin. Though the Seth Thomas firm survives to the present it is no longer a manufacturing concern, but markets clocks that are assembled from purchased components.

## THE ANSONIA CLOCK COMPANY

The Ansonia Clock Company developed from the enterprises of Anson G. Phelps, a native of Simsbury, Connecticut, who became a wealthy importer of tin, brass, and copper in New York City. In 1844, Phelps built a copper-rolling mill on the Naugatuck river two miles north of Derby, Connecticut, at a place he called "Ansonia" after his given name.

On May 7, 1850, the Ansonia Clock Company was incorporated at Derby, Connecticut, with a capital of one hundred thousand dollars. Theodore Terry and Franklin C. Andrews were associated with Phelps in the concern. Both had been in partnership from 1842 to 1850 with Terry's brother Ralph in the manufacture of brass clocks. Another brother, Samuel Steele Terry, who had been a wheel and pinion maker for the firm of Terry & Andrews, also went to Ansonia in 1850 to work for the firm, where he worked until his death (1867).

In 1851, Phelps, Terry, and Andrews advertised their firm in the Connecticut Business Direc-

**201.** "Philosopher" model offered from *c.* 1885 until after 1915 by Ansonia Clock Co., Brooklyn, NY. Retail price in 1886 was $36.50. (*American Clock & Watch Museum*)

202

203

**202.** "Gravity" model, powered by its own weight, sold by
Ansonia Clock Co. in 1926 for $13.50. **203.** Pocket sundial
sold for $1 by Ansonia in 1926. (*Am. Clock & Watch Museum*)

tory as the "Ansonia Clock Company, Manufacturers and Dealers in Clocks and Time-Pieces, of every description, Wholesale and Retail, Ansonia, Ct." After 1852, Theodore Terry also conducted a clockmaking enterprise under his own name, but apparently used Ansonia's facilities.

In 1854, the company factory burned at a loss of twenty thousand dollars, and Phelps moved his Derby mill to Ansonia, merging it with the existing Ansonia mill. The company was renamed the Ansonia Brass & Copper Company and it made clocks there from 1854 to 1878. In 1878 the Ansonia Clock Company was again formed to take over manufacture and a year later all clockmaking operations were moved to Brooklyn, New York.

The timing proved to be ill chosen, for the newly established factory burned some months after the move. In a letter written by the E. Ingraham Company of Bristol on November 1, 1880, it is mentioned that the Ansonia Clock Company factory "burned to the ground last week."

By 1881, however, a new factory had been built in Brooklyn, the business was expanded considerably, and many new styles of clocks were added to its production. By January, 1883, the company had sales offices in New York, Chicago, and London. It also had launched production of the novelty and figurine clocks for which it became well known.

By 1914, the company had agents in Australia, New Zealand, Japan, China, and India and exported a large quantity of merchandise to these and eighteen other countries. By that time, its line of clocks (including now a few models of nonjeweled watches) was probably the most diversified in the industry. After World War I its products gradually declined in quality and quantity.

In a lecture given at Swampscott, Massachusetts, on April 13, 1968, Mr. Edward Ingraham, former president of the E. Ingraham Company, noted that Ansonia's sales tactics were, on the whole, undependable:

> After a clock meeting, possibly about 1910, in which members of the industry agreed to establish certain prices, our then Sales Manager, Elmer E. Stockton, caught one of their officials telephoning to customers evidently offering deals at 'old pricing.' [Stockton] evidently confirmed this because he went after all of Ansonia's principal accounts and ended up taking away all of that business from Ansonia, which having lost its volume business, went down and out.

In a letter written to the E. Ingraham Company on September 24, 1937, it was stated:

> In March, 1929, the Ansonia Clock Company voluntarily placed itself under the supervision of a Creditors' Committee. During the Summer of that year active manufacturing was discontinued and

by the end of the year the bulk of the clockmaking machinery and certain dies and patterns were sold and shipped out to the Russian government. The remaining assets of the Company, principally real estate, have been conserved under the same Creditors' Committee. . . . As the Company is still in existence and theoretically might be refinanced and resume manufacturing operations, we feel that it should not be regarded as defunct.

Unfortunately, the company was never revived and, as far as clockmaking activities were concerned, was defunct after the summer of 1929.

205

204. "Bee" alarm clock with box, by Ansonia Clock Co., Brooklyn, NY, c. 1890. (Am. Clock & Watch Mus.) 205. One-day timepiece, New Haven Clock Co., 1884. Escapement involves action of small metal bead on string, suspended from center-post bracket. Bead winds and unwinds by swinging around each outer post, hence the name "flying pendulum" clock. Though a poor timekeeper, its action is fascinating to observe. (Courtesy, Mrs. Helen Watters Riga)

## THE NEW HAVEN CLOCK COMPANY

Incorporation of the New Haven Clock Company took place on February 17, 1853, with a capital of twenty thousand dollars. Hiram Camp was chosen president. The firm was formed to produce cheap brass movements for the Jerome Manufacturing Company. Two years later the Jerome Manufacturing Company went into bankruptcy and serious problems arose. Its property, including the plant, tools, and finished clocks, was to be sold by the executors. The New Haven Clock Company, however, was able to raise the funds necessary to purchase the defunct company, and after 1856, it expanded its operations and began to manufacture complete clocks.

By 1880, the company boasted sales offices in Chicago; Liverpool, England; and Yokohama, Japan. Its catalog listed its own clocks and also carried items made by F. Kroeber of New York, E. Ingraham & Company of Bristol, and E. Howard Company of Boston. By 1885, it had discontinued the marketing of clocks by other domestic companies, but did offer a number of imported clocks.

A short time later the company's own line of clocks had grown to such a degree that it did not offer additional items. During the latter part of the century, the number of models it offered grew tremendously, possibly to its detriment. According to Edward Ingraham, the New Haven Clock Company had a difficult time making money. "As far back as 1910, I recall my father and Mr. Stockton discussing New Haven and remarking that no company can make money in the clock business with such an extensive line as New Haven showed in their catalog."

In 1880, the company also ventured into the manufacture of nonjeweled pocket watches; wristwatches were added in 1917. The company was a major producer of inexpensive watches until 1956, when production was ceased.

On March 22, 1946, the company was succeeded by a corporation called the New Haven Clock and Watch Company. Its financial situation grew worse and on December 6, 1956, the company filed a petition for corporate reorganization

206

207

under the Federal Bankruptcy Act. The company reorganized in February of 1958, but in December of 1959, it was decided that it was impossible to continue manufacturing on a profitable basis. An auction was held in March of 1960, and the complete manufacturing facilities of the company were sold.

## THE SETH THOMAS CLOCK COMPANY

Unlike many of his associates, Seth Thomas was a good businessman and managed to build a sound concern. Thomas was wise enough to diversify his financial interests and he acquired a considerable amount of land early in his career. In addition to his clockmaking activities, he established a cotton factory in 1834, which was profitably operated until the Civil War. When the financial panic hit Connecticut in 1837 and pushed many in the clock business into bankruptcy, Thomas was able to continue, being aided by both the cotton factory and by farming operations that were conducted on his landholdings.

Thomas was often reluctant to launch into new production methods and designs, being content with established procedures that had proved successful in the past. However, when the bronze looking-glass clocks replaced the pillar and scroll design and later when wood clocks were replaced by the cheaper brass ones, he was forced to change his methods of manufacture in order to retain his customers.

By 1844, Thomas had discontinued making the wood clock and had put his nephew, Marcus Prince, in charge of his entire movement-making operations. Prince had been trained in brass-clockmaking procedures by Hiram Camp. Brass-clock production proved profitable for Thomas; by June of 1850, the company was producing 24,000 brass clocks annually, which were valued at sixty thousand dollars.

In about 1852, Thomas again expanded his operations and built a brass-rolling mill, which was incorporated as the Thomas Manufacturing Company on July 20, 1853. The factory burned several years later but was rebuilt and, by 1860, was producing over 170 tons of brass and German silver annually. The mill continued to provide brass for Thomas' clockmaking concern until it was sold on May 21, 1869, to Holmes, Booth & Atwood Manufacturing Company of Waterbury, Connecticut, for four hundred thousand dollars.

Nearing the age of sixty-eight, and feeling the infirmities of old age coming upon him, Thomas organized the Seth Thomas Clock Company, a joint stock corporation, in order to avoid cessation of production on his death. He deeded $58,688 worth of property and estate to the company (which was incorporated on May 3, 1853). Thomas remained as president and major shareholder

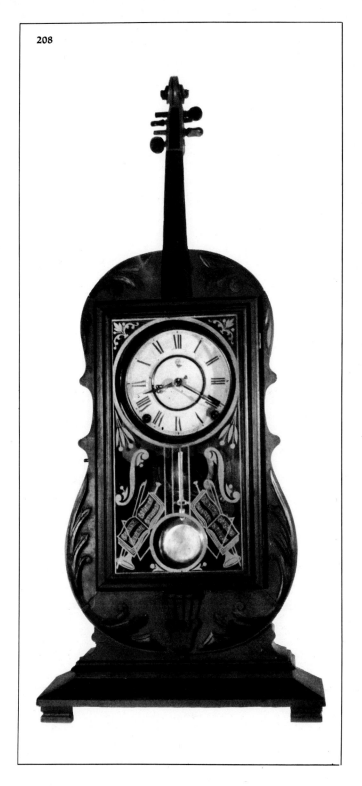

208

**206.** Hiram Camp (1811–93), nephew of Chauncey Jerome and president of New Haven Clock Co. for 40 years. **207.** Seth Thomas (1785–1853), founder of Seth Thomas Clock Co. and one of America's best-known clock manufacturers. **208.** Rare violin-case clock made *c.* 1890 by Seth Thomas Clock Co., Thomaston, CT. For unknown reasons, interesting case design was abandoned after only a few were produced. (*All, Edward Ingraham Library*)

until his death at age seventy-three in Plymouth Hollow on January 28, 1859.

Thomas was one of the richest men in Connecticut when he died, and even his long-time competitor, Chauncey Jerome, acknowledged his abilities:

> Seth Thomas was in many respects a first-rate man. He never made any improvements in manufacturing; his great success was in money making. He always minded his own business, was very industrious, persevering, honest; his word was as good as his note, and he always determined to make a good article to please his customers.

Plymouth Hollow's townspeople also respected Thomas, for he had provided industries that were essential to the early growth of the town. Six years after his death, by June of 1865, they renamed the town "Thomaston" in his honor; it was incorporated as such ten years later.

After Thomas' death, the company was run by his sons Aaron, Edward, and Seth, Jr. The business was expanded and many new models of spring-driven clocks were added. Calendar clocks were introduced about 1862 and became an important part of its manufacture until 1917, when production was ceased.

On October 17, 1865, a company known as Seth Thomas' Sons & Company was formed for the manufacture of balance-wheel, or marine, escapement movements. It also produced finely made pendulum movements of eighteen-day duration in an effort to compete with the superb French clock movements. Although they were among the finest spring-driven movements produced in America at that time, they could not approach the excellence of French workmanship. The firm was consolidated with the Seth Thomas Clock Company on January 31, 1879.

By June of 1880, the company claimed a half million dollars in capital investment and was producing seven hundred twenty-nine thousand dollars' worth of clocks annually. It employed 640 men, 123 women, and 71 children; ran a ten-hour workday; and paid a skilled mechanic three dollars a day and an ordinary laborer a dollar fifty a day.

In 1882, the decision was made to go into the production of jeweled pocket watches, making the firm the first in Connecticut to venture into high-

**209.** Two blacksmiths from foundry section of Seth Thomas Clock Company's tower clock shop, c. 1900. (*Courtesy, Seth Thomas Clock Company*)

172

grade watchmaking. Watches were made until 1915.

The company made a continual effort to achieve excellence in its production and introduced many styles of regulators. In 1879 and 1880 it began a line of high-grade regulators with mercury pendulums and continued to produce them until about 1910. In 1888, a high-precision clock, especially made for observatory use, was introduced; it was offered until 1913. The production of tower clocks was also an important aspect of the firm's business.

On January 1, 1931, the Seth Thomas Clock Company became a division of the General Time Instruments Corporation, later known as General Time Corporation. Seth E. Thomas, Jr., great grandson of the company's founder, remained as chairman of the board of directors until his death on June 5, 1932, at which time the company's leadership passed out of the hands of the Thomas family for the first time.

Although World War II seriously affected the company, it was able to continue with some production. After the war it was decided that the manufacturing of movements was no longer profitable and it was phased out; movements were purchased thereafter from foreign and domestic sources.

In 1955, the company sustained serious damage from the devastating flooding that occurred in Connecticut. The damage was so severe that production was stopped and the Thomaston factory closed.

In 1956, it was decided to reopen the factory and carry on the Seth Thomas name. On May 14, 1970, General Time lost a stockholder's fight in the courts and its business, which also included Westclox, was taken over as a division of Talley Industries of Seattle, Washington. Though its mode of manufacture has changed drastically, the concern, still active, remains the longest established American clockmaking company.

**210.** Early one-hundred-number punch time clock by Dey Time Register Co., Syracuse, NY, *c.* 1890. Movement by Seth Thomas Clock Co. (*American Clock & Watch Museum*)

## THE WATERBURY CLOCK COMPANY

The Waterbury Clock Company was a major producer of clocks from 1857 to 1944 and of an inexpensive watch from 1880 to the present. Its beginnings stemmed from Benedict & Burnham, the brass manufacturing company that became associated with the Jerome Manufacturing Company in 1850, but became dissatisfied and sold out. Hiram

Camp noted, however, that "as the Waterbury people in this way had been led to see that in the manufacture of clocks, an opening was made for large quantities of brass, they were more easily led to engage in the business in after years." This later involvement resulted in the formation of the Waterbury Clock Company, a joint stock company organized on March 27, 1857, with a capital of sixty thousand dollars.

213

**211.** "Dewey" model oak kitchen clock made by E. Ingraham Company, Bristol, CT, *c.* 1905. Rotary press used to impress design into steam-softened wood. **212.** Four-dial street clock as manufactured by Seth Thomas Clock Co. from *c.* 1870 to 1929; 15 ft . tall. **213.** "Defender" model oak wall clock by Waterbury Clock Co., Waterbury, CT, *c.* 1901, retailing for $16.50. **214.** Regulator No. 4, made by William L. Gilbert Clock Co., Winsted, CT, *c.* 1885. (*All, American Clock & Watch Museum*)

First located in the Benedict & Burnham shops, the clock company secured larger facilities in 1873 on North Elm Street in Waterbury. The company made a modest number of clocks of its own design for about twenty years, but it was primarily concerned with selling its own movements in figurine-shaped cases made of cast iron and bronze that had been purchased from other sources.

In 1880, the company ventured into the manufacture of nonjeweled watches and produced most of the watches sold by R. H. Ingersoll & Brother until 1914. Its watchmaking activities have survived to the present as a part of Timex.

By 1881, the company was acting as selling agent for the Ithaca Calendar Clock Company of Ithaca, New York; it continued to promote the Ithaca product until 1891, when it introduced its own line of perpetual calendar models. In 1887, the company boasted employment of over 300 workers; the number had grown to over 3,000 employees by 1917. The output at that time was 23,000 clocks and watches daily.

In 1900, company operations were again expanded and two five-story additions were built onto the factory; the following year three additional five-story buildings were built. By 1907, another building was needed and another five-story facility was erected. During the years 1909 and 1910 one hundred thousand dollars was spent on still further additions.

Waterbury's financial position changed considerably during the next twenty years. The company went into receivership during the Depression, and in 1933 its case shop and materials were sold at auction. In 1944, the company was sold to United States Time Corporation.

## THE E. INGRAHAM COMPANY

Elias Ingraham (1805–85), founder of the company, was a native of Marlborough, Connecticut, and came to Bristol in May of 1828 to work for George Mitchell, a leading merchant in the town. Ingraham had served a five-year apprenticeship as a cabinetmaker and, while working in the cabinetmaking shop of Daniel Dewey of Hartford, had become acquainted with Solomon Hinman, an agent for George Mitchell.

Mitchell was looking for someone to make a new style of clock case worthy of competing with the stenciled-column case that had been introduced by Chauncey Jerome. Mitchell asked Ingraham to come to Bristol and the *Bristol Herald* of June 26, 1890, recounted some of the events that followed:

> Elias Ingraham worked for George Mitchell at case making a little more than two years, and during the first year, 1828, he invented what was called

the carved case with carved mahogany columns, carved lion-paw feet and corner blocks over the columns in which there was a turned rósette, a fret urn on each block, and a basket of fruit carved between the blocks. On some of these cases were bronze columns and tips instead of carvings. Mr. Ingraham made this style of case, except for the carvings, for over two years for Mr. Mitchell, turning out some eight or nine hundred the second year, doing the work mostly himself.

In October of 1830, Elias Ingraham went to work for Chauncey and Lawson C. Ives, who had begun to manufacture the eight-day brass clock invented by Joseph Ives. On October 20, Ingraham charged the firm $5.62 "To Form Pattern and Making New-Fashioned Cases." This particular case, commonly called a triple decker, was a long Empire-style case with three sections, which often had carved columns and animal-paw feet. In the following three years, Ingraham made almost six thousand cases for the firm of C. & L. C. Ives.

Ingraham, in partnership with William G. Bartholomew, purchased a small piece of land from Ira Ives in November of 1831 and erected a cabinetmaking shop, specifically for making clock cases. In September of 1832, he sold his interest in the shop to Jonathan Clark Brown.

In September of 1835, Ingraham purchased another shop. Here he manufactured chairs, mirrors, and clock cases. When his business suffered losses in the financial panic two years later, he borrowed money from Chauncey Ives. By 1840, he had borrowed eight thousand dollars from Ives and subsequently petitioned for bankruptcy.

The firm of Brewster & Ingrahams was formed in 1844, Elias and his brother Andrew going into partnership with Elisha Curtis Brewster. Noah L. Brewster, Elisha's son, represented the firm in England. Epaphroditus Peck, who had formerly worked in this capacity for Chauncey Jerome, made an agreement on April 6, 1848, to act as agent in England for the firm. After fulfillment of the contract he remained in England as an agent until his death on September 30, 1857.

Elias Ingraham designed the sharp Gothic clock case about 1845 and early examples with four columns were produced by Brewster & Ingrahams. His style, somewhat modified and commonly called the "steeple" case, became one of the most popular small shelf styles ever produced.

On July 24, 1852, the firm of Brewster & Ingrahams was dissolved and a new firm known as E. & A. Ingraham was formed. Andrew Ingraham sold half of his interests in the firm to Edmund Clarence Stedman, the famous banker-poet of New York, who became the New York sales representative for the company, now named Ingrahams & Stedman.

On December 6, 1855, the Ingraham factory in

**215.** Seth Thomas Clock Company's finest Victorian tall clock, No. 2784, made *c.* 1905 for $650. Westminster chimes; 100 inches tall. **216.** Quarter-hour "Sonora" chime clock made by Seth Thomas Clock Co., *c.* 1915, retailing for $25. Patented "Adamantine" finish is colored Celluloid applied as veneer. **217.** Miniature "Venetian" model by E. Ingraham & Co., *c.* 1860. Only 11½ inches tall. **218.** E. Ingraham's "Doric, gilt column" offered in 1880 for $4.25 plus 50 cents for alarm. (*All, American Clock & Watch Museum*)

Bristol burned with serious losses. The following announcement was sent to customers:

Bristol, December 10th, 1855

To our customers:

Gentlemen: In consequence of a disastrous fire which totally consumed our Factory on the morning of the 6th inst. and in which a large amount of superior stock was destroyed, we shall perhaps for a short time be unable to fill all the orders you are sending us, with Clocks of our own manufacture.

Our loss by the fire is about $30,000, of which $20,000 was safely insured. We shall immediately procure another Factory, and continue our business with the same workmen as heretofore, and hope within six weeks to be finishing as many goods as ever. In the meantime, our New York Warehouse is open, and all orders will be promptly filled, we trust, to your satisfaction.

Soliciting a continuance of your custom, we are,

Gentlemen,

Very respectfully yours,

E. & A. INGRAHAM CO.
Bristol

INGRAHAMS & STEDMAN
New York

In March of 1856, Stedman sold his interest in the New York firm to the Ingrahams and the sales firm was dissolved.

The previous January, Elias Ingraham had moved to Ansonia, Connecticut. A few clocks were sold with the label E. & A. Ingraham & Company, Ansonia, Connecticut, but the firm was entirely disbanded before the end of the year.

Elias returned to Bristol and, with his son

219

**219.** View inside E. Ingraham Company factory in Bristol, CT, *c.* 1914. **220.** Sharp Gothic or steeple clock made by Brewster & Ingrahams, *c.* 1844, with Charles Kirk's patent cast-iron backplate eight-day spring movement. **221.** "Doric, Mosaic" model offered by the E. Ingraham Co. for $5.25 in 1880. **222.** Elias Ingraham (1805–85), case maker by trade and founder of the E. Ingraham Company. He designed many popular case styles for 19th-century Connecticut clocks. (*All, E. Ingraham Library, American Clock & Watch Museum*)

Edward (1830–92), organized the firm Elias Ingraham & Company in 1857. From 1861 to 1880 the name E. Ingraham & Company was used.

From 1881 to 1884, the firm was known as The E. Ingraham & Company; in 1884, it was incorporated as The E. Ingraham Company; in 1958, the name was changed to The Ingraham Company.

In 1885, the company introduced clocks with black-painted or japanned cases. They proved successful and over 220 different models based on the style were eventually introduced by the firm. Nonjeweled pocket watches were added to its line in 1914 and wristwatches in 1930. Eight-day lever-movement clocks were produced after 1915, and electric clocks after 1931. The production of pendulum clocks was discontinued in 1942.

In 1941, the company opened a new plant in Toronto, Canada; another was established at Elizabethtown, Kentucky, in 1954, and a third in Laurinburg, North Carolina, in 1959.

In November of 1967, the company was sold to McGraw-Edison, a conglomerate, and though clockmaking activities ceased at Bristol, electric and battery clocks continued to be produced at the Laurinburg factory.

## THE WILLIAM L. GILBERT CLOCK COMPANY

William Lewis Gilbert (1806–90) began a lifelong career in the clockmaking business when he purchased a clock shop with his brother-in-law, George Marsh, in December of 1828. The firm of Marsh, Gilbert & Company was active in Bristol and Farmington, Connecticut, until about 1834, when it moved to Dayton, Ohio, and began marketing wood clocks.

Returning to Bristol about 1835, Gilbert formed a partnership with John Birge in the firm Birge, Gilbert & Company and marketed Empire-cased shelf clocks with Joseph Ives's patent movements. The firm was dissolved about 1837 and Gilbert went into partnership with Chauncey and Noble Jerome and Zelotas Grant in 1839 as Jerome, Grant, Gilbert & Company; it manufactured and vended Jerome's inexpensive brass-movement clocks.

Later, Gilbert moved to Winchester, Connecticut, where with Lucius Clarke he purchased a clock factory on October 29, 1841, from the widow of Riley Whiting. Along with Ezra Baldwin, the men formed Clarke, Gilbert & Company for the

**225**

**226**

**223.** Eight-day shelf clock by Brewster & Ingrahams, Bristol, CT, *c.* 1852. **224.** One-day steeple clock with brass springs by Brewster & Ingrahams, *c.* 1847. **225.** Four-column sharp Gothic designed by Elias Ingraham and produced by Brewster & Ingrahams *c.* 1845. **226.** Four-column ogee-top Gothic case with rippled molding, made by Brewster & Ingrahams *c.* 1850. **227.** "Grecian, Mosaic" model offered from 1871 to 1883 by the E. Ingraham Co. It retailed for $6.50 in 1880. (*All, American Clock & Watch Museum*)

**227**

production of the cheap brass clock. In 1845, Clarke sold out his interests to Gilbert, who continued as W. L. Gilbert & Company. In 1848, Clarke repurchased his interests and the two men continued until 1851 as Gilbert & Clarke.

In 1851, the firm again became known as W. L. Gilbert & Company and, in 1866, a joint stock company, the Gilbert Manufacturing Company, was formed. It continued in business until April 2, 1871, when the entire Winsted factory burned.

On July 5, 1871, a new corporation, known as the William L. Gilbert Clock Company, was formed and a month later construction was begun on two four-story brick buildings. The business expanded and experienced successful growth under the general managership of George B. Owen. Owen came to Winsted about 1880 and served as manager for about twenty years. A talented case designer, Owen conducted a separate business under his own name in both Winsted and New York for many years.

During the first decade of the twentieth century several buildings were added, but the reces-

sion of 1907 seriously hurt the business. After 1912, the company was financially pressed, but in 1914 its creditors allowed the firm to continue. Its general manager was able to put the company back onto a profitable basis during the 1920s and all debts were paid by 1925.

Sorely hit by the depression of 1929, the company was forced into receivership by September of 1932. The E. Ingraham Company of Bristol wanted to buy Gilbert's entire business and attempted to do so in partnership with the Western Clock Company of La Salle, Illinois, but the project went unrealized. The company was able to terminate the receivership after two years and the name was changed to the William L. Gilbert Clock Corporation.

During World War II, the U.S. government permitted Gilbert to continue manufacturing clocks—specifically alarm clocks—because the company did not use the metal so important to the war effort. By 1940, it was manufacturing papier-mâché items, and alarm clock cases could be made from pressed paper pulp rather than metal.

228

**229**

**230**

**231**

**228.** "Monarch" model black-enameled case mantle clock by E. Ingraham Company, Bristol, CT, *c.* 1901. Painted marbleized wood columns. **229.** Movement factory of E. N. Welch Mfg. Co., Forestville, CT, *c.* 1895. In March, 1899, this shop was destroyed by fire. **230.** Jonathan C. Brown (1807–72), once Bristol's largest brass clock manufacturer, went bankrupt in 1856, and E. N. Welch purchased the factory. **231.** "Parliament" model wall clock with Daniel J. Gale's multiple dial, or astronomical calendar. This clock retailed for $17.50 in 1878. (*All, Edward Ingraham Library, American Clock & Watch Museum*)

Financial problems continued to plague the company after the war, and in 1953, it began to manufacture adding machines in an effort to stimulate profits. The company was taken over by the General Computing Machines Company in 1957, and the name was changed to the General-Gilbert Corporation. On December 23, 1964, the clock division of the corporation, which had not produced a profit for thirteen years, was sold to the Spartus Corporation of Chicago, Illinois, and Louisville, Mississippi, for five hundred thousand dollars.

## THE E. N. WELCH MANUFACTURING COMPANY/THE SESSIONS CLOCK COMPANY

Founder Elisha Niles Welch (1809–87) was originally in business with his father, George Welch, who ran an iron foundry in Bristol and supplied weights and bells for clocks. In 1831, Welch joined Thomas Barnes, Jr., to form Barnes & Welch; the company marketed wood-movement shelf clocks until 1834.

Welch became a partner with Jonathan C. Brown and Chauncey Pomeroy in the Forestville Manufacturing Company of Bristol in 1841. Welch thereafter had considerable financial interests in the various J. C. Brown enterprises, which included the Forestville Hardware and Clock Company and the Forestville Clock Manufactory.

Fire destroyed the main factory of J. C. Brown's Forestville Hardware and Clock Company in January, 1853; by 1856 he was bankrupt. Welch purchased both Brown's businesses and the case-making shop of Frederick S. Otis, and began to produce clocks as E. N. Welch, "successors to the old establishment late J. C. Brown."

Welch carried on the clockmaking concern under his own name until July 6, 1864, when a joint stock company was organized under the name of E. N. Welch Manufacturing Company. It was formed for "the combining and manufacture of various kinds of metals, rolling the same and converting them into various articles for sale such as plate or sheet brass, clocks and clock movements." Stock was sold for twenty-five dollars per share; Elisha Welch purchased 2,800 shares, while his son James Hart Welch and sons-in-law Andrew Fuller Atkins and George Henry Mitchell each purchased 400. Fifteen days later, Welch sold the corporation two clock factories and shops with steam engines, boilers, and fixed machinery for $29,700. The firm remained successful for about twenty-five years, becoming the largest clock manufacturer in Bristol.

In the spring of 1868, Elisha Welch, Solomon Spring, James Welch, George Mitchell, and Andrew Atkins became partners in the firm of Welch, Spring and Company. Welch gave a clock factory he had purchased from Elisha and Charles

232. "Ionic" gilt wall timepiece with alarm, made by E. Ingraham Co., retailed for $7.50 in 1880 (plus $1 for gilt). (*American Clock & Watch Museum*)

H. Manross to the new firm in March of 1868, "reserving to the E. N. Welch Mfg. Co. all the machinery and tools in said factory used in the manufacture of clock springs." On April 23, 1868, Solomon Crosby Spring (1826–1906) sold his clock factory on Riverside Street to the new firm for ten thousand dollars. (The factory had formerly been owned by Birge, Peck & Company and, after 1864, by S. C. Spring & Company.)

Welch, Spring and Company produced a higher-grade line of clocks than most of the companies in Bristol at that time. The movements were exceptionally well made and the cases were nicely designed. Unfortunately, quality does not guarantee profit, and in 1884, the company was absorbed by the E. N. Welch Manufacturing Company. Solomon Spring became superintendent of the company and remained with it in that capacity until the business was discontinued temporarily in 1893.

Elisha Welch died in Forestville on August 2, 1887; the following October his son James became president. Due to poor management and a slack in local economy, the company's financial condition deteriorated and, in 1893, their biggest creditor, the Bristol Brass and Clock Company, sought the appointment of a receiver "on the ground of its embarrassed financial condition." Realizing its situation, the company voluntarily agreed to the appointment of a receiver in the person of Edward A. Freeman of Plainville, Connecticut, in October of 1893. Clock production was discontinued for nearly three years, but by November 27, 1895, Freeman, having settled all claims against the company, was discharged. The company resumed operations in February of 1897.

The production of a cheaper line of clocks, first introduced in 1893 to create a profit margin, was resumed. But to no avail. Many customers had been lost in the interim and financial difficulties began to mount. In March of 1898, twenty-five thousand dollars had to be borrowed to continue operations. Another serious blow fell in 1899 when, in March of that year, the movement factory was destroyed by fire; the case factory was similarly destroyed in December.

A modern brick factory complex was constructed and in use by April of 1900. The funds borrowed for this rebuilding added an extra burden to the critical financial situation.

James Welch died in January of 1902, and at the directors' meeting on January 31, "the matter of finances was discussed at length." On July 5 of that year it was noted that the mortgage was due, unpaid bank notes were past due, liabilities were maturing, and suits had been threatened. The company had absolutely no funds. At that meeting it was voted "that the affairs and business of this company be wound up and it discontinued."

Meanwhile, William E. Sessions, who was president and principal owner of the Sessions Foundry Company of Bristol, and his nephew Albert L. Sessions had been actively buying company stock. On July 24, 1902, W. E. Sessions was elected president of the company and A. L. Sessions became treasurer. In August they borrowed sixty-five thousand dollars to revitalize the company and on January 9, 1903, the corporate name was changed to the Sessions Clock Company.

Sessions continued the production of many clocks in the Welch line, especially the black mantle clock and the oak-cased kitchen clock. The 1930s brought forth further financial troubles, which reached a peak when the electric clock received public acceptance. In about 1936, the company discontinued the manufacture of spring-wound clocks and concentrated on producing electric clocks.

In 1956, the company name was changed to The Sessions Company. It operated successfully for many years under the management of W. K. Sessions, Sr., but in 1958 it sustained a loss of over a million dollars.

In March of 1958, the company was sold to Consolidated Electronics Industries Corporation of New York and continued to manufacture at Forestville, Connecticut, for another decade as a subsidiary of that firm. In August of 1968, the inventory, equipment, and tools of the clockmaking division of Sessions was purchased by United Metal Goods Company of Brooklyn, New York, a company that manufactured electric clocks and percolators. Production ceased at Forestville in 1968 and two years later the empty buildings were sold.

In 1958, W. K. Sessions, Jr., formed a business known as the New England Clock Company. The firm was first located in Bristol and later moved to Farmington, Connecticut. It has continued successfully, though it does not produce its own movements as the early Sessions company had done.

**233.** Twenty-four-inch dial "Corrugated Gilt Gallery" timepiece by E. Ingraham Company, Bristol, CT, retailed for $45 in 1880. (*American Clock & Watch Museum*)

## THE DECLINE OF THE INDUSTRY

The years 1880 to 1920 were a "Golden Age" for the giants. Generally, they enjoyed good profits, good sales on domestic and foreign markets, constant improvements and refinements in manufacturing techniques, and greater volume production. The following half century, however, saw these companies and much of the remainder of the industry in a steady decline toward an ultimate demise.

Certainly, the decline of this great industry was not caused by any one factor, but by a series of them. Mr. Edward Ingraham (1887–1972), president of the E. Ingraham Company during most of this period, observed:

At this writing, in March, 1935, business is fair. We are working under a strain, trying to maintain a large sales volume while the administration is unfriendly to industrialists and we are pressed with fears of inflation and unfavorable legislation.

Many companies were affected by the depression of the 1930s, some being forced into receivership. The depression's effects were compounded by the inflation that followed. During World War II, much of the industry was shut down for from two and a half to three years. As Ingraham wrote: "In February, 1942, the War Production Board issued orders that we cease and liquidate all clock and watch production by July 30, 1942. . . . This meant no work for our entire plant except war work." Companies were forced to reduce person-

nel and much of their machinery lay idle and eventually deteriorated.

At the end of the war the industry was faced with multiple trials. Besides having to expend tremendous amounts of money to recondition or replace their machinery, they had to rehire and retrain workers, find new sources for raw materials, and reestablish their markets. They were also faced with rising labor costs as a result of the growing strength of unions.

At the same time, with the reduction of import tariffs, foreign competition was increasing. German and Japanese industries were growing—with the aid of American funds—and using cheaper labor, thereby reducing further the cost of their goods.

American management was also to blame for not diversifying, for not spending an adequate amount of funds on research for the development of more modern equipment. Eventually they had to concede that they could no longer compete.

Of the giants, Seth Thomas alone survives as a division of General Time Corporation, a Talley Industry. Though the names Ingraham and Sessions survive as trademarks on some electric clocks, they are no longer companies.

Following are several firms that have survived. Though their modes of manufacturing may have changed drastically in the past fifty years, they have tried to carry on an industry that nears extinction in America.

### THE CHELSEA CLOCK COMPANY

The Chelsea Clock Company of Chelsea, Massachusetts, was formed in 1897 as successor to the Boston Clock Company, a concern that had been producing high-grade marine clocks from 1888 to 1897. The Chelsea company continued the manufacture of high-grade marine and pendulum movements and did not attempt to compete on a volume basis with the Connecticut manufacturers. It was a well-managed concern and had a profitable business. Its production in latter years included fine ships' bell-striking clocks and barometers.

For over seventy years, the Chelsea Clock Company conducted business without change of management or control. On December 31, 1969, the business, sold to Automation Industry of Los Angeles, California, was run under a division of Keynon Marine in Guilford, Connecticut. The Chelsea Clock Company has the rare distinction of being one of the few existing concerns to have continued making its own clock movements.

### THE HERSCHEDE HALL CLOCK COMPANY

In 1904, the Herschede Hall Clock Company was incorporated in Cincinnati, Ohio. For many years the company produced fine tall clocks and at times ventured into the manufacture of mantle clocks. It produced its own movements, which are among the finest movements of their type produced in the country. In about 1928, the company ventured into production of the electrically wound tall clock, but later returned to weight-driven models.

In 1960, this family-controlled concern was sold to a firm of cabinetmakers in Starkville, Mississippi, and clockmaking operations were moved there and continued. Herschede survives as one of the few companies in the United States that still produces its own movements.

### THE LUX MANUFACTURING COMPANY

Paul Lux, a native of Germany, started the Lux Clock Company in a small shop in Waterbury, Connecticut, in March of 1914. In January of 1917, the firm was incorporated as the Lux Manufacturing Company, with a capital of fifty thousand dollars. The firm successfully produced clocks and clock movements under the management of Lux and his sons and grandsons. The Lux company was especially well known for its production of small novelty clocks, many of which were marketed by a firm called the Keebler Clock Company.

Though their principal operation was at Waterbury, Lux built another plant in Lebanon, Tennessee, in about 1950. In June of 1961, the Lux Manufacturing Company was taken over on an exchange-of-stock basis by the Robertshaw-Fulton Controls Company and continues in business as a division of that firm.

### WESTCLOX

In 1884, Charles Stahlberg went to LaSalle-Peru, Illinois, from Waterbury, Connecticut, and there received backing to start making clocks on a small scale. On December 23, 1885, the United Clock Company was formed and began to produce about fifty alarm clocks a day. The infant company lasted two years before going into bankruptcy.

In 1895, F. W. Matthiessen, president of the Matthiessen & Hegeler Zinc Company of LaSalle, acquired the plant and organized the Western Clock Manufacturing Company. The company specialized in the manufacture of alarm clocks, but also made small back-wind one-day marine-movement clocks for novelty and porcelain cases. Nonjeweled watch production also played an important part in the firm's growth. By 1903, the firm claimed to be producing over a million alarm clocks a year.

Prior to 1925, the firm became known as the Western Clock Company and, in 1930, it became a division of General Time Instruments Corporation. In 1936, the company was renamed Westclox, a name that had formerly been a trademark.

Westclox continues business under General Time Instruments Corporation, which is a division of Talley Industries of Seattle, Washington.

**234.** Rotary pendulum timepiece patented by John C. Briggs in 1855, but manufactured by E. N. Welch Mfg. Co., c. 1878. Only 7 inches tall. (*Courtesy, Henry C. Wing, Jr.*)

*Part IV:*

*Watches:*
*1800–1970*

Watches are portable time-keeping devices. Many early examples are as large as some present-day clocks, but today, watches are usually small and delicate in nature, yet durable enough to withstand the normal abuse of daily use.

Pocket watches were the standard of watchmaking until the twentieth century, though smaller models had been introduced in the late nineteenth century designed to be worn by ladies on a neck chain or as a pendant. Wristwatches were not introduced until World War I, and they were not generally accepted by gentlemen until after 1930.

A watch consists of a series of small wheels, pinions, and arbors held together by plates. Its movement is powered by springs and regulated by an escapement that must be of the balance-wheel style, rather than the pendulum, so that the watch will continue to run when moved or turned

in various positions. Many watches also have jewels, which are small pieces of hard minerals inserted into the watch plates at the points of pivot of the arbors. Being harder, the jewel will wear less than a pivot hole drilled into the brass plate.

The watch was developed in Europe after 1500. It is doubtful that watches were constructed in America before 1773, perhaps not before 1809. Machine-made watches were first attempted in 1838 and successfully made after 1850, when many firms were formed specifically for the purpose. Some lasted only a short time; others achieved enormous success and produced millions of watches. After 1875, less-expensive watches were introduced, some eventually selling for under a dollar. Between 1850 and the 1950s, when the industry began to decline in America, it is not unreasonable to believe that the total number of watches made was well over a billion.

236

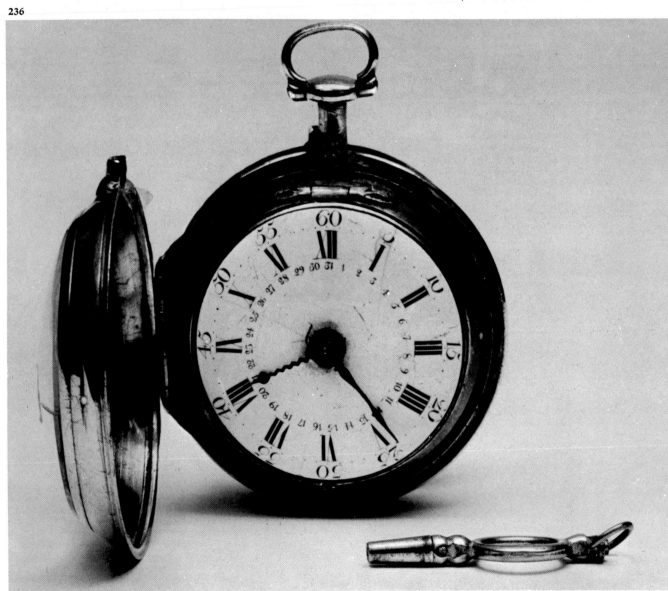

*Preceding pages:* **235.** New England Watch Company's "Cavour" model, *c.* 1908. Duplex escapement, art nouveau case only 1 inch diameter. (*Am. Clock & Watch Museum*)

**236.** Verge-escapement key-wound pocket watch with calendar by Thomas Harland, Norwich, CT, *c.* 1800. (*Courtesy, Henry Francis du Pont Winterthur Museum*)

# THE BEGINNINGS

Initial development of the watch is credited to Peter Henlein (1479–1542) of Nuremburg, Germany.

In the *Cosmography of Pomponius Mela* (published *c.* 1511), edited by Jean Coquille, is the following description:

> In these days, ingenius things are invented. As Peter Hele, still a very young man, performs works that astonish even the most learned scientists. For, from a little iron, he makes timepieces containing many small wheels that, no matter how they are turned about, both indicate time and beat forty hours, even though carried on the chest or in the pocket.

From other records it has been ascertained that "Peter Hele" was Peter Henlein, who became a master locksmith at Nuremburg in 1509. On his death in 1542, Henlein was called an *urmacher* or watchmaker.

Watchmaking later spread throughout Europe and England. Centers of fine watchmaking were established during the seventeenth and eighteenth centuries, especially in London, Paris, and Geneva. Initially, a watch was made by several craftsmen: rough castings were made by one artisan and the parts were finished and assembled by the watchmaker, who then engraved his name on the finished product. Cases were made by an artisan in the case-making trade. Since the parts were finished individually and by hand, they were never interchangeable, even as parts of watches produced by one maker.

Colonial America had many artisans who considered themselves watchmakers. David Johnson of Boston was taxed as a watchmaker in 1687 and many men advertised as such thereafter.

It is almost certain, however, that they did not construct watches; rather, they sold and repaired watches imported from England and Europe.

Watches are occasionally found bearing the name of an American "watchmaker," but close examination indicates that the name had been engraved by the importer. (For example, the names of Effingham Embree of New York and Ephraim Clark of Philadelphia often appear. Customs documents exist, however, that prove both men brought in crates of watches from England during the 1790s.)

In 1838, the Pitkin brothers of East Hartford, Connecticut, attempted to produce watches by machine methods, thus paving the way for others. During the latter half of the nineteenth century, the American watch industry became the greatest in the world. Economic trends of the present century, however, have forced the surrender of that honor to the Swiss.

There is evidence that Thomas Harland (1735–1807) was the earliest watchmaker in America. Harland, an English-trained clockmaker, settled at Norwich, Connecticut, in 1773. He advertised on December 9, 1773, that he "makes in the neatest manner and on the most approved principles, horizontal, repeating, and plain gold watches in gold, silver, metal or covered cases." He also noted "watch wheels and fuzees of all sorts and dimensions, cut and finished upon the shortest notice, neat as in London and at the same price."

It is not known whether Harland actually made watches or just engraved his name on imported examples, but he certainly had the ability to make watches. He perhaps made a few after his arrival and later found it more economical to import them. In later advertisements, such as the one dated January 9, 1800, he no longer claimed to make watches, but had "for sale at his shop in Norwich, an assortment of Warranted Watches, vis. English silver Watches, cap'd and jeweled; day of month and seconds, in silver and gilt cases; second-hand watches, various sorts; French gold and silver Watches, day of month, seconds, and plain."

Further evidence that Thomas Harland, Sr., made watches is found in an obituary that appeared in the *Connecticut Gazette* of April, 1807: "Died at Norwich, Mr. Thomas Harland, age seventy-two, Goldsmith; *he is said to have made the first watch ever manufactured in America.*"

After 1800, Harland's watch business was being conducted by his son, Thomas, Jr. On the younger Harland's death in 1806, his estate papers listed 117 watches. All were noted as being of foreign manufacture, except for one that carried the name of Philip Sadler of Baltimore (though it was probably a foreign-made watch too).

Luther Goddard (1762–1842) of Shrewsbury, Massachusetts, made ten purchases at the estate auction in 1807. He bought two French gold-case watches at twenty-eight dollars and ten dollars and five silver watches for less than ten dollars apiece. He also spent fifty cents for a pair of small rollers, a dollar for two dozen old seals, and ten dollars for a set of watch tools. Goddard began producing watches at Shrewsbury two years later; it is probable that he had received some watchmaking instructions from the Harlands.

Goddard began his business in a small shop about eighteen feet square. He bought hands, dials, hairsprings, mainsprings, balance verges, fusee chains, and pinions from Boston importers. The plates, wheels, and other brass parts were cast at the Shrewsbury shop and the watches assembled there. The plates and watch cocks were fire-gilded and engraved by an engraver in nearby Marlborough. Goddard's watches were made in a typical English style; however, his casting, his

**237.** English verge watch (No. 608) imported by Effingham Embree, NY, NY, c. 1795; he engraved his name on the watches and sold them. *(Am. Clock and Watch Museum)*

**238.** Watch papers. Advertisements often inserted in cases after repairing. Note Joshua Wilder's with Massachusetts shelf clock. *(American Clock & Watch Museum)*

**239.** No. 293, by L. Goddard & Son, Shrewsbury, MA, c. 1814. Some parts were imported, but major portion was made in America. *(Courtesy, Henry C. Wing, Jr.)*

plate finishing, and the quality of the engraving were not as fine as on imported watches.

One of Goddard's apprentices, William H. Keith, later wrote: "His tools consisted mainly of a tooth-cutting engine, a common foot lathe, brass pivot turns, an upright tool, and sinking, depthing, grooving, and hairspring tools; and the usual variety of pliers, tweezers, files, and other appliances in use by watch repairers, all of which were of English manufacture."

Goddard's first watches were marked "L. Goddard"; after taking his son Parley into the business, he used the name L. Goddard and Son. The business was apparently unprofitable, for after 1814, he again began importing watches.

In 1817, Goddard moved to nearby Worcester and opened a watch-repairing business. Less than 530 watches had been finished when he moved; his sons Parley and Daniel finished another 70 watches thereafter.

On July 16, 1817, the following notice appeared in the *Worcester National Aegis:*

PUBLICK NOTICE

Luther Goddard with his son Daniel Goddard have taken and opened the shop opposite Mr. D. Waldo's Brick Store in Worcester, for the purpose of making and repairing Watches, where they keep many Watches & Eight Day Time Pieces—all warranted good—together with an assortment of Silver & Gold Ware, Chains, Keys, Seals, and Trinkets, for Cash or approved Credit.
Worcester, July 16, 1817

The eight-day timepieces were probably made by Goddard's cousin Simon Willard, who advertised in the same newspaper on September 25, 1822, that "he has authorized L. Goddard & Son to sell his new Patent Alarm Time Pieces."

In 1828, Goddard moved to Preston, Connecticut, and by 1830, he had moved to Norwich. He later returned to Massachusetts, where he died on March 24, 1842, at the age of eighty-one.

By 1835, though few watches had been made in America and none had been made by machine methods, the Pitkin brothers, Henry (1811–46) and James Flagg (1812–70), of East Hartford, Connecticut, were developing a watch they hoped could be made successfully in quantity. Henry, as well as two older brothers, John O. and Walter, had been apprenticed as a silversmith and watch repairman, probably under Jacob Sargeant of Hartford. The youngest brother, James, was trained by his older brothers.

The Pitkins ran a shop in East Hartford for the manufacture of silver articles; they later opened a retail store in downtown Hartford. The store was destroyed by fire in 1833. They took over Sergeant's shop shortly thereafter and began experimentation with the machine-made watch. One of their four apprentices, Nelson P. Stratton, later

240

241

240. Pear-cased watch (No. 194) by Luther Goddard, Shewsbury, MA, c. 1812. Crudely finished plates. Goddard may have been first to make American watches, though Thomas Harland may have preceded him. *(Courtesy, Henry C. Wing, Jr.)* 241. Example (No. 164) of America's first machine-manufactured watch by H. & J. F. Pitkin, made at East Hartford, CT, c. 1839. *(Courtesy, Henry C. Wing, Jr.)*

**242.** Backplate of watch in illus. 236. Engraved "Thos. Harland, No. 481," *c.* 1800. This example probably imported, after Harland found domestic manufacture unprofitable. (*Courtesy, Henry Francis du Pont Winterthur Museum*)
**243.** Patent model of Jacob D. Custer's watch, made at Norristown, PA, 1843. (*Courtesy, Smithsonian Institution*)

became involved in the Boston Watch Company, American Watch Company, and Nashua Watch Company. He began working for the Pitkins in 1836. By this time they were making the tools and machinery necessary for the production of their American lever watch.

In their experimentation, the brothers attempted standardization so that the watch parts would be interchangeable. They cut the wheels in stacks and as uniformly as possible, though final hand-finishing was found to be necessary. They tried to avoid using foreign-made parts, but dials, hands, hairsprings, mainsprings, and jewels, when used, had to be obtained from importers.

The first fifty watches were marked "Henry Pitkin," but later examples were engraved "H. & J. F. Pitkin." No place of origin was engraved on the East Hartford-made watches, though the words "Detached Lever" appeared on the balance bridge. An American flag was engraved on the backplate. Watch number 164 is extant and Ambrose Webster (1832–94), a historian of the watchmaking business, claimed in 1890 to be the owner of watch number 90.

In October of 1841, the brothers moved their watch factory to New York in hopes of finding a better market in the city. Unfortunately, Pitkin & Company was not successful, for its watches were too expensive to compete with imports.

During the summer of 1846, Henry had a nervous breakdown and on September 8, while being taken to Bloomingdale Sanitarium in New York, he fell or jumped from the Croton Aqueduct, then under construction, and was killed.

After his death, the oldest brother, John, came to New York and with James formed the firm Pitkin & Brother. They manufactured watch cases, but not watches, and sold imported watches. The manufacture of cases was discontinued about 1850 and James continued to import and sell watches until 1865.

It is believed the Pitkins manufactured about four hundred watches. Those made in New York, marked "Detached Lever/Pitkin & Co./New York," were quite different from those made earlier in Connecticut. Watch number 367 is extant; watch number 378 was illustrated on the cover of the 1884 edition of the *Jeweler's Journal*, but its present location is unknown.

Another maker was Jacob Detweiler Custer (1805–72) of Norristown, Pennsylvania. He developed a number of unusual clock-movement styles during his career. On February 4, 1843, he was granted a patent for a watch of his own design; the patent model with its original key is in the United States National Museum in Washington, D.C. Custer apparently made few, perhaps only a dozen, of these watches. Watch number 7, a fusee watch—basically nonjeweled—is known.

## THE BOSTON WATCH COMPANY

Successful production of a machine-made American watch was achieved after 1850 through the efforts of Aaron L. Dennison and Edward Howard, among others.

Aaron Lufkin Dennison (1812–95), a native of Freeport, Maine, was trained as a clockmaker and jeweler by James Carey of Brunswick, Maine. In 1833, he went to Boston. He first worked for Currier & Trott, jewelers, then set up a watch-repairing business near the corner of Washington and Milk Streets. A short time later he worked as a watch repairman for Jones, Low & Ball of Boston. Jubal Howe, a former apprentice of Luther Goddard, was in charge of the watch-repair department and Dennison undoubtedly learned some of Goddard's watchmaking techniques from Howe.

After a brief tenure in New York, Dennison returned to Boston and in 1839, on Washington Street, established the firm of Dennison, Adams & Company as dealers in watches, tools, and materials. In 1846, he moved to another location on Washington Street and with Nathan Foster organized the firm of A. L. Dennison & Company.

Though Dennison first manufactured boxes for the jewelry trade, he became increasingly interested in the manufacture of watches. In January of 1850, he wrote:

> It is now about ten years since I first began to entertain the notion that the manufacture of watches might be introduced into this country with advantage, but I had supposed that in order to compete with the cheap labors of the old countries, Yankee ingenuity would have to be taxed to a considerable extent to produce a favorable result.
>
> For the first five or seven years of the above period, I contented myself with simply entertaining the opinion. . . . Once I recollected . . . to Mr. Willard in Congress St. that I believed that ten or twenty years would not elapse before American-made watches of a medium quality could be afforded for one-half the price of English manufacture, to which, as I expected, he expressed dissent. . . . Of course, whether this is correct remains to be proved, but after a still further consideration of the subject I am of the opinion that the final result will be as likely to produce the articles at one-quarter the price of importing as it is to exceed the first estimate by any degree.

Dennison became acquainted with Edward Howard, then in partnership with David Porter Davis in the manufacture of clocks and balances. He impressed Howard with his ideas on the potential of watch manufacturing and was given a small room in the Howard & Davis factory at Roxbury, Massachusetts, where, in 1849, he began to experiment and develop machinery for watch production. Howard & Davis provided him with

244

245

**244.** Edward Howard (1813–1904), watch and clock manufacturer for 50 years whose name is usually associated with high-grade precision timekeepers. (*Courtesy, Dana J. Blackwell*) **245.** Watch movement (No. 1546) made by Boston Watch Co., Waltham, MA, *c.* 1856, with trademark "Dennison, Howard & Davis." (*Courtesy, Dana J. Blackwell*)

ten thousand dollars and Samuel Curtis, a successful Boston gilder, dial maker, and ornament painter, invested another twenty thousand dollars. A new two-story brick building had been built for his use by the end of 1850.

Dennison's first model, an eight-day watch with two mainspring barrels, proved to be an unreliable timekeeper, because the barrels were too small to carry sufficient spring to maintain a constant rate. Dennison did not give up the idea of an eight-day watch. He told two of his employees, Oliver Marsh and his brother David, that if they would design two eight-day models after working hours, the company would furnish the materials, tools, and facilities. They finished the project by the fall of 1852. Dennison, though hoping to produce a hundred, managed to complete but twenty. These, in handsome gold cases made by Dubois & Company of New York, were given to company officials. Edward Howard's watch, number 1, is now preserved in the Smithsonian Institution. Number 3 was presented to David P. Davis, and it is assumed that Aaron Dennison had number 2. These watches were engraved "Howard, Davis & Dennison, Boston."

While the Marsh brothers were developing the eight-day models, Dennison was working on a thirty-six-hour model patterned after a standard English design. When the models were completed, Dennison found he could not gild them properly. Nelson P. Stratton, a third employee, was sent to Coventry, England, in 1852 to acquire the skill. Having done so, he returned and the first of Dennison's thirty-six-hour watches were placed on the market.

The firm name, originally the American Horologue Company, was changed at that time to Warren Manufacturing Company in honor of General Joseph Warren of Roxbury, who had been killed at the Battle of Bunker Hill in 1775. Approximately a hundred movements were finished that spring and sold with the name "Warren, Boston" engraved on the plates. By early 1854, another thousand movements had been finished that bore the trademark "Samuel Curtis, Roxbury." These first movements, with silver cases, cost the company about eighteen dollars each to produce.

In September of 1853, the company name was changed to the Boston Watch Company. By then the Roxbury factory had proved inadequate and a new site was chosen at Waltham, Massachusetts. The new building was completed and ready to operate by October of 1854. Aaron Dennison was manager of the plant, and Edward Howard manager of the finances. By this time some thirty watches were being produced a week.

After moving to Waltham, the Boston Watch Company began its production with watch number 1,000. Approximately four thousand watches

246. Eight-day watch engraved "Howard, Davis & Dennison, Boston, No. 3," which was personal watch of David P. Davis. Made in 1852. 247. Gold-cased Waltham watch presented to Dutch sea captain K. Wytsma by the President of the United States in 1865 for saving the crew of the sinking American barquentine *Hattie Morrison*. *(Courtesy, Henry C. Wing, Jr.)*

were engraved "Dennison, Howard & Davis, Waltham." About a hundred carried instead the name of Fellows & Schell of New York, a firm that gave financial aid to the company in 1856.

In that year, as the country moved into a financial recession, business slowed, and the Boston Watch Company, unable to meet its obligations, went into receivership in March of 1857. During May of that year, its property was auctioned off for $56,500.

## THE WATCH INDUSTRY GROWS

Though the Boston Watch Company did not survive, its establishment and subsequent development of watch manufacturing methods set a pattern that was followed by other companies. Once the potential of watch manufacturing had been realized, new firms began to be formed. Many survived only a few years and many, in fact, exhausted their resources before watches were even put on the market. But names such as Wal-

tham, Howard, Elgin, Hampden, and Illinois are remembered as successful producers of millions of machine-made watches.

In 1936, the United States entered into the Reciprocal Trade Treaty, which lowered duties on Swiss watches by 50 percent. It was an unfortunate happenstance for the American watch industry. During and after World War II, while American firms were suffering from postwar inflation, rising wages, and a need for capital to modernize production, the Swiss continued to flood the American market with watches. Within twenty years, the American jeweled watch industry had ceased to exist.

## THE AMERICAN WALTHAM WATCH COMPANY

Royal Elisha Robbins (1842–1902), a partner in Robbins & Appleton, watch importers of New York, purchased the Boston Watch Company in May of 1857 for $56,500. Additional backing was received from the firm of Tracy & Baker of Philadelphia, from whom the defunct company had been acquiring gold watch cases. Dennison continued with the firm as superintendent.

After the acquisition, the firm became known as Tracy, Baker & Company. The following month, Baker left the firm and it was reorganized as Appleton, Tracy & Company. On January 1, 1859, the company was merged with the Waltham Improvement Company, a landholding company that had been organized in March of 1853 to promote the building of the Boston Watch Company factory in Waltham. Officially incorporated on February 4, 1859, the new firm became the American Watch Company.

Dennison left the company after difficulties with the new owners. He had become convinced that more watches could be sold if cheaper models could be made, but the company's management did not want to invest in the necessary experimentation. Dennison persisted, but on January 3, 1862, the Board of Directors held a special meeting in which the members voted to discharge Dennison and forbid his admission to the factory workshops. Dennison brought suit against the company. It was settled out of court in November of 1863, and Dennison turned his attention to the Tremont Watch Company.

In 1885, the firm was reorganized under the name of the American Waltham Watch Company and realized a profitable business until after World War I. In 1921, the net losses of the firm were half a million dollars and in 1922, they increased to two and a half million, at which time the company became insolvent.

In 1923, the firm was again reorganized and became known as the Waltham Watch and Clock Company, merging its interests in a local clock manufacturing firm known as the Waltham Clock

Company, which had been purchased in 1913. In 1925, the company name was changed to the Waltham Watch Company. Production of pendulum clocks had been more or less discontinued by that time; electric clocks and speedometers continued to be made until about 1940.

Between its inception in 1860 and the end of its production of watches in 1957, the company had produced over thirty-four million watches. Although watches are still sold with the Waltham name, they usually contain Swiss movements.

## THE NASHUA WATCH COMPANY

Mr. B. D. Bingham of Nashua, New Hampshire, who had been running a watch and jewelry business and occasionally making some clocks and regulators, became interested in watch production. While in Waltham, he and Nelson P. Stratton approached Leonard White Noyes (1779–1867), a horological promoter of Nashua, for financial support. Noyes agreed to help and a company was formed with a hundred thousand dollars capital.

By 1862, some fifty-three thousand dollars had been spent and funds were exhausted. Stratton persuaded the American Watch Company to purchase the business for fifty-three thousand dollars, and approximately a thousand of the remaining Nashua Watch Company movements were finished and sold, though their plates were engraved with the Appleton, Tracy & Company trademark.

## E. HOWARD AND COMPANY

Edward Howard returned to Roxbury after leaving the Boston Watch Company. In 1857, he reinstated the old watch factory, which was being used by the firm of Howard & Davis. Here Howard worked with the receiver, Charles E. Rice, until 1858, when his creditors were paid off. Some watches were produced at this time with the name Howard & Rice.

On December 11, 1858, Edward Howard and his cousin, Albert Howard, went into partnership as E. Howard & Company. During much of 1859, Edward worked to develop a new watch model, which was placed on the market the next spring.

On March 24, 1861, a joint stock company known as the Howard Clock & Watch Company was formed with one hundred and twenty thousand dollars capital. Albert Howard was chosen president, Edward Howard superintendent and treasurer. The firm had to borrow money to keep operating and by 1863 was in serious financial trouble. On May 6, 1863, the directors decided to close the factory and dispose of the company's assets.

Edward Howard delayed the disposition and was eventually able to form another company, the Howard Watch & Clock Company, on October 2,

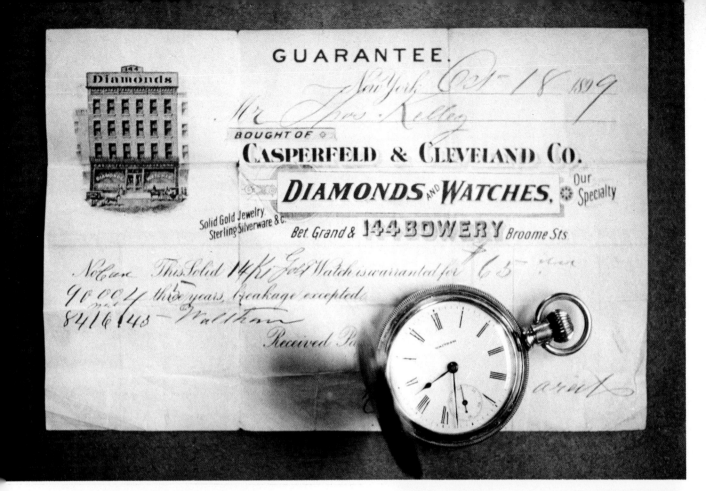

**248.** Waltham model 83, 7 jewel, No. 8416145, with its original 1899 bill of sale for $65 in 14K gold case. **249.** Waltham promotional advertisement. **250.** Waltham model 99, 15 jewel, No. 8669978, made *c.* 1898, with unusual hunting case allowing time to be seen without opening front cover. (*All, American Clock & Watch Museum*)

**251.** Pocket chronometer (No. 1) by Waltham with backplate engraved "Franklin C. Adams, Waltham, MA," and dated 1874. **252.** Masonic movement by Dudley Watch Co., Lancaster, PA, c. 1922. (*Both, courtesy, Henry C. Wing, Jr.*) **253.** Seth Thomas Clock Company's model 5, "Maiden Lane," No. 205573, with 17·jewels, made c. 1903. (*American Clock & Watch Museum*)

1863, with himself as president. Some new movement designs were adopted and the company realized a profit. In 1869, land was purchased adjoining the watch factory and a clock factory was built.

On December 1, 1881, a new company, called the E. Howard Watch & Clock Company, was formed with a capital of two hundred and fifty thousand dollars. Edward Howard remained as president, but retired in 1882 and the company purchased his interests in the firm for eighty-one thousand dollars. The company manufactured watches until 1903, when it sold the use of the trademark "Edward Howard" to the Keystone Watch Case Company of Philadelphia. About 854,000 watches had been produced. In 1905, the Keystone Company purchased the factory of the defunct United States Watch Company at Waltham, Massachusetts, and produced watches there until 1927.

### THE TREMONT WATCH COMPANY

After leaving the American Watch Company in 1862, Aaron L. Dennison, in partnership with A. O. Bigelow of the Boston jewelry firm of Bigelow, Kennard & Company, organized the Tremont Watch Company in Boston. Dennison proposed that to make a less-expensive watch, the watch parts could be made in Switzerland, where labor costs were cheaper, then brought to the American factory and assembled into finished watches. He went to Switzerland and set up a shop in Zurich, where gears for the trains and balances were made. They were shipped to the company factory at Melrose, Massachusetts, where the plates and

spring barrels were made and the watches were assembled.

Prospects seemed good at first, but when the initial investment of fifty thousand dollars had been exhausted, the stockholders refused to invest further and the factory was closed in 1868. Dennison returned to Boston to try to revive the company but failed. He went to England, where he remained until his death in 1895.

### THE NEWARK WATCH COMPANY

Napoleon Bonaparte Sherwood (1822–72), an employee of E. Howard & Company of Boston, started a watch factory with the financial aid of Fellows & Schell of New York, jewelers and importers. A room was rented in New York in April of 1863, and Sherwood, with six machinists, began to build machinery. Through an apparent disagreement, Sherwood left the company in 1864 or 1865 and was replaced by Arthur Wadsworth, an Englishman.

Louis S. Fellows died in 1866, and the firm, now Robert Schell & Company, was moved to Newark, New Jersey. Though the firm name was not changed, the trademark, "Newark Watch Company," is generally used in connection with its business.

In 1867, its watches were put on the market and about four hundred were sold that year. About a thousand were produced in 1868 and fifteen hundred the following year. Schell, however, found the business unprofitable, and ceased production about 1870. The factory was sold in January of 1871 to Paul Cornell of Chicago for one

hundred and twenty-five thousand dollars' worth of stock in the Cornell Watch Company.

## THE CORNELL WATCH COMPANY

In 1870, Paul Cornell, a Chicago lawyer and real estate investor, organized the Cornell Watch Company with a capital of two hundred thousand dollars. A new building was erected at a cost of seventy-five thousand dollars, and in August of 1871, machinery was moved into it from Newark. Ten grades of watches were produced, and a ladies' watch was attempted, but proved unsuccessful. The business did not prosper, and by 1873, there was serious thought given to disposing of it.

Cornell, however, realizing the potential of using the cheap labor provided by Chinese immigrants in California, persuaded William C. Ralston, a wealthy San Francisco banker, to purchase the company for one hundred thousand dollars. Cornell remained a stockholder. About sixty employees moved to San Francisco, where a new company, the Cornell Watch Company of San Francisco, was organized with a capital of two hundred and fifty thousand dollars. The attempt to employ Chinese laborers eventually failed, however, for the regular employees, in opposition to the plan, went on strike for ten days.

New machinery was built and prospects appeared good. But in November of 1875, after Ralston committed suicide, it was discovered that the company was indebted to the Bank of California for almost seventy-eight thousand dollars. The payroll could not be met and operations were suspended in January of 1876.

## THE CALIFORNIA WATCH COMPANY

A new company, called the California Watch Company, was organized under new management. It located in Berkeley, California, and construction of a factory was begun. By mid-1876, the company was producing watches but, lacking funds, was in financial trouble. The employees had to be paid in watch movements, which they could then trade for necessities from local stores. Production was ceased by the summer of 1876.

The following January, Albert Troller purchased the unfinished material and leased the buildings for four months in order to finish and sell the remaining movements. The machinery was eventually taken over by the creditors and sold to the Independent Watch Company of Fredonia, New York, among others.

Troller moved to Chicago in 1877 and in 1880, together with Paul Cornell and others, organized the Western Watch Company. The company, lasting only four months on its capital of ten thousand dollars, made very few watches.

## THE ROCKFORD WATCH COMPANY

When the Cornell Watch Company was in the process of moving from Chicago to California, Charles W. Parker, a former employee, persuaded some of the Cornell investors to back a venture he proposed to start in Rockford, Illinois. A capital of one hundred fifty thousand dollars was raised and the company was organized in March of 1874.

A building was secured, machinery and tools were purchased, and the factory was operative within a month. Many of the employees were those of the Cornell Company who had not wanted to move to California. In 1875, a new factory was built and by May, 1876, watches were being put on the market.

Considerable success was enjoyed by the firm for many years. It catered to the railroad trade and adopted a train on the dial as a trademark. The firm failed in 1896 and was operated by receivers until 1901, when it was reorganized as the Rockford Watch Company and continued in business until 1915.

## THE UNITED STATES WATCH COMPANY

In 1863, the United States Watch Company was formed in Newark, New Jersey. James H. Gerry of Waltham was engaged to make its machinery. The firm was officially organized in 1864 with a capital of five hundred thousand dollars by Frederick A. Giles, of Giles, Wales & Company, a New York jeweler concern, who was chosen president. The company's factory, built in Marion, New Jersey, at a cost of one hundred and twenty-five thousand dollars, began operations in 1865.

A number of different movement styles were made by the firm, but it failed to prosper and by 1872 it was in receivership. Production continued at the factory, though the firm name was changed to the Marion Watch Company. The movements produced thereafter were of poor quality.

By the time the factory was closed in 1874, Giles, Wales & Company had lost over three-quarters of a million dollars. William A. Wales later went to Auburndale, Massachusetts, where he failed in another watch business.

## THE FITCHBURG WATCH COMPANY

Sylvanus Sawyer of Fitchburg, Massachusetts, was one of the stockholders of the United States Watch Company of Marion, New Jersey, when it went bankrupt. Wanting to start a factory in his own town, he invested forty-five thousand dollars, leased a building, purchased some machinery, and hired the superintendent and some workmen from the former Marion factory. Operations began in 1875.

Within three years, the factory was producing twenty watches a day, though a company had yet to be formed. Upon reviewing his financial situation, Sawyer decided not to continue. Two years later, most of the machinery was disposed of and Sawyer went on to form the Sawyer Watch Tool Company.

## E. F. BOWMAN

Ezra F. Bowman (1852–1901), a Lancaster, Pennsylvania, retail jeweler and watch repairman, wanted to make a fine watch. He hired William H. Todd, an experienced watchmaker who had worked for the National Watch Company and the Lancaster Watch Company, to design and supervise its production. Though 300 watches were started, only 50 had been completed after two and a half years. Disillusioned, Bowman sold his machinery to J. P. Stevens of Atlanta, Georgia, in 1882, and returned to his jewelry business. In 1887, he founded the Bowman Technical School of Lancaster, which continues to offer training in clock and watch repair.

## THE J. P. STEVENS WATCH COMPANY

Josiah Percy Stevens (1852–1929), an Atlanta, Georgia, jeweler, invented a watch regulator that was patented on September 19, 1881. Stevens decided to buy rough parts from the Hampden Watch Company and have them finished at Atlanta, using his patented regulator.

In June of 1882, Stevens bought the machinery of E. F. Bowman of Lancaster, Pennsylvania, built a factory, and began operations in Atlanta. The J. P. Stevens Watch Company was then formed with a capital of one hundred thousand dollars. On June 10, 1884, the jewelry firm of J. C. Stevens and Company purchased the watch company stock and the operation was moved to a larger building in Atlanta.

On the death of J. C. Freeman, a large investor in both businesses, manufacturing was discontinued and Stevens sold his interest to Freeman's heirs. The machinery was disposed of in 1887.

## THE ELGIN NATIONAL WATCH COMPANY

In 1863, John C. Adams of Chicago and Nelson P. Stratton of the American Watch Company of Waltham, Massachusetts, met to consider the formation of a watch factory to serve the growing market in the western states. (Adams, devoted to the idea of watch manufacturing, later assisted in the formation of the Illinois Springfield Watch Company, the Adams & Perry Manufacturing Company, and the Fredonia Watch Company.) The company did not materialize at that time, but during the following spring, Patten Sargeant Bartlett and Ira G. Blake, both of the American Watch Company, visited Chicago and the idea was again discussed.

On August 27, 1864, the proposition became a reality. The National Watch Company was incorporated with a capital of one hundred thousand dollars. On February 15, 1865, the company was reorganized under a special Illinois charter with a capital of half a million dollars, and Benjamin W. Raymond became the first president.

The site for a new factory was chosen at Elgin, Illinois; the land was donated by the town's residents. Machinery was purchased in the East and installed upon completion of the building in January of 1865.

On April 1, 1867, the first watches were introduced. The company enjoyed almost immediate success and within the year built an addition to the original factory. By 1869, the company's capital was raised to two million dollars. Additional buildings and a boiler house were erected in 1874, and four years later, another large extension was added. In 1881, two additional buildings were needed.

On May 12, 1874, the company name was changed to the Elgin National Watch Company. By June of 1886, 2,300 workers were employed and 1,200 watch movements were being made a day. By 1953, nearly fifty million watches had been made. Manufacture of watches was discontinued by the firm in 1964.

### THE NEW YORK WATCH COMPANY

In 1864, Don J. Mozart (1820–77), a native of Italy, interested several New York businessmen in investing in the manufacture of a three-wheel watch he had invented. The venture, called the New York Watch Company, was organized at Providence, Rhode Island, with a capital of one hundred thousand dollars. Two years later, since no watches had been completed because of difficulties with the escapement, the directors decided that the Mozart watch could not be successfully produced.

In 1866, the New York Watch Company was reorganized and Mozart left the firm and went to Ann Arbor, Michigan. The following year, two buildings were purchased in Springfield, Massachusetts; the company was moved there and reorganized with three hundred thousand dollars capital. In 1868, James H. Gerry, formerly of the United States Watch Company, was hired as superintendent.

Fire destroyed the factory on April 25, 1870, but most of the stock and machinery were saved. Another building was moved onto the site and remodeled for factory use. After 1873, business began to slow and in 1875, the factory was closed. Reorganized as the New York Watch Manufacturing Company, the firm survived for only another year.

### THE HAMPDEN WATCH COMPANY

Reorganized in June of 1877 as successor to the defunct New York Watch Company, the Hampden Watch Company of Springfield, Massachusetts, conducted a fairly successful business. In 1881, a new brick building was erected and in 1886, John C. Dueber, a watch case manufacturer, purchased controlling interest in the firm. In 1888, the operation was moved to Canton, Ohio.

In 1889, Dueber also moved his original company, the Dueber Watch Case Works, to Canton, but the two companies operated independently until 1923, when they were merged as the Dueber-Hampden Watch Company. In September of 1925, the company was sold to a group of Cleveland businessmen for over a million dollars; in 1927, it went into receivership; and in 1930, its operations ceased and its machinery and tools were sold to Amtorg, a Russian buying agency, for three hundred and twenty-five thousand dollars. Twenty-one former employees were hired to train the Russians in manufacturing procedures; they left for Russia on February 25, 1930, to help establish the Soviet Watch Factory in Moscow.

### THE MOZART WATCH COMPANY

After failing to produce a marketable watch for the New York Watch Company, Don J. Mozart went to Ann Arbor, Michigan, where he experimented further with his design. As a result of his efforts, the Mozart Watch Company was formed in 1866 with a capital of two hundred thousand dollars. Mozart was appointed superintendent and given stock as payment for the use of his patents.

Production of Mozart's three-wheel watch continued to prove problematic, and though four years passed, a watch had yet to be created for the waiting market. It was decided in 1870 to discontinue the effort. About thirty watches had been finished and ten of these were specially designed for the stockholders. One contained an interesting notation on the backplate:

> Made expressly for ever faithful George Doty, stockholder of Mozart Watch Company, at a cost of $2,500. Under Don J. Mozart's patent of December 24, 1868 – Mozart Watch Company, Ann Arbor, Michigan. Number 5.

**254.** No. 549 of one thousand movements made by the Boston Watch Co. in 1854 that carried the trademark "Samuel Curtis, Roxbury." (*Courtesy, Henry C. Wing, Jr.*)

The company's machinery and tools were later purchased by the Rock Island Watch Company. Mozart returned to the watch repairing and jewelry business, but in December of 1874 had a mental breakdown and was committed to the Kalamazoo County Mental Hospital. After being judged incurable, he was transferred to the county almshouse at Ann Arbor, where he died on March 15, 1877.

### THE ROCK ISLAND WATCH COMPANY

In February of 1871, the Rock Island Watch Company was organized with a capital of one hundred thousand dollars, and the machinery of the Mozart Watch Company of Ann Arbor, Michigan, was acquired. The price, set at forty thousand dollars, was paid in notes and stock in the new concern.

George B. McElwain, a Chicago jeweler who had been instrumental in organizing the company, attempted to make a watch similar to Mozart's, except for its balance arrangement. A factory was opened at nearby Milan, Illinois, and the machinery was moved there. The Rock Island Watch Company, however, became defunct long before a watch reached the market. The Mozart Watch Company eventually took the machinery back and received a five thousand dollar settlement for the damage it had received from being improperly stored. The machinery was later sold to the Freeport Manufacturing Company.

### THE FREEPORT MANUFACTURING COMPANY

During 1874, a stock company for the manufacture of watches was formed in Freeport, Illinois, with capital set at two hundred and fifty thousand dollars. The factory, newly constructed, was destroyed by fire on October 21, 1875, and most of the machinery was ruined. Because of the loss, the company failed without having put a watch on the market.

### THE ILLINOIS SPRINGFIELD WATCH COMPANY

In January of 1869, the Illinois Springfield Watch Company was formed—mainly through the efforts of John C. Adams—with a capital of one hundred thousand dollars. In April of 1870, six employees from the National Watch Company at Elgin rented a shop in Springfield, Illinois, and began making machine tools. A three-story building was built in Springfield in 1870, and the first watches were completed in 1872. In 1873, a New York sales office was formed to counteract the initial difficulty encountered in marketing them. At the end of the first year of production, 125 workers were employed at the factory and twenty-five watches were being produced each day.

A general slowing of the economy occurred in 1873, and the company was left with many unsold watches. It began borrowing money to meet expenses, and by 1875, the company's liabilities

**256.** Colorful dial from Seth Thomas ladies' watch. (*Courtesy, Christopher Brooks*) **257.** "Tuxedo" model, No. 822364, duplex-escapement watch by the New England Watch Co., *c.* 1905. (*American Clock & Watch Museum*)

amounted to just about one hundred thousand dollars.

Financial struggles continued until 1879, when the firm was reorganized as the Springfield Illinois Watch Company. Several additions were made to its factory, and during the next four years the company's financial condition became stable.

From 1885 to 1927, the firm's name was the Illinois Watch Company; in those years, over five and a half million watches were made. The firm was then purchased by the Hamilton Watch Company, who ran the factory until about 1933. At that time the Springfield factory was disbanded, half the machinery was sold, and the other half was moved to Hamilton's factory at Lancaster, Pennsylvania.

## THE ADAMS & PERRY MANUFACTURING COMPANY

In April of 1874, John C. Adams of Chicago came to Lancaster, Pennsylvania, and with E. H. Perry formed the Adams & Perry Manufacturing Company. Approximately seventy-eight thousand dollars of an authorized one hundred thousand dollars capital was subscribed by seventy stockholders and the firm was incorporated on September 26, 1874. (Adams, in disagreement with Perry as to method of manufacture, eventually resigned from the firm.)

Production began in July of 1875, and movements were first completed in April of 1876, but by that time the company was in serious financial difficulty.

On June 10, 1876, the company went into receivership. Purchasers were sought but none wished to pay the price demanded. William H. Todd, a former employee of the National Watch Company, had evaluated the stock and machinery and reported that for twenty thousand dollars some eight hundred watch movements could be completed for sale.

## THE LANCASTER WATCH COMPANY

On the basis of Todd's favorable report, the Lancaster Watch Company was formed in August of 1877. Only a few of the old movements were finished, but plans were made for a new model that could be made and sold as a cheaper watch.

On October 31, 1878, the company was reorganized as the Lancaster, Pennsylvania, Watch Company with a capital of one hundred and sixty thousand dollars. Financial troubles persisted and on May 9, 1879, still another company was formed, adopting the former name—the Lancaster

256  257

Watch Company. The new company took lease of the property of the Lancaster, Pennsylvania, Watch Company for three years, at the end of which time the companies were merged.

During 1883, the Lancaster factory was closed and reopened several times; by 1884, the company's debts were approaching one hundred thousand dollars. Abram Bitner of Lancaster, assuming the liabilities, purchased over 5,600 shares of stock of the available 8,000 shares at ten cents on the dollar.

In 1886, the firm was purchased by the Keystone Standard Watch Company, which had been formed to take over the Lancaster business. Subsequent production was sold to Atkinson Brothers of Philadelphia, who were distributors. The Keystone Company went into bankruptcy in 1890, and its assets were sold in 1892. The buyers also purchased the defunct Aurora Watch Company and merged both companies into the Hamilton Watch Company, which was incorporated on June 15 of that year. Machinery was moved from Aurora, Illinois, to Lancaster, Pennsylvania, and an addition was built onto the Keystone factory.

In 1893, the first Hamilton watch was put into production. The company, aiming sales at the railroad trade, adopted two slogans: "Hamilton—The Railroad Timekeeper" and "Hamilton, The Watch of Railroad Accuracy." The firm enjoyed success for many years.

On January 1, 1928, Hamilton purchased the Illinois Watch Company of Springfield, Illinois, and the following year, the company merged with the Sangamo Electric Company of Springfield to form the Hamilton–Sangamo Corporation. Electric clocks were made by the latter firm until it was sold to General Time Instruments Corporation in 1931. Hamilton ceased watch production at the start of World War II.

### THE DUDLEY WATCH COMPANY

William Wallace Dudley (1851–1928), a Canadian by birth, was first a model maker for the Waltham Watch Company. He later worked for the Illinois, Trenton, and South Bend watch concerns and, in 1906, was hired as designer and manufacturing superintendent at the Hamilton Watch Company in Lancaster, Pennsylvania.

Dudley was an active Mason and in 1918 developed a watch with movement bridge plates in the form of Masonic symbols. He was granted a design patent for his watch on June 20, 1923. To produce the watch, Dudley and two other Lancaster men, George W. Adams and John D. Wood, formed the Dudley Watch Company on June 7, 1920, with a modest capital of five thousand dollars, and acquired a two-story building.

Plates and winding mechanisms for the watches were made at the Lancaster factory, but the escapement and gear trains of the first models were purchased from the Waltham Watch Company. Watches first produced had nineteen jewels and ranged in price from a hundred and twenty-five to two hundred and fifty dollars.

Sales were not good, so a second model was developed. It was similar to some Hamilton products, but most of the escapements and gear trains were imported from Switzerland. Sales were still poor and a third model, with floral engravings on the bridge rather than Masonic symbols, was designed but did not reach the production stage.

On March 3, 1925, a receiver was appointed for the bankrupt firm. Dudley returned to Hamilton and worked as a mechanic until 1931, when he retired at the age of eighty. After the creditors were paid off, the Dudley operation was taken over by P. W. Baker & Company, who operated the watch division until 1935. The firm's products were mainly Swiss imports, though a few Masonic watches were assembled from the old Dudley Watch Company stock.

### THE COLUMBUS WATCH COMPANY

In 1876, Dietrich Gruen and William J. Savage began importing Swiss watch movements and installing them in American-made cases engraved with their firm name, the Columbus (Ohio) Watch Manufacturing Company. They later decided to manufacture their own movements and on November 18, 1882, the Columbus Watch Company was incorporated with one hundred and fifty thousand dollars capital.

The building formerly used by Gruen and Savage was purchased and a second building was added. In August of 1883, the first watch movements were finished. The firm went into receivership in 1894, and struggled financially until 1902, when it was sold to the Studebaker family of South Bend, Indiana, who formed the South Bend Watch Company.

Dietrich Gruen (1847–1911) left the Columbus Watch Company about 1894 and went into partnership with his sons Fred and George. In 1900, their firm was incorporated as The D. Gruen, Sons & Company.

Gruen's movements were first imported from Dresden; by 1904, the company was using Swiss movements. In 1916, construction of a Swiss-style factory building was begun on a site later known as Time Hill in Cincinnati. In 1955, the Gruen family sold its interests and the firm became known as Gruen Industries, Inc. The operation was moved to New York in 1958.

### THE SOUTH BEND WATCH COMPANY

In 1902, George, J. M., and Clement Studebaker, Jr., members of the family who founded the Studebaker wagon and automobile business, purchased the Columbus Watch Company of Columbus, Ohio, and formed the South Bend Watch Company, with Clement, Jr., as president. Capital was set at one hundred and thirty-two thousand dollars, and the following August a factory was built near South Bend, Indiana. On March 28, 1903, production was begun.

Charles T. Higginbotham, who had previously been a superintendent with the Seth Thomas Clock Company and the Columbus Watch Company, continued with the firm as a consulting superintendent. Several fine watches were offered and the company enjoyed a good reputation.

In 1923, the Studebaker Watch Company was incorporated as a separate company to sell watches and jewelry by mail order. Business declined during the late 1920s and by November of 1929, it was decided to terminate the business. By the end of 1932, all assets had been sold to satisfy the firm's creditors.

## THE INDEPENDENT WATCH COMPANY

E. D. and C. M. Howard, two brothers from Fredonia, New York, were in business under the name of Howard Brothers in the 1870s, selling Swiss watches by mail order. Later they purchased American watches from various manufacturers and sold them under the name of the Independent Watch Company.

They eventually decided to manufacture their own watches, and the Independent Watch Company was formed in 1880 with a capital of one hundred and fifty thousand dollars. Machinery was purchased from the California Watch Company, additional machinery and some unfinished stock from the United States Watch Company.

With Charles S. Moseley as superintendent, the new company started by completing the United States Watch Company movements. James Dangerfield succeeded Moseley in 1881, and he designed a new movement that was put on the market in 1883. But sales were poor; resistance to the Independent watches seemed to be due to their confusion with the Swiss mail-order watches sold under the same name.

In 1883, C. M. Howard met John C. Adams of Chicago, who went to Fredonia to evaluate the situation. He found the workmanship mediocre and the machinery in poor condition. He suggested closing the factory, overhauling the old machinery, and installing some new. To help pay for the improvements, Adams took many of the finished movements and disposed of them as best he could. On reopening, the company's name was changed to the Fredonia Watch Company.

Sales, however, continued to lag and in the summer of 1885, it was decided to relocate the factory and raise new capital. Residents of Peoria, Illinois, were interested in having the factory and promised to furnish one hundred thousand dollars. The Peoria Watch Company was incorporated on December 19, 1885. A factory building was erected on six acres of donated land and in use by June of 1886. The firm was successful for several years, but failed about 1895.

## THE UNITED STATES WATCH COMPANY OF WALTHAM

In 1879, two brothers named Nutting from Waltham, Massachusetts, began making watch tools and machinery. They were joined by Charles Vander Woerd, formerly of the American Watch Company, and in 1882, a firm was organized as the Waltham Watch Tool Company. Woerd, a native of the Netherlands, was an ingenious mechanic and had been prominently associated with several American watch firms after 1844.

After a company decision to manufacture watches, Woerd gained the support of E. C. Hammer and, in 1884, with a capital of fifty thousand dollars, the United States Watch Company of Waltham was formed. The first watch produced, designed by Woerd, because of its extremely large mainspring barrel, had a domed portion in the plate to accommodate the center wheel and required a special case. The movement proved unpopular and the model was dropped in November of 1887, at which time Woerd left the firm.

Granville Nutting succeeded Woerd as superintendent, a conventional watch design was adopted, and the capital was raised to one hundred and fifty thousand dollars. The firm failed in May of 1896, and in May of 1901 was purchased by some New Jersey backers who, in 1905, sold the factory to the Keystone Watch Case Company of Philadelphia.

## THE SETH THOMAS CLOCK COMPANY

In 1882, a decision was made by the Seth Thomas Clock Company of Thomaston, Connecticut, to begin producing pocket watches. In the summer of 1883, George Heath was engaged as a master mechanic and Herman A. T. Reinicke as a master watchmaker. Under Heath's supervision, about fifty machinists began to make the tools and machinery necessary for watch production.

In 1883, construction was begun on a four-story addition to the company's original marine shop. When actual production began in 1884, eighteen different models were manufactured, each in four grades and using from seven to twenty-eight jewels.

Reinicke was succeeded in 1886 by Charles T. Higginbotham, who had been with the Hampden Watch Company of Springfield, Massachusetts. Seth Thomas watches of the finest grade carried the "Maiden Lane" trademark. With the exception of the "Centennial" model, introduced about

**258.** E. Ingraham Company's 1939 New York World's Fair Commemorative nonjeweled watch retailed for $1.50 with fob. *(American Clock & Watch Museum)*

1913, movements were not cased at the factory. By 1915, when production of watches was ceased, over four million watches had been made.

### THE CHESHIRE WATCH COMPANY

George J. Capewell, with the assistance of Arthur E. Hotchkiss, started a watch manufacturing concern in Cheshire, Connecticut, in 1883. The company originally planned to manufacture a cylinder-escapement watch with lantern pinions, which had been designed by Hotchkiss, but it was found to be impractical.

Daniel A. A. Buck, formerly with the Waterbury Watch Company, was engaged as superintendent. During his two years of employment, Buck designed a lever-escapement watch with the

pendant attached to the movement so the movement could be removed from the case by the pendant when the bezel was off.

Many of the company's watches were marketed by the Appleton Wisconsin Watch Company, which had been formed in 1887 for that purpose. The Cheshire firm ceased operation about 1894; some of its models were later sold to the New England Watch Company.

### THE NEW HAVEN WATCH COMPANY

W. E. Doolittle, patentee of a watch movement, helped organize the New Haven Watch Company in October of 1883 with a capital of one hundred thousand dollars. A building was leased the following January on Day Street in New Haven.

Connecticut, for production consideration. The company felt, however, that the design was not perfected and turned down the offer. Hopkins then offered his invention to George Merritt of Boston, who was also interested in the production of a cheap watch. Merritt supplied funds for its further development, but seeing no practical results, eventually withdrew his help.

In 1876, Hopkins received backing from William Bentley Fowle (1826–1902) of Auburndale, Massachusetts. Machinery formerly used by the defunct United States Watch Company was purchased and production was begun.

The first of the Auburndale rotary watches were placed on the market in 1877; they cost ten dollars each, a price far higher than Hopkins had foreseen. They were stem-wound watches with lever escapements and usually with five jewels.

Hopkins' original estimate that he would need sixteen thousand dollars to set up an operation capable of producing two hundred watches a day was far out of line. By the time his watches were placed on the market, some one hundred and forty thousand dollars had been spent. The Waterbury watch, which proved quite cheap to manufacture, was being developed at this time, and the Auburndale backers decided to discontinue operations. About a thousand rotary watches were supposedly made; number 507, however, is the highest serial number known.

William B. Fowle, because of his considerable investment, did not wish to see the entire operation cease. On May 28, 1878, William A. Wales patented a timer, which the company produced until 1881, though without much success. In the same year, Chauncey Hartwell, the company's superintendent, developed two other low-priced models. These, named after W. B. Fowle's two sons, were the "Lincoln," a key-wound model, and the "Bentley," a stem-wound version.

In November of 1879, the Auburndale Watch Company was incorporated with a capital of five hundred thousand dollars, with William B. Fowle as president. But by 1883, Fowle's fortune was gone and the company made a voluntary assignment. In February of 1884, the machinery was sold.

## THE BENEDICT & BURNHAM MANUFACTURING COMPANY

The Benedict & Burnham Manufacturing Company of Waterbury, Connecticut, was incorporated in 1843 to supply brass for local button makers. Realizing the potential use of brass in the clock and watch industry, the firm, in 1857, formed the Waterbury Clock Company and also became interested in watch production.

The company was first offered J. R. Hopkins' low-cost watch by E. A. Locke, but it turned down the offer on the ground that the design was not

**261.** Special issue watch engraved "George Washington Exhibition Watch, Philadelphia, 1876." Apparently made by Marion Watch Co., though that firm reputedly closed in 1874. *(Courtesy, Henry C. Wing, Jr.)* **262.** Cornell Watch Co., No. 14650, made *c.* 1873 in Chicago, IL. *(American Clock & Watch Museum)* **263.** Auburndale Watch Company's "Lincoln" key-wind watch No. 653, made *c.* 1882. *(Courtesy, Henry C. Wing, Jr.)*

**263**

ready for production. The events that followed were recorded by Charles S. Crossman in the *Jeweler's Circular and Horological Review* (*c.* 1887):

Meanwhile, Mr. Locke had not given up the idea of bringing out a cheap watch. He was positive that there was a field for a cheap watch, as at that time no Swiss watch in either nickel or silver cases were on the market that sold for less than seven dollars retail, while toy watches running for a few seconds sold at thirty-five cents each. He argued there must be a happy medium somewhere in the neighborhood of three or four dollars. . . . While walking along the street in Worcester, Massachusetts, in the spring of 1877, Mr. Locke saw a tiny steam engine in the window of a watch repairer's shop. He went in and entered into conversation with the proprietor, Mr. D. A. Buck. There he learned that this engine, weighing fifteen grains, had been exhibited at the Centennial Exhibition by the side of the mammoth Corliss engine, and had been made by Mr. Buck with his watchmaker's tools. This engine, with its boiler, governor, and pumps all complete, stands on a space one-eighth of an inch square, or less than the area of a gold dollar. It is five-eighths of an inch high and is composed of one hundred and forty-eight distinct parts held together by fifty-two screws. Three drops of water fill the boiler to its proper capacity.

After viewing the machine, Locke was convinced that Daniel Azro Ashley Buck was an exceptional mechanic and discussed the idea of a cheap watch with him. Buck completed a watch model, sent it to Locke and Merritt, who had been invited into the venture, and was paid a hundred dollars. The model was a rotary with a chronometer escapement similar to that of Hopkins' watch, but was also considered too unfinished to be successfully produced.

Buck finished an improved model in 1877. The watch was a rotary—the movement turning one revolution each hour—and had a duplex escapement, which Buck felt was the real innovation toward low-cost production. The watch had only fifty-eight parts, about half the number in normal watches, and no jewels. The mainspring was nine feet long and coiled around the entire back of the case behind the movement. It took 150 half turns of the stem to wind the watch, which is why it was nicknamed the "long wind." Patents were granted to Buck for his watch on May 21, 1878, and on December 16, 1879.

During January of 1878, Locke, Merritt & Buck presented the improved model to Benedict & Burnham. It was tested and found to be satisfactory. Backing needed in order to go into production was adjudged to be eight thousand dollars.

In December of 1878, the first watches were put on the market and sold for $3.50 each. At first they were sold in colored celluloid cases; later, nickel-plated brass cases were used. The dials on the watches were open, so many of the moving parts were visible. The watches were made and sold successfully under the name of the Benedict & Burnham Manufacturing Company until the formation of the Waterbury Watch Company.

## THE WATERBURY WATCH COMPANY

Finding Benedict & Burnham's facilities inadequate for its growing watch business, a joint stock corporation known as the Waterbury Watch Company was formed on March 1, 1880, with a capital of four hundred thousand dollars. The principle stockholders were Charles Benedict, Gordon W. Burnham, Charles W. Dickinson, George Merritt, Edward A. Locke, and Daniel A. A. Buck. Benedict was chosen president, a position he held until his death in 1881. He was succeeded by Burnham.

In April of 1880, ground was broken for a new brick building, the main part of which was four stories with a single-story wing and a three-story wing. Manufacturing was begun in May, a year later, and six hundred watches were made each day. Within a few years the number had increased to a thousand.

By 1885, the company had introduced two additional series of watches, the three being called A, B, and C. The company called them the "ABC of Horology." The firm claimed every watch was run for six consecutive days before leaving the factory and would run for twenty-eight hours with each winding. It also stated that factory charges for repair would never exceed fifty cents per watch.

In 1882, the company attempted manufacture of a pin-anchor-escapement watch designed for them by Herman A. T. Reinicke. About ten thousand were begun, but few were finished. The next year, Reinicke left Waterbury and became a model maker for the Seth Thomas Clock Company.

In 1884, Daniel Buck left the Waterbury Watch Company to work as superintendent of the Cheshire (Connecticut) Watch Company. His "long-wind" watch was discontinued by Waterbury in 1891 and a short-wind version introduced.

In 1898, the Waterbury Watch Company was reorganized as the New England Watch Company. Care should be taken not to confuse the Waterbury Watch Company with the Waterbury Clock Company, both of whom were making nonjeweled watches. Even though both were started by the Benedict & Burnham Manufacturing Company, they were operated independently. The Waterbury Clock Company was the firm that supplied R. H. Ingersoll & Brother of New York with many of its watches. The Waterbury Watch Company did *not* make watches for Ingersoll, but the situation becomes somewhat confusing because Ingersoll purchased the defunct New England Watch Company (which had formerly been the Waterbury Watch Company) in 1914.

## THE NEW ENGLAND WATCH COMPANY

On July 1, 1898, the Waterbury Watch Company was reorganized as the New England Watch Company with a capital of six hundred thousand dollars. The new company continued production of low-priced watches, but was not always financially solvent.

Until 1904, the firm produced mainly duplex-escapement watches without jewels. They introduced a small four-jewel ladies' watch at that time and, in about 1907, a seven-jewel pocket watch. The ladies' watch, the "Elfin," was the smallest watch then made in America and because of its size was probably worn as a pendant or on a neck chain.

In about 1909, the company brought out a seven-jewel chronograph, which was what Mr. George Tetro, a foreman at the New England factory, said "really . . . sank them." Mr. Tetro also noted that the company made the best duplex watch in the country.

Lesser firms often sold the New England Watch Company's products. These included the Holly Watch Company of Jersey City, New Jersey; the Atlas Watch Company of Chicago; the Cambridge Watch Company of Boston; and the Columbia Watch Company, later known as the Suffolk Watch Company, of Boston.

In peak years, the company had almost 750 workers. By 1906, its capital had been increased to seven hundred and fifty thousand dollars, and later to a million dollars, but by 1912, its financial situation deteriorated, and on July 17, the company went into receivership.

On November 25, 1914, a bid of seventy-six thousand dollars was accepted from R. H. Ingersoll & Brother of New York and the business, which had been inventoried at three hundred and twenty-five thousand dollars, was sold. The Ingersoll firm used the factory and manufactured watches until its bankruptcy in 1922. The final owners, the Waterbury Clock Company, dismantled the factory.

## R. H. INGERSOLL & BROTHER

Robert Hawley Ingersoll (1859–1928) and Charles Henry Ingersoll (1865–1948), natives of Delta, Michigan, formed a partnership in 1881 in New York City that developed into a mail-order business. In 1892, finding sales good for a cheap watch they were offering, they decided to have some specially made.

The first was made by the Waterbury (Connecticut) Clock Company. It was an improvement of the "Jumbo" model that had been designed for Waterbury by Archibald Bannatyne. Ingersoll sold almost ten thousand of them. In 1893, the brothers commissioned Waterbury to make them a similar

watch with a specially designed case to sell at the Columbian Exposition, which was being held in Chicago that year to commemorate the four hundredth anniversary of the landing of Christopher Columbus. The case was impressed with pictorial designs of Columbus' three ships surrounded by likenesses depicting Columbus, an American Indian, and Columbia, with the Exposition Building at the bottom.

Business continued to be good and Ingersoll approached Waterbury in 1894 with an order for half a million watches for the following year. In 1896, the smaller "Yankee" model, which was the first to sell for a dollar, was introduced. The company later adopted the slogan, "The watch that made the dollar famous," which thereafter linked the name of Ingersoll with the dollar watch in the public's mind.

In 1898, one million watches were sold. The brothers subsequently sold their mail-order business and devoted their time to marketing the watches that were still being supplied to them by the Waterbury Clock Company.

In 1899, Robert Ingersoll went to England to arrange for an outlet for their watches, and in 1902, they issued a special commemorative watch of the South African or Boer War especially for the English and South African trade. In 1904, Simonds Stores, Ingersoll's English distributors, went out of business, and in January, 1905, the company opened its own office in London. By 1911, watches were being assembled in London from parts made by the Waterbury Clock Company, and in 1915, the London branch became known as Ingersoll Watch Company. The Ingersoll enterprises in England continued successfully even after the demise of the American firm.

R. H. Ingersoll & Brother conducted a successful marketing business right up to the time of World War I. They had accumulated considerable cash and in 1908 had acquired the defunct factory of the Trenton (New Jersey) Watch Company. Here they manufactured their own jeweled watch movements, which perhaps contributed to the deterioration of their assets.

In about 1914, the Waterbury Clock Company terminated its contract to supply Ingersoll with nonjeweled watches. The brothers, seriously in need of a source for cheap watches, purchased the bankrupt New England Watch Company later that year. They paid seventy-six thousand dollars for the factory in Waterbury, Connecticut, and began to manufacture their own nonjeweled watches. By 1917, they had almost seven hundred employees.

During World War I, many of their better watchmakers had been called into service; manufacturing was continued, but with less skilled personnel. The company's policy of guaranteeing watches remained unchanged and more and more

265. America's first successful inexpensive watch sold for $3.50 when introduced in December of 1878. Watch, developed by Daniel A. A. Buck, had only 58 parts. *(Courtesy, Edward Ingraham Library)*

watches were returned for repair, the expense of which was a major factor in the ultimate failure of the firm.

By 1920, the financial situation had become so critical that the company was forced to borrow money from a bank. The company continued to lose money and eventually it was taken over by the bank. In the first six months under the management of New York bankers, it lost over eight hundred thousand dollars more, and in 1922, it went into receivership. Charles Ingersoll tried to encourage the E. Ingraham Company to buy the business, but the firm did not want to assume the liabilities. It is not known whether he approached other clock companies, but it is probable.

After the failure of R. H. Ingersoll & Brother, the firm was taken over by the Waterbury Clock Company and watches were produced and sold under the name of The Ingersoll–Waterbury Company. The new company survived the Depression, and in 1933 introduced the popular Mickey Mouse watch, which sold for $1.33. The watch, though popular, was priced so low that it did not bring in much money. The machinery used was antiquated and in poor condition and the quality of the products manufactured by the new company was, for the most part, inferior.

In 1944, the Ingersoll–Waterbury Company

**266.** Nine-foot-long coiled spring that gave Buck's watch the nickname the "long wind"; 150 half turns needed to wind. (*Courtesy, Edward Ingraham Library*)

**267.** Movement of Buck's rotary-movement duplex-escapement watch produced by Benedict & Burnham Mfg. Co., Waterbury, CT. (*Courtesy, Edward Ingraham Library*)

was purchased by United States Time Corporation. Under the leadership of Joakim Lehmkuhl, who had fled Norway during Hitler's invasion in 1940, the company prospered. The Ingersoll trademark was continued until 1951, when the Timex trademark was adopted. Timex has since become a highly successful business with wide distribution of its products. The company manufactures mechanical, electric, and quartz watches.

### THE BANNATYNE WATCH COMPANY

Archibald Bannatyne (1852–1931), a native of Scotland, came to America at the age of twenty-five and began working for the Waterbury Clock Company. He was a master mechanic at the time the company developed the "Jumbo" model clock-watch, which it began to produce in 1880. After twenty-eight years of service, Bannatyne resigned from the company to start a firm for the manufacture of a smaller, stem-wind pocket watch that could retail for $1.50.

In November of 1905, the Bannatyne Watch Company was organized at Waterbury, Connecticut, with a capital of one hundred thousand dollars. The factory was located at 31–37 Canal Street. By 1911, approximately three hundred and fifty thousand watches had been produced, but in July of that year, the company failed. Nearly a year

later, the assets of the company, including machinery, tools, and stock, were purchased by the E. Ingraham Company and moved to Bristol, where they became the nucleus of the company's successful watch production.

After the failure of his company, Bannatyne worked for the Ansonia Clock Company of Brooklyn, New York, from which he retired in 1920.

### THE E. INGRAHAM COMPANY

With the purchase of the Bannatyne Watch Company in 1911, the E. Ingraham Company of Bristol, Connecticut, who had been manufacturing clocks for half a century, began to make pocket watches.

In 1930, the company developed a wristwatch and in November of that year put out about fifty samples. Two years had been spent in making models. The first were round, but later a tonneau (barrel) shape was adopted. To reduce the cost the second hand was often not added to the dial face.

In January of 1931, the wristwatches were put on the market; they sold to the retailer for $3.21 and to the public for $5.00 or more. By the end of the first year, two thousand watches were being produced each day. The company's competitors in the nonjeweled wristwatch market at that time were the Ingersoll–Waterbury Company and the New Haven Clock Company.

Ingraham's pocket watch, which was basically the watch developed by Archibald Bannatyne, was produced—with minor changes in movement design—until the company ceased production of watches in 1967. By that time over sixty-five million pocket watches and over fifteen million wristwatches had been produced.

## THE NEW HAVEN CLOCK COMPANY

In 1880, the New Haven Clock Company also began production of nonjeweled pocket watches. Its earlier models were wound from the back and were quite large, as were those being made by the Waterbury Clock Company.

In 1917, New Haven added wristwatches to its line. Wristwatches, considered to be feminine, were not generally accepted by men until World War I, when they were found to be far easier for soldiers to carry than pocket watches.

In 1946, the company was reorganized under the name of the New Haven Clock & Watch Company, but its watch production declined seriously after that time. During the 1950s, many of its watch movements were made in Switzerland, being so marked on their backplates. In 1956, the company went into bankruptcy and discontinued watch manufacture. It claimed to have produced over forty million watches since 1880.

## THE E. N. WELCH MANUFACTURING COMPANY

In about 1890, the E. N. Welch Manufacturing Company developed a small, back-wind timepiece movement for use in some of its novelty clocks. The movement was only two and a half inches long, one and a fourth inches wide, and half an inch deep. It was put in a large watch case and sold as a commemorative timepiece for the Columbian Exposition in Chicago in 1893. The clock-watch was impressed on the back of the case with a scene depicting the landing of Columbus.

Other than this special issue, the company did not manufacture watches. Production of the Columbus watch also was apparently brief; the company went into receivership in 1893 and did not resume production of its line of clocks until about January of 1896.

## WESTCLOX

In about 1899, the Western Clock Manufacturing Company of LaSalle, Illinois, began production of nonjeweled watches. The company had been manufacturing various styles of small-lever-escapement clocks and found that its methods were adaptable to pocket watch manufacture.

Three models had been introduced by 1909, and in that year the trademark "Westclox" was adopted. It became the company name in 1936. Some five years after watch production had begun, a hundred watches were being produced a day. The number increased over the years until, in 1974, production was about thirteen thousand watches a day.

## THE ANSONIA CLOCK COMPANY

Not to be outdone by the Waterbury and New Haven Clock companies, the Ansonia Clock Company of Brooklyn, New York, introduced a nonjeweled pocket watch in 1904. Up to ten models were produced with the same basic movement design. These were priced at from one to four dollars, though most sold for about two dollars. Approximately ten million watches were produced between 1904 and 1929, the year the company discontinued business.

## THE NEW YORK AND INTERNATIONAL WATCH COMPANIES

Two other companies were formed for the production of nonjeweled watches, but both were short-lived. The New York Watch Company, also known as the New York City Watch Company, was located at 43 Downing Street and produced pocket watches from 1890 to 1897. An interesting feature of its watches was the use of crank winding. The feature was invented by S. Schisgall and patented by him on October 2, 1894. The watches appear to be common stem-wind models, but the crown does not turn; the whole pendant is, in fact, a crank that is pulled counterclockwise along the rim of the watch for winding.

Another firm, the International Watch Company of Newark, New Jersey, made open-faced watches from 1902 to about 1907. It used the trademarks Berkshire, Madison, and Mascot.

## SWISS IMITATIONS

Once American machine-made watches had achieved popularity and success, it was not long before they were copied, especially by the Swiss. Some, though made in American styles, were sold openly as foreign watches; others were marked so as to deceive the public. Often words such as "American Watch," "The Pennsylvania," "California," or "Manhattan" were put on foreign-made dials or plates to associate the watch with American manufacture. False company names were also engraved on some watches. Companies such as the Brooklyn Watch Company, the Ohio Watch Company, and the Roxbury Watch Company were nonexistent. Two fictitious firms, the Bristol Watch Company and the New England Watch Company, engraved Bristol, Connecticut, on their products as the supposed place of manufacture. Though Bristol was associated with clock and watch production, no watches were made there before 1912.

Sometimes a foreign firm was able to mislead the public by changing the spelling of a name

**268.** Clock-watch produced by E. N. Welch Mfg. Co. for the Columbian Exposition held in Chicago in 1893. Huge watch is 1⅜ inches thick, 2¾ inches in diameter. *(Henry C. Wing, Jr.)*

familiar on American watches. Examples might be the use of P. Z. Bartzlett or P. S. Bartlets (instead of P. S. Bartlett), Waldham (instead of Waltham), and Morian Watch Company (instead of Marian Watch Company).

On March 3, 1971, Congress passed a law requiring the country of origin to be plainly marked on watches legally brought into the United States. Though some were brought in illegally, the number of imitations that reached the Ameri-

can market was thereafter greatly diminished.

Of course, many companies existed that legitimately marketed watches containing Swiss movements. Such a firm was the Non-Magnetic Watch Company of America, which was formed about 1890 to market Charles August Paillard's non-magnetic balance watches. But the Swiss-made movements were marked as such. The Philadelphia Watch Company, incorporated on October 23, 1868, with Eugene Paulus as president, is

**269**

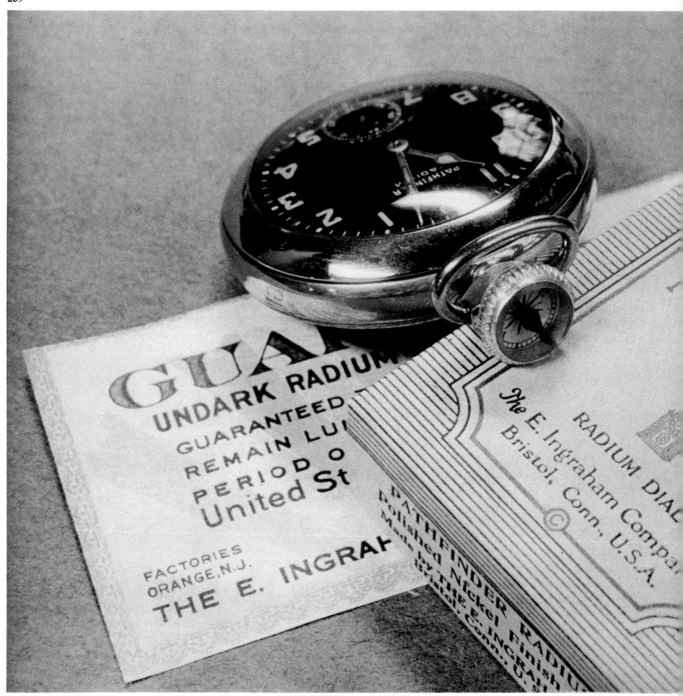

thought to have operated in the same way, though the origin of its movements is unknown.

Indeed, today one finds "Swiss Made" a common notation on the dials of watches that have been placed on the market by established American firms. Unfortunately, because of the keen competition and economic conditions in American industry, most of these firms have had to close down their operations in this country and purchase movements made overseas in order to exist.

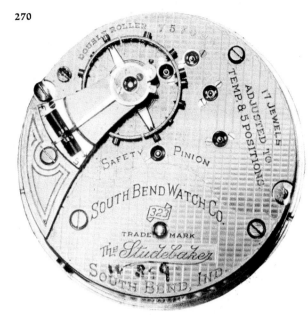

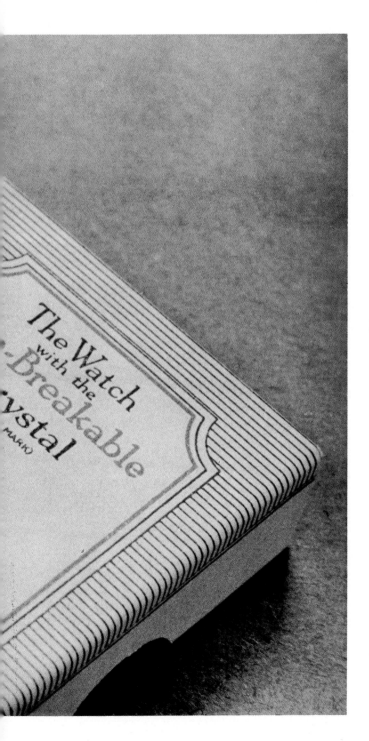

**269.** E. Ingraham's "Pathfinder" model with radium dial and compass pendant. Retail cost was $3.36 in 1929. **270.** South Bend Watch Company's "Studebaker" model, No. 757098, 17 jewel, made *c.* 1907. Adjusted for temperature and five positions. **271.** New Haven Clock Company's nonjeweled back-wind pocket watch, dated Jan. 23, 1900, on backplate. (*All, American Clock & Watch Museum*)

# Clockmakers & Watchmakers in America

| Tall Clocks* | Connecticut | | | | Delaware | Kentucky |
|---|---|---|---|---|---|---|
| | Bristol, Plymouth, Waterbury | Fairfield, New Haven & vicinity | Hartford & vicinity | Other | | |
| **1700** | | |  **272.** By Seth Youngs, Windsor, CT (c. 1745) | | | |
| | | **Ebenezer Parmele** (1690–1777) Guilford, CT | | | | |
| | | **Macock Ward** (1702–83) Wallingford, CT | | | **William Furniss** (fl. c. 1740) Wilmington, DE | |
| | | **Abel Parmele** (1703–c. 1766) New Haven, CT; Branford, CT, after 1741 | | | **Benjamin Chandlee** (1685–c. 1750) Philadelphia, PA (1702–12); Nottingham, MD (1712–41); Wilmington, DE (after 1741) | |
| **1750** | | **John Davis** (fl. c. 1750) Stratford and Fairfield, CT | **Seth Youngs** (1711–61) Hartford, CT (1735–42); Windsor, CT (1742–60) | | **273.** Dial from MA clock shown in illus. 44 | |
| | | **John Whitear** (d. 1762) Fairfield, CT | **Ebenezer Balch** (1723–1808) From Boston, MA; Hartford, CT (c. 1744); Wethersfield, CT (1756) |  | | |
| | | **John Whitear, Jr.** (1738–73) Fairfield, CT | **William Burr** (fl. c. 1760) Fairfield, CT | | | |
| | | | **Samuel Rockwell** (1722–73) Providence, RI; Hampton, VA; Philadelphia, PA; Middletown, CT (1760–73) | | | |
| | | **Isaac Doolittle** (1721–1800) New Haven, CT | **Benjamin Youngs** (Shaker) (1736–1818) (Son of Seth, Sr.) From Windsor, CT; Schenectady, NY, after 1766; Watervliet, NY | | | |
| | | | **Benjamin Cheney, Jr.** (wood) (1725–1815) East Hartford, CT (3 sons to Northfield, MA, Windsor and Woodstock, VT) | | **George Crow** (fl. 1754–70) Wilmington, DE | |
| | | | | | **Duncan Beard** (fl. c. 1767) Appoquinimink Hundred, DE | |

*(Brass clockmakers unless otherwise noted)

| Maine | Maryland | Massachusetts | | | | |
|---|---|---|---|---|---|---|
| | | Boston | Amesbury, Bradford, Lynn, Newburyport, Salem | Grafton, Lexington, Roxbury, Worcester | Other | |
| | | **James Batterson** (fl. *c.* 1707) Boston, New York, Philadelphia, and Charleston, SC | | | | 1700 |
| | | **John Brand** (fl. *c.* 1711–14) Boston, MA | | | | |
| | | **Thomas Badely** (fl. *c.* 1712–20) Boston, MA | | | | |
| | | **Joseph Essex** (fl. *c.* 1712) Boston, MA. | | | | |
| | | **William Claggett** (1696–1749) Boston, MA (*c.* 1714–16); Newport, RI (1716–49) | | | | |
| | | **Benjamin Bagnall** (*c.* 1689–1773) Boston, MA | | | | |
| | | **Benjamin Bagnall, Jr.** (fl. *c.* 1720) Boston, MA | | | | |
| | | **Samuel Bagnall** (fl. *c.* 1720) (Son of Benjamin) Boston, MA | | | | |
| | **Benjamin Chandlee** (1685–*c.* 1750) Philadelphia, PA (1702–12); Nottingham, MD (1712–41); Wilmington, DE (after 1741) | **James Bichault** (fl. *c.* 1729) Boston, MA | | | | |

**274. By Isaac Doolittle, New Haven (*c.* 1745)**

| Maine | Maryland | Boston | Amesbury, Bradford, Lynn, Newburyport, Salem | Grafton, Lexington, Roxbury, Worcester | Other | |
|---|---|---|---|---|---|---|
| | | | **Jonathan Mulliken** (fl. *c.* 1735) Bradford and Falmouth, MA | | **Henry Harmson** (fl. *c.* 1733–37) Marblehead, MA | |
| | | **James Atkinson** (fl. *c.* 1744–54) Boston, MA | **Samuel Mulliken** (1720–56) From Bradford, MA; Newburyport, MA, after 1740 | | | |
| | **John Powell** (fl. *c.* 1745) Baltimore, MD | **Ebenezer Balch** (1723–1808) From Boston, MA; Hartford, CT (*c.* 1744); Wethersfield, CT (1756) | **Jonathan Blaisdell** (1709–1802) Amesbury, MA, and East Kingston, NH | | | |
| | | | | | **Richard Manning** (*c.* 1710–74) Ipswich, MA | 1750 |
| | **John Finley** (fl. *c.* 1754) Baltimore, MD | | **David Blaisdell** (1712–56) Amesbury, MA | | | |
| | | **Gawen Brown** (fl. 1749–1801) Boston, MA | | | | |
| | **Patrick Sinnott** (fl. *c.* 1761) Baltimore, MD | | **Isaac Blaisdell** (1738–91) (Son of David) From Amesbury, MA; Chester, NH, after 1762 | | | |
| | **William Thompson** (fl. *c.* 1762) Baltimore, MD | | **Nathaniel Mulliken** (1722–67) From Bradford, MA; Lexington, MA, after 1751 | | | |
| | **Benjamin Chandlee, Jr.** (1723–91) Nottingham, MD | **Thomas Clark** (fl. *c.* 1764) Boston, MA | | | | |
| | **William Faris** (1728–1804) Annapolis, MD | | | | | |
| | **John Burrage** (fl. *c.* 1769) Baltimore, MD | **James Ashby** (fl. 1769–73) Boston, MA | | | | |

| Tall Clocks* | Connecticut | | | | Delaware | Kentucky |
|---|---|---|---|---|---|---|
| | Bristol, Plymouth, Waterbury | Fairfield, New Haven & vicinity | Hartford & vicinity | Other | | |
| **1770** | | Hezekiah Hotchkiss (1729–71) New Haven, CT | | | | |
| | | Nathan Howell (1740–84) New Haven, CT | Timothy Cheney (brass and wood) (1731–95) East Hartford, CT | | | |
| | | Silas Merriman (1734–1805) New Haven, CT | Enos Doolittle (fl. 1772) Hartford, CT | John Avery (1732–94) Preston, CT | | |
| | | Richardson Minor (1736–97) Stratford, CT | | Thomas Harland (1735–1807) Norwich, CT, after 1773 | Christopher Weaver (fl. c. 1775) Georgetown, DE | |
| | | Joseph Buckley (1755–1815) Fairfield, CT | | | George Crow, Jr. (fl. 1770–1802) Wilmington, DE | |
| | | | Miles Beach (1743–1828) Litchfield, CT; Hartford, CT (1785–88) | Reuben Ingraham (1743–1811) From Preston, CT; Plainfield, CT, after c. 1790 | | |
| | | | | Benjamin Hanks (1755–1824) Litchfield, CT (c. 1780–90); Mansfield, CT; Albany, NY | | |
| | | | | Gurdon Huntington (1763–1804) Windham, CT (1784–89); Walpole, NH (1789–1804) | | |
| | | | | Peregrine White (1747–1834) Woodstock, CT | | |
| **1790** | | | Daniel Burnap (1759–1838) East Windsor, CT (1786–1805) | Thomas Jackson (1727–1806) Portsmouth, NH; Preston, CT (c. 1775–1806) | | |
| | | | | John Avery (1762–1843) Plainfield, CT; Bridgewater, NY, after c. 1796 | | |
| | | | | William Stillman (b. 1767) From Westerly, RI; Burlington, CT (1789–92); Westerly, RI (1792–1809) | | |
| | | G. Bradford Whiting (1764–1844) | | Timothy Barnes (brass and wood) (1749–1825) Litchfield, CT | | |
| | | Isaac Marquand (1766–1838) | | | | |
| | | Whiting & Marquand (1790–1800) Fairfield, CT | | Asa Sibley (1764–1829) Woodstock, CT (c. 1785–1800); Walpole, NH; Rochester, NY | | George Smart (fl. c. 1795) Lexington, KY |
| | Gideon Roberts (wood) (1749–1813) Bristol, CT | Isaac Doolittle, Jr. (1759–1821) New Haven, CT | | Ezra Dodge (1766–98) New London, CT | Jonas Alrichs (1759–1802) Wilmington, DE | Edward West (1757–1827) Stafford County, VA (until 1788); Lexington, KY (c. 1790) |
| | Eli Terry (brass and wood) (1772–1852) Plymouth, CT | John Clark (fl. c. 1777–1811) Danbury, CT | Jacob Sargeant (1761–1843) From Mansfield, CT; Springfield, MA (1787–95); Hartford, CT (1795–c. 1835) | Phineas Pratt (1747–1813) Saybrook, CT | | Henry Hyman (fl. c. 1800) Lexington, KY |
| | | | Martin Cheney (fl. c. 1801) (Son of Benjamin, Jr.) From East Hartford, CT; Windsor, VT | Wooster Harrison (b. 1772) Trumbull, CT (1795–1800); Newfield, CT (after 1800) | | |
| | | Simeon Jocelin (1746–1823) New Haven, CT | David Greenleaf, Jr. (1765–1835) Hartford, CT | Nathaniel Shipman (1764–1853) Norwich, CT | | |
| | | Comfort Starr Mygatt (1763–1823) Danbury, CT (c. 1783–1807); Canfield, OH (after 1807) | Russell Cheney (fl. c. 1806) (Son of Benjamin, Jr.) From East Hartford, CT; Woodstock, VT | | | |
| | | | Asahel Cheney (brass and wood) (Son of Benjamin, Jr.) From East Hartford, CT; Northfield, MA (c. 1806); Royalton, VT (1808–16); Rochester, VT (after 1816) | | Thomas Crow (fl. 1808–24) (Son of George) West Chester, PA (1808–10); Wilmington, DE (1810–24) | |

*(Brass clockmakers unless otherwise noted)

| Maine | Maryland | Massachusetts | | | | |
|---|---|---|---|---|---|---|
| | | Boston | Amesbury, Bradford, Lynn, Newburyport, Salem | Grafton, Lexington, Roxbury, Worcester | Other | |
| | | | | | John Bailey (brass and wood) (1730–1810) Hanover, MA | 1770 |
| | Jacob Moehler (fl. c. 1773) Baltimore, MD | Charles Geddes (fl. c. 1773) Boston, MA | Nicholas Blaisdell (1743–c. 1800) (Son of David) Amesbury, MA (1764–74); Newmarket, NH (1774–c. 1776); Portland, ME (after 1776) | Nathaniel Mulliken, Jr. (1752–76) Lexington, MA | | |
| | | | Daniel Balch (1735–89) From Bradford, MA; Newburyport, MA, after 1757 | | | |
| Paul Rogers (fl. c. 1775) Berwick, ME | Benjamin Banneker (1731–1806) Baltimore, MD | | David Blaisdell, Jr. (1736–94) Amesbury, MA | | Preserved Clapp (b. 1731) Amherst, MA | |
| Nathaniel Hamlen (wood) (1741–1834) From Oxford, ME; Augusta, ME, after c. 1780 | Rudolph Spangler (1738–1811) Hagerstown, MD, and York, PA | | Jonathan Mulliken (2d) (1746–82) (Son of Samuel) Newburyport, MA | | Jonas Fitch (wood) (1741–1808) Pepperell, MA | |
| Nicholas Blaisdell (1743–c. 1800) (Son of David) Amesbury, MA (1764–74); Newmarket, NH (1774–c. 1776); Portland, ME (after 1776) | | | | Benjamin Willard, Jr. (1743–1803) Grafton, Lexington, and Roxbury, MA | | |
| Benjamin Snow (fl. c. 1783) Augusta, ME | | | | Joseph Mulliken (1765–1802) (Son of Nathaniel) From Lexington, MA; Concord, MA, after 1775 | | |
| | Hyrum Faris (1769–1800) Annapolis, MD | | | | | |
| | David Evans (fl. c. 1789) Baltimore, MD | | | | | |
| | William Faris, Jr. (b. 1762) From Annapolis, MD; Norfolk, VA (1790–95); Edenton, NC (1797–c. 1800) | | | | | 1790 |
| | Goldsmith Chandlee (c. 1751–1821) (Son of Benjamin, Jr.) Nottingham, MD, and Winchester, VA | | John Bailey, Jr. (1751–1823) From Hanover, MA; Lynn, MA | | | |
| | Eli Bentley (b. 1752) Taneytown, MD, and Chester County, PA | | | Simon Willard (1753–1848) From Grafton, MA; Roxbury, MA, after 1783 | | |
| | Charles Faris (1764–1800) Annapolis, MD | | | John Mulliken (b. 1754) Lexington, MA | | |
| Nathan Adams (1755–1825) Wiscasset, ME | Ellis Chandlee (1755–1816) (Son of Benjamin, Jr.) Nottingham, MD | | | Ephraim Willard (b. 1755) Boston, MA, and Roxbury, MA | Jacob Sargeant (1761–1843) From Mansfield, CT; Springfield, MA (1787–95); Hartford, CT (1795–c. 1835) | |
| Lebbeus Bailey (1763–1827) North Yarmouth, ME, after 1791 | | | Michael Carlton (1757–1836) Bradford and Haverhill, MA | Aaron Willard (1757–1844) Roxbury, MA | Calvin Bailey (1761–1835) (Son of John) Hanover, MA | |
| Jonathan Bemis (fl. c. 1800) Paris, ME | Isaac Chandlee (1760–c. 1813) (Son of Benjamin, Jr.) Nottingham, MD | | Daniel Balch, Jr. (1761–1835) Newburyport, MA | (Samuel) Taylor & Edwards (fl. c. 1801)         (wood) Worcester, MA | Abraham Edwards (wood) (1761–1840) Ashby, MA | |
| Enoch Burnham (fl. c. 1800) Paris and Portland, ME | William McParlin (fl. c. 1800) Annapolis, MD | | Samuel Mulliken (2d) (1761–1847) From Newburyport, MA; Salem, MA; Lynn, MA | | Calvin Edwards (wood) (1763–96) Ashby, MA | |
| Robert Eastman (fl. c. 1805) Belfast, ME | Thomas F. Adams (fl. after 1804) From Baltimore, MD; Petersburg, VA (1804–9); Edenton, NC (after 1809) | | | Jonathan Winslow (wood) (1765–1847) New Salem, Warren, and Worcester, MA; Springfield, MA, after 1820 | Asa Munger (brass and (1777–1851)         wood) From Ludlow, MA; Herkimer, NY (1803–18); Auburn, NY (after 1818) | |
| Frederick Wingate (1782–1864) From Haverhill, MA; Augusta, ME, after 1804 | | | David Wood (1766–c. 1824) Newburyport, MA | | Frederick Wingate (1782–1864) From Haverhill, MA; Augusta, ME, after 1804 | |
| Samuel Edwards (wood) (Son of Abraham) From Ashby, MA; Gorham, ME (1808–30) | | | | | Asahel Cheney (brass and (Son of Benjamin, Jr.) wood) From East Hartford, CT; Northfield, MA (c. 1806); Royalton, VT (1808–16); Rochester, VT (after 1816) | |

| Tall Clocks* | Connecticut | | | | Delaware | Kentucky |
|---|---|---|---|---|---|---|
| | Bristol, Plymouth, Waterbury | Fairfield, New Haven & vicinity | Hartford & vicinity | Other | | |
| **1810** | Joseph Ives (wood) (1782–1862) Bristol, CT (c. 1810) | | Daniel White Griswold (wood) (1767–1844) East Hartford, CT | Ziba Blakeslee (1768–1834) Newton, CT | | |
| | Lamson, Sperry & Co. (wood) (1810–17) Waterbury, CT | | | Elisha Cheney (brass and wood) (1770–1847) (Son of Benjamin) Berlin, CT | | |
| | Ebenezer and Solomon Griggs (wood) (fl. c. 1810) Bristol, CT | | | Edward Ells (1773–1832) From Preston, CT; Middlebury, VT, after 1810 | | B. B. and T. K. Marsh (fl. c. 1810) Paris, KY |
| | Levi Lewis (wood) (fl. c. 1810) Bristol, CT | | | | | |
| | Dr. Titus Merriman (wood) (fl. c. 1810) Bristol, CT | | | | | |
| | John Rich (wood) (fl. c. 1810) Bristol, CT | | | | | |
| | Gideon Roberts, Jr. (wood) (fl. c. 1810) Bristol, CT | | | | | |
| | Samuel Hoadley (wood) (1776–1858) From Waterbury, CT; Winchester, CT, after 1803 | | | | | |
| | Luther Hoadley (wood) (1781–1813) From Waterbury, CT; Winchester, CT | | | | | |
| | Heman Clark (wood) (1783–1838) Plymouth, CT (1805–23); Salem Bridge, CT (1823–35) | | | | | |
| | William Leavenworth (wood) (1759–1836) Waterbury, CT (1812–18); Albany, NY (1818–23) | | | | Samuel McClary (fl. 1803–16) Wilmington, DE | |
| | Mark Leavenworth (wood) (1774–1849) Waterbury, CT | | | | Jacob Alrichs (1775–1857) Wilmington, DE | |
| | Lemuel Harrison (wood) (1765–1857) Waterbury, CT | | | | | |
| | Seth Thomas (wood) (1785–1859) Plymouth, CT | | | | | |
| | Silas Hoadley (wood) (1786–1870) Plymouth, CT | | | | | |
| | Elias Roberts (wood) (1779–1841) (Son of Gideon) Bristol, CT | | | | | Asa Blanchard (fl. 1808–32) Lexington, KY |
| **After 1820** | Ephraim Downs (wood) (1787–1860) Plymouth and Waterbury, CT; Cincinnati, OH | | | Riley Whiting (wood) (1785–1835) Winchester, CT | | |
| | Chauncey Boardman (wood) (1789–1857) Bristol, CT | | | | Ziba Ferris, Jr. (1786–1875) Wilmington, DE | |
| | | | | | Charles Canby (1792–1883) Wilmington, DE | |

**275.** By Nathaniel Dominy, E. Hampton, NY (c. 1790)—illus. 32 shows movement

*(Brass clockmakers unless otherwise noted)

| Maine | Maryland | Massachusetts | | | | |
| --- | --- | --- | --- | --- | --- | --- |
| | | Boston | Amesbury, Bradford, Lynn, Newburyport, Salem | Grafton, Lexington, Roxbury, Worcester | Other | |
| Samuel Ranlet (1780–1867) From Augusta, ME; Monmouth, ME, after 1809 | Jacob Spangler (1767–1843) (Son of Rudolph) Hagerstown, MD, and York, PA | William Cummens (1768–1834) Boston, MA | | | Samuel Edwards (wood) (Son of Abraham) From Ashby, MA; Gorham, ME (1808–30) | 1810 |
| Paine Wingate (1767–1833) Augusta, ME, with brother Frederick (1811–17); Haverhill, MA (1817–33) | | Elnathan Taber (1768–1854) Boston, MA | Samuel Mulliken (3d) (b. 1769) From Newburyport, MA; Hallowell, ME | | John Osgood (1770–1840) Andover, MA | |
| Samuel Mulliken (3d) (b. 1769) From Newburyport, MA; Hallowell, ME | | | | | | |
| | | | Benjamin Balch (1774–1860) From Newburyport, MA; Salem, MA, after 1796 | | Alexander Tarbell Willard (1774–1850) (wood) Ashby, MA | |
| Daniel Noyes Dole (1775–1841) Wiscasset, ME | | | | | | |
| Nathaniel Mulliken (1776–1847) (Grandson of Samuel) From Newburyport, MA; Hallowell, ME | | | Nathaniel Mulliken (1776–1847) (Grandson of Samuel) From Newburyport, MA; Hallowell, ME | | Nathaniel Munroe (1777–1861) from Concord, MA; Baltimore, MD (1816–40) | |
| Abner Rogers (b. 1777) Berwick, ME | | | | Luther Goddard (1762–1842) Shrewsbury, MA, 1809–17; Worcester, MA, 1817–28; Preston, CT, 1828–30; Norwich, CT, 1830–42 | Paine Wingate (1767–1833) Augusta, ME, with brother Frederick (1811–17); Haverhill, MA (1817–33) | |

276. By Jesse Emory, Weare, NH (c. 1810)

| Maine | Maryland | Massachusetts | | | | |
| --- | --- | --- | --- | --- | --- | --- |
| | Nathaniel Munroe (1777–1861) from Concord, MA; Baltimore, MD (1816–40) | | | | | After 1820 |
| James Carey (1790–1865) Belfast and Brunswick, ME | | Benjamin Franklin Willard (1803–47) (Son of Simon) Boston, MA | | | Joshua Wilder (1786–1860) Hingham, MA | |
| Reuben Brackett (1791–1867) From Berwick, ME; Vassalboro, ME (1820–27); Unity, ME (after 1827) | | | | | John Edwards (wood) (b. 1787) (Son of Abraham) Ashby, MA | |
| Benjamin Swan (1792–1867) Augusta, ME; Hallowell, ME | | Simon Willard, Jr. (1795–1874) Boston, MA | | | | |

| Tall Clocks* | New Hampshire | New Jersey | New York | North & South Carolina | Ohio |
|---|---|---|---|---|---|
| **1700** | | | Everardus Bogardus (fl. *c.* 1700) New York, NY | | |
| | | | James Batterson (fl. *c.* 1707) Boston, New York, Philadelphia, and Charleston, SC | James Batterson (fl. *c.* 1707) Boston, New York, Philadelphia, and Charleston, SC | |
| | | | | Delonguemaire (fl. *c.* 1720) South Carolina | |
| | | Isaac Pearson (1685–1749) Burlington, NJ | Anthony Ward (fl. *c.* 1724) From Philadelphia, PA; New York, NY | Joseph Massey (fl. 1722–36) Charleston, SC | |
| | | | | John Harris (fl. 1729–39) Charleston, SC | |
| | | | | James Hillard (fl. 1730–49) Charleston, SC | |
| | | | John Bell (fl. *c.* 1734) New York, NY | Thomas Goodman (fl. 1733–38) Charleston, SC | |
| | | | | Peter Mowrove (fl. 1735–39) Charleston, SC | |
| | | Joseph Hollingshed (fl. 1740–75) Burlington, NJ | Bartholomew Barwell (fl. 1749–60) New York, NY | | |
| **1750** | Elisha Purington, Jr. (fl. *c.* 1750–68) Kensington, NH | Aaron Miller (fl. *c.* 1750) Elizabeth, NJ | | | |
| | Caleb Shaw (1717–91) Kensington, NH | William Crow (1715–58) Salem, NJ | | | |
| | Jonathan Blaisdell (1709–1802) Amesbury, MA, and East Kingston, NH | Stephen Tichenor (fl. *c.* 1760) Newark, NJ | | Marcel Boloquet (fl. *c.* 1760) New Bern, NC | |
| | Isaac Blaisdell (1738–91) (Son of David) From Amesbury, MA; Chester, NH, after 1762 | | | | |
| | | | Isaac Heron (fl. *c.* 1765–78) New York, NY | | |
| | Thomas Jackson (1727–1806) Portsmouth, NH; Preston, CT (*c.* 1775–1806) | | Benjamin Youngs (Shaker) (1736–1818) (Son of Seth, Sr.) From Windsor, CT; Schenectady, NY, after 1766; Watervliet, NY | | |
| | Jonathan Purington (1732–1816) Kensington, NH | Morgan Hollingshead (b. 1732) Morristown, NJ | | William Lee (fl. *c.* 1768) Charleston, SC | |
| | Abner Jones (fl. *c.* 1775) Weare, NH | Cornelius Miller (d. 1779) (Son of Aaron) Elizabeth, NJ | | | |
| | Ephraim Potter (wood) (fl. *c.* 1775) Concord, NH | | | | |

*(Brass clockmakers unless otherwise noted)

| Pennsylvania | | Rhode Island | Vermont | Virginia | |
| Philadelphia | Other | | | | |
| --- | --- | --- | --- | --- | --- |
| **Samuel Bispham**<br>(fl. *c.* 1696)<br>Philadelphia, PA | | | | | |
| **Abel Cottey**<br>(1655–1711)<br>Philadelphia, PA | | | | | 1700 |
| **James Batterson**<br>(fl. *c.* 1707)<br>Boston, New York, Philadelphia,<br>and Charleston, SC | | | | | |
| **Peter Stretch**<br>(1670–1746)<br>Philadelphia, PA, after 1702 | | | | | |
| **Benjamin Chandlee**<br>(1685–*c.* 1750)<br>Philadelphia, PA (1702–12);<br>Nottingham, MD (1712–41);<br>Wilmington, DE (after 1741) | **Dr. Christopher Witt**<br>(1675–1765)<br>Germantown, PA, after 1708 | | | | |
| **Anthony Ward**<br>(fl. *c.* 1724)<br>From Philadelphia, PA;<br>New York, NY | | | | | |
| | **Christopher Sauer**<br>(1693–1758)<br>Germantown, PA, after 1731 | | | | |
| **Joseph Wills**<br>(1700–59)<br>Philadelphia, PA, after 1725 | **Augustine Neisser**<br>Georgia (1736–40);<br>Germantown, PA (1740–80) | **William Claggett**<br>(1696–1749)<br>Boston, MA (*c.* 1714–16);<br>Newport, RI (1716–49) | | | |
| **John Wood**<br>(fl. *c.* 1734–61)<br>Philadelphia, PA | **John Fisher**<br>(fl. after 1749)<br>York, PA | **Samuel Rockwell**<br>(1722–73)<br>Providence, RI; Hampton,<br>VA; Philadelphia, PA;<br>Middletown, CT (1760–73) | | | |
| | **Frederick Solliday**<br>(fl. after 1750)<br>Bedminster, PA | **Isaac Anthony**<br>(fl. *c.* 1750)<br>Newport, RI | | | 1750 |
| | **Valentine Urletig**<br>(fl. 1758–83)<br>Reading, PA | **James Wady**<br>(fl. *c.* 1750)<br>Newport, RI | | | |
| **Samuel Rockwell**<br>(1722–73)<br>Providence, RI; Hampton,<br>VA; Philadelphia, PA;<br>Middletown, CT (1760–73) | **William Campbell**<br>(fl. *c.* 1763)<br>Carlisle, PA | | | **Samuel Rockwell**<br>(1722–73)<br>Providence, RI; Hampton,<br>VA; Philadelphia, PA;<br>Middletown, CT (1760–73) | |
| | **Joshua Humphrey**<br>(fl. *c.* 1764–73)<br>Chester County, PA | | | **Thomas Walker**<br>(fl. *c.* 1760–80)<br>Fredricksburg, VA | |
| | **Richard Chester**<br>(fl. *c.* 1765)<br>Hanover, PA | | | | |
| | **Jacob Gorgas**<br>(1728–98)<br>From Germantown, PA;<br>Ephrata, PA, after 1763 | | | **James Craig**<br>(fl. *c.* 1770)<br>Williamsburg, VA | |
| **Jacob Godschalk**<br>From Towamencin, PA;<br>Philadelphia, PA, after 1769 | **Isaac Thomas**<br>(1721–1802)<br>Chester County, PA | | | **Robert Egan**<br>(fl. *c.* 1770)<br>Williamsburg, VA | |
| **David Rittenhouse**<br>(1732–96)<br>Norristown, PA (1749–70);<br>Philadelphia, PA (after 1770) | **Isaac Jackson**<br>(1734–1807)<br>Chester County, PA | **Edward Spaulding**<br>(1732–85)<br>Providence, RI | | | |
| | **George Hoff**<br>(fl. 1765–1816)<br>Lancaster, PA | | | | |

**277.** By Daniel Balch, Bradford, MA (*c.* 1756)

| Tall Clocks* | New Hampshire | New Jersey | New York | North & South Carolina | Ohio |
|---|---|---|---|---|---|
| **1775** | **Nicholas Blaisdell** (1743–*c.* 1800) (Son of David) Amesbury, MA (1764–74); Newmarket, NH (1774–*c.* 1776); Portland, ME (after 1776) | **Moses Ogden** (1736–1814) Newark, NJ<br><br>**Benjamin Reeve** (1737–1801) Greenwich, NJ<br><br>**Lebbeus Dod** (1739–1816) Mendham, NJ | **Nathaniel Dominy** (1737–1812) East Hampton, NY | | |
| | | **John Hollingshead** (b. 1745) (Son of Joseph) Burlington and Mt. Holly, NJ | | | |
| | **Jeremiah Fellows** (1749–1837) Kensington, NH | **Isaac Brokaw** (1746–1826) Elizabeth, NJ; Rahway, NJ, after *c.* 1790 | | **John James Himeley** (fl. 1786–1809) Charleston, SC | |
| | **Gurdon Huntington** (1763–1804) Windham, CT (1784–89); Walpole, NH (1789–1804) | **Jacob Hollingshead** (b. 1747) (Son of Joseph) Salem, NJ | | **De St. Leger** (fl. *c.* 1790) New Bern, NC | |
| | **Benjamin Clark Gilman** (fl. *c.* 1790) Exeter, NH | **Joseph Hollingshed, Jr.** (b. 1751) Burlington, NJ | **Amos Jewett** (Shaker) (wood) (1753–1834) New Lebanon, NY | **Patrick Magann** (fl. *c.* 1790) Charleston, SC | **Thomas Lyman** (fl. after 1791) Marietta, OH |
| | **Nathan Hale** (1771–1849) Rindge, NH (*c.* 1791); Chelsea, VT (*c.* 1797) | **Hugh Hollingshead** (1753–86) Morristown and Mt. Holly, NJ | **Andrew Billings** (fl. *c.* 1795) Poughkeepsie, NY | | |
| | **Jesse Emory** (wood) (1759–1838) Weare, NH | **Aaron Lane** (1753–1819) Bound Brook and Elizabeth, NJ | **Benjamin Hanks** (1755–1824) Litchfield, CT (*c.* 1780–90); Mansfield, CT; Albany, NY | **Nathan Tisdale** (fl. *c.* 1795) New Bern, NC | |
| | **James Purington** (b. 1759) (Son of Jonathan) From Kensington, NH; Marietta, OH, after 1816 | | **John Avery** (1762–1843) Plainfield, CT; Bridgewater, NY, after *c.* 1796 | **William Faris, Jr.** (b. 1762) From Annapolis, MD; Norfolk, VA (1790–95); Edenton, NC (1797–*c.* 1800) | |
| **1800** | **James Fellows** (fl. *c.* 1800) (Son of Jeremiah) Kensington, NH | | **Asa Sibley** (1764–1829) Woodstock, CT (*c.* 1785–1800); Walpole, NH; Rochester, NY | | **Samuel and Robert Best** (fl. *c.* 1800) Cincinnati, OH |
| | **Abel Hutchins** (1763–1853) Concord, NH | | | | **Richard Jackson** (fl. *c.* 1800–40) Jefferson County, OH |
| | **Timothy Chandler** (1760–1848) Concord, NH | | | | |
| | **Levi Hutchins** (1761–1855) Concord, NH | | | | |
| | **Richard Blaisdell** (1762–90) (Son of Isaac) Chester, NH | | | | |
| | **Asa Sibley** (1764–1829) Woodstock, CT (*c.* 1785–1800); Walpole, NH; Rochester, NY | | | | |
| | **Stephen Hassam** (1764–1861) Charlestown, NH | | | | |
| | **Jedediah Baldwin** (fl. 1794–1810) From Hanover, NH; Rochester, NY, after 1810 | | | **William Hillard** (fl. *c.* 1805) Fayetteville, NC | |
| | **Robinson Perkins** (wood) (1766–1837) Jaffrey, NH (1790–1810); Fitzwilliam, NH (after 1810) | | | **William Dye** (fl. *c.* 1805) Fayetteville, NC | |

*(Brass clockmakers unless otherwise noted)

| Pennsylvania | | Rhode Island | Vermont | Virginia | |
|---|---|---|---|---|---|
| Philadelphia | Other | | | | |
| | Christian Forrer (1737–83) Lampeter, PA (1754–74); Newberry, PA (after 1774) | | | | 1775 |
| | Rudolph Spangler (1738–1811) Hagerstown, MD, and York, PA | | | | |
| | Benjamin Rittenhouse (b. 1740) Norristown, PA | | | | |
| | Elisha Kirk (fl. 1780–90) York, PA | | | | |
| | Samuel Hill (1765–1809) Harrisburg, PA | | | | |
| | John Jackson (1746–95) Chester County, PA | | | Edward West (1757–1827) Stafford County, VA (until 1788); Lexington, KY (c. 1790) | |
| | John Keim (1749–1819) Reading, PA | Benjamin Dudley (fl. c. 1790) Newport, RI | | William Faris, Jr. (b. 1762) From Annapolis, MD; Norfolk, VA (1790–95); Edenton, NC (1797–c. 1800) | |
| John Wood, Jr. (1736–93) Philadelphia, PA | Daniel Rose (1749–1827) Reading, PA | Calvin Wheaton (fl. c. 1790) Providence, RI | | John Weidemeyer (fl. c. 1790–1820) Fredericksburg, VA | |
| | Eli Bentley (b. 1752) Taneytown, MD, and Chester County, PA | Godfrey Wheaton (fl. c. 1790) Providence, RI | | Goldsmith Chandlee (c. 1751–1821) (Son of Benjamin, Jr.) Nottingham, MD, and Winchester, VA | |
| | Christian Bixler, Jr. (fl. 1785–1830) Easton, PA | | | | |
| | Samuel Davis (fl. 1797–1826) Pittsburgh, PA | Caleb Wheaton (1757–1827) Providence, RI | | | |
| Griffith Owen (fl. 1790–1814) Philadelphia, PA | John Hoff (d. 1822) (Son of George) Lancaster, PA | Barton Stillman (fl. c. 1800) Westerly, RI | | Caleb Bentley (fl. c. 1800) Leesburg, VA | 1800 |
| | | William Stillman (b. 1767) From Westerly, RI; Burlington, CT (1789–92); Westerly, RI (1792–1809) | Martin Cheney (fl. c. 1801) (Son of Benjamin, Jr.) From East Hartford, CT; Windsor, VT | James Galt (fl. c. 1800) Williamsburg, VA | |
| | | Willet Stillman (1777–1826) Westerly, RI | | John Woltz (fl. c. 1800) Shepherdstown, VA | |
| | Alexander Cooke (fl. c. 1802) Canonsburg, PA | | | | |
| | Mordecai Thomas (fl. c. 1802) (Son of Isaac) Chester County, PA | | | | |
| | | | | Thomas F. Adams (fl. after 1804) From Baltimore, MD; Petersburg, VA (1804–9); Edenton, NC (after 1809) | |
| | | Paul Stillman (fl. 1782–1810) Westerly, RI | | Jacob Craft (1765–1825) Shepherdstown, VA | |
| | Jacob Hostetter (1754–1831) Hanover, PA; Lisbon, OH (after 1822) | | Russell Cheney (fl. c. 1806) (Son of Benjamin, Jr.) From East Hartford, CT; Woodstock, VT | | |

| Tall Clocks* | New Hampshire | New Jersey | New York | North & South Carolina | Ohio |
|---|---|---|---|---|---|
| **1800** (continued) | | John Brokaw (b. 1767) (Son of Isaac) Elizabeth, NJ | | | Joseph Hough (fl. *c.* 1806) Butler County, OH |
| | Edward S. Moulton (fl. 1807) Rochester, NH | Benjamin Norton Cleveland (1767–1841) Newark, NJ | | | Philip Price (fl. *c.* 1806) Cincinnati, OH |
| | Timothy Gridley (wood) (fl. *c.* 1808) Sanbornton, NH | Aaron Brokaw (fl. *c.* 1800) (Son of Isaac) Rahway, NJ | | | Comfort Starr Mygatt (1763–1823) Danbury, CT (*c.* 1783–1807); Canfield, OH (after 1807) |
| | | | | Thomas F. Adams (fl. after 1804) From Baltimore, MD; Petersburg, VA (1804–9); Edenton, NC (after 1809) | |
| **1810** | Samuel Foster (brass and wood) (fl. *c.* 1810) Amherst, NH | Smith Burnet (1770–1830) Newark, NJ | Nathaniel Dominy, Jr. (1770–1852) East Hampton, NY | | Abner, Amasa, and Ezra Read (wood) (fl. 1810) Xenia, OH |
| | John Robie (fl. after 1810) Hanover, NH | Stephen Dod (1770–1853) (Son of Lebbeus) Newark, NJ | Jedediah Baldwin (fl. 1794–1810) From Hanover, NH; Rochester, NY, after 1810 | | |
| | | George Hollingshead (1771–1820) (Son of Morgan) Woodstown, NJ | | | |
| | | Cornelius Brokaw (1772–1857) (Son of Isaac) Rahway, NJ | Calvin Wells (Shaker) (1772–1853) Watervliet, NY | | Daniel Symmes (1772–1827) Cincinnati, OH |
| | | Abner Dod (1772–1847) (Son of Lebbeus) Newark, NJ | Benjamin Seth Youngs (1774–1855) Watervliet, NY | | |
| | | | | William Tisdale (fl. *c.* 1816) New Bern, NC | James Purington (b. 1759) (Son of Jonathan) From Kensington, NH; Marietta, OH, after 1816 |
| | Abijah Gould (brass and wood) (1777–*c.* 1841) Hollis, NH | | Asa Munger (brass and wood) (1777–1851) From Ludlow, MA; Herkimer, NY (1803–18); Auburn, NY (after 1818) | | Thomas Best (fl. 1808–26) Warren County, OH |
| | | Daniel Dod (1778–1823) Mendham and Elizabeth, NJ | William Leavenworth (1759–1836) Waterbury, CT (1812–18); Albany, NY (1818–23) | | Humphrey Griffith (1791–1868) Huntington, PA (1818–19); Lebanon, OH (1819–24); Indianapolis, IN (1825–34) |
| **1820** | | Joakim Hill (1783–1869) Flemington, NJ | | | Ephraim Downs (wood) (1787–1860) Plymouth and Waterbury, CT; Cincinnati, OH |
| | | | | | Oliver Roberts (brass and wood) (fl. *c.* 1815) Lancaster, PA; Eaton, OH |
| | Simeon Cate (wood) (1790–1835) Sanbornton, NH | | | | Luman Watson (wood) (1790–1841) Cincinnati, OH |
| | James C. Cole (1791–1867) Rochester, NH | | | George W. Hillard (fl. *c.* 1823) Fayetteville, NC | Jacob Hostetter (1754–1831) Hanover, PA; Lisbon, OH (after 1822) |
| | | | | | Joseph Budd (fl. *c.* 1830) Hamilton, OH |
| | | | Isaac Newton Youngs (brass and wood) (1793–1865) Mt. Lebanon, NY | | Jacob Jameson (fl. *c.* 1830) From Lancaster, PA; Springfield, OH |
| | | | Felix Dominy (1800–68) East Hampton, NY | | |

*(Brass clockmakers unless otherwise noted)

| Pennsylvania | | Rhode Island | Vermont | Virginia | |
|---|---|---|---|---|---|
| Philadelphia | Other | | | | |
| | **Jacob Spangler**<br>(1767–1843)<br>(Son of Rudolph)<br>Hagerstown, MD, and<br>York, PA | | | | **1800**<br>**(continued)** |
| | **Christian Eby**<br>(fl. *c.* 1799–1837)<br>Manheim, PA | | **John Peabody**<br>(fl. *c.* 1808)<br>Woodstock, VT | | |
| | **Thomas Crow**<br>(fl. 1808–24)<br>(Son of George)<br>West Chester, PA (1808–10);<br>Wilmington, DE (1810–24) | | **Asahel Cheney** (brass and wood)<br>(Son of Benjamin, Jr.)<br>From East Hartford, CT;<br>Northfield, MA (*c.* 1806);<br>Royalton, VT (1808–16);<br>Rochester, VT (after 1816) | | |
| | **Benedict Darlington**<br>(fl. *c.* 1810)<br>Chester County, PA | | **Jacob Kimball**<br>(fl. *c.* 1810)<br>Montpelier, VT | | **1810** |
| | **Jacob Hendel**<br>(fl. *c.* 1810)<br>Carlisle, PA | | **Edward Ells**<br>(1773–1832)<br>From Preston, CT;<br>Middlebury, VT, after 1810 | | |
| | **Frederick Heisely**<br>(1759–1843)<br>From Lancaster, PA;<br>Harrisburg, PA, after 1811 | | **Nathan Hale**<br>(1771–1849)<br>Rindge, NH (*c.* 1791);<br>Chelsea, VT (*c.* 1797) | | |
| | **James Thomson**<br>(fl. 1812–25)<br>Pittsburgh, PA | | | | |
| **John J. Parry**<br>(1773–1835)<br>Philadelphia, PA | | | | | |
| | **Oliver Roberts** (brass and wood)<br>(fl. *c.* 1815)<br>Lancaster, PA; Eaton, OH | | | | |
| | **George Beatty**<br>(1781–1862)<br>Harrisburg, PA | | | | |
| | **Humphrey Griffith**<br>(1791–1868)<br>Huntington, PA (1818–19);<br>Lebanon, OH (1819–24);<br>Indianapolis, IN (1825–34) | | | | |
| | | | | **William Cowen**<br>(fl. *c.* 1820)<br>Richmond, VA | **1820** |
| | | | | **George Downing**<br>(fl. *c.* 1820)<br>Richmond, VA | |
| | | | | **John Fasbender**<br>(fl. *c.* 1820)<br>Richmond, VA | |
| | **Jacob Detweiler Custer**<br>(1805–72)<br>Norristown, PA | | | | |
| | **Jacob Jameson**<br>(fl. *c.* 1830)<br>From Lancaster, PA;<br>Springfield, OH | | | | |
| | **Samuel Solliday**<br>(fl. to 1833)<br>Doylestown, PA | | | | |
| | **Joseph Bowman**<br>(1799–1892)<br>Lampeter, PA | | | | |
| | **John Erb**<br>(b. 1814)<br>Conestoga Center, PA | | | | |

278. By Simeon Jocelin, New Haven (*c.* 1800)

# Shelf Clocks

| | Connecticut | | | Massachusetts |
|---|---|---|---|---|
| | **Bristol** | **Plymouth, Salem Bridge, Waterbury** | **Other** | |
| **Pre-1800** | | | | **Simon Willard** (1753–1848) From Grafton, MA; Roxbury, MA, after 1783 **Aaron Willard** (1757 1841) Roxbury, MA **John Bailey, Jr.** (1751–1823) From Hanover, MA; Lynn, MA |
| **1800** | | | | **Daniel Balch, Jr.** (1761–1835) Newburyport, MA |
| | | | | **David Wood** (1766–c. 1824) Newburyport, MA |
| | | | | **William Cummens** (1768–1834) Boston, MA |
| | | | | **Elnathan Taber** (1768–1854) Boston, MA |
| | | **Eli Terry** (wood) (1772–1852) Plymouth, CT | | **Thomas Hutchinson Balch** (1771–1817) (Son of Daniel) Newburyport, MA |
| | **Dr. Titus Merriman** (wood) (fl. c. 1817) Bristol, CT | | **F. & E. Sanfords** (wood) (fl. c. 1818) Goshen, CT | |
| | | | **Norris North** (wood) (1788–1875) From Waterbury, CT; Torrington, CT (1823–31) | |
| | **Joseph Ives** (1782–1862) Bristol, CT (1810–24, 1830–39, 1844–62); Brooklyn, NY (1824–30); Plainfield, CT (1839–43) | **Heman Clark** (brass) (1783–1838) Plymouth, CT (1805–23); Salem Bridge, CT (1823–35) | **Bishop & Bradley** (brass and wood) (1824–32) Watertown, CT | |
| **1825** | | **Seth Thomas** (brass and wood) (1785–1859) Plymouth, CT | **Riley Whiting** (wood) (1785–1835) Winchester, CT | |
| | | **Mark Leavenworth** (wood) (1774–1849) Waterbury, CT | **Judson Williams Burnham** (brass) (1793–1857) Salisbury, CT | |
| | | **Silas Hoadley** (brass and wood) (1786–1870) Plymouth, CT | **Lucius Brown Bradley** (brass) (1800–70) Watertown, CT | |
| | | | **Ethel North** (wood) (1800–73) From Waterbury, CT; Torrington, CT | |

**279.** By Ephraim Downs, Bristol (c. 1830)

| New Hampshire | New York | Ohio | Pennsylvania | |
|---|---|---|---|---|
| | | | | Pre-1800 |
| | **Andrew Billings**<br>(fl. *c.* 1795)<br>Poughkeepsie, NY | | | |
| | | | | 1800 |

**Levi Hutchins**
(1761–1855)
Concord, NH

280. Terry Clock Co. "Parlour" model (*c.* 1875)

281. By Joseph Ives, Bristol (*c.* 1820)

**Frederick Heisely**
(1759–1843)
From Lancaster, PA;
Harrisburg, PA, after 1811

| | | | | 1825 |

**Asa Munger**
(1777–1851)
From Ludlow, MA;
Herkimer, NY (1803–18);
Auburn, NY (after 1818)

**Joseph Ives**
(1782–1862)
Bristol, CT (1810–24, 1830–39,
1844–62); Brooklyn, NY (1824–30);
Plainfield, CT (1839–43)

**Christian Bixler, Jr.**
(fl. 1785–1830)
Easton, PA

# Shelf Clocks

| | Connecticut | | | Massachusetts |
|---|---|---|---|---|
| | **Bristol** | **Plymouth, Salem Bridge, Waterbury** | **Other** | |
| **1825** *(cont.)* | **Ephraim Downs** (wood) (1787–1860) Bristol, Plymouth, and Waterbury, CT | | | **John Bailey III** (brass) (1787–1883) From Hanover, MA; New Bedford, MA, after 1824 |
| | **C(hauncey) & L(awson) Ives** (brass and wood) (1823–37) Bristol, CT | | | |
| | **Chauncey Boardman** (brass and wood) (1789–1857) Bristol, CT | | | |
| | **Elisha Hotchkiss, Jr.** (brass and wood) (1789–1882) Bristol and Burlington, CT | | | |
| **1830** | **Samuel Terry** (wood) (1774–1853) Plymouth, CT (1818–28); Bristol, CT (1828–35) | **Henry Terry** (1801–77) (Son of Eli) Plymouth, CT | | |
| | | **Sylvester Clark** (brass) (Brother of Heman) (1801–81) From Salem Bridge, CT; Milford, CT | **Olcott Cheney** (wood) (1796–1860) (Son of Elisha) Berlin and Middletown, CT | **Rodney Brace** (wood) (1790–1862) North Bridgewater, MA (1831–35) |
| | **Chauncey Jerome** (brass and wood) (1793–1868) Bristol and New Haven, CT | | | **David Studley** (fl. *c.* 1834) From Hanover, MA; North Bridgewater, MA, after 1834 |
| | | | | **Luther Studley** (fl. *c.* 1834) North Bridgewater, MA |
| | | | **Herman Northrop** (wood) (1801–90) (Partner of B. F. Smith) Goshen, CT | |
| | | | **Benjamin F. Smith** (wood) (1803–65) (Partner of H. Northrop) Goshen, CT | |
| | | **Silas B. Terry** (brass) (1807–76) Plymouth, CT (1831–50); Terryville, CT (1850–59) | **Edwin Hodges** (wood) (1810–84) Torrington, CT | |
| | **Ralph Ensign Terry** (brass) (1804–92) (Son of Samuel) Bristol, CT | **Richard Ward** (brass) (1787–1854) Salem Bridge, CT | **Edward Hopkins** (wood) (1797–1867) (Partner of A. Alfred) Harwinton, CT | **Daniel Pratt, Jr.** (brass and wood) (1797–1871) Reading, MA |
| | **John Burnham Terry** (brass) (1806–70) (Son of Samuel) Bristol, CT | | **Augustus Alfred** (wood) (1806–64) (Partner of E. Hopkins) Harwinton, CT | |
| | | **Eli Terry, Jr.** (wood) (1799–1841) Plymouth, CT | | |
| | **Noble Jerome** (brass and wood) (1800–61) Bristol, CT | **Spencer, Wooster & Co.** (brass) **Spencer & Hotchkiss** (fl. *c.* 1840) Salem Bridge, CT | **Asaph Hall** (wood) (1800–42) Goshen, CT (assembly plant in Clinton, GA) | |
| **1850** | After this date, the seven major clock companies (see p. 241) manufactured the majority of shelf clocks. | | | |

| New Hampshire | New York | Ohio | Pennsylvania | |
|---|---|---|---|---|
| | | | | 1825 (cont:) |
| | | | | 1830 |

Luman Watson (wood)
(1790–1841)
Cincinnati, OH

Jacob Detweiler Custer
(1805–72)
Norristown, PA

John Scharf
(fl. after 1836)
Selinsgrove, PA

282. By Hotchkiss & Benedict, Auburn, NY
(c. 1835)—made with convict labor

1850

# Specialized Clocks

| | Banjo & New Hampshire-style Mirror Clocks | Dwarf Tall Clocks ("Grandmother") | Marine Clocks | Tower Clocks |
|---|---|---|---|---|
| 1700 | | | | **Peter Stretch** (1670–1746) Philadelphia, PA, after 1702 <br><br> **Joseph Essex** (fl. c. 1712) Boston, MA <br><br> **Dr. Christopher Witt** (1675–1765) Germantown, PA, after 1708 <br><br> **Benjamin Bagnall** (c. 1689–1773) Boston, MA <br><br> **Ebenezer Parmele** (1690–1777) Guilford, CT <br><br> **Macock Ward** (1702–83) Wallingford, CT |
| 1750 | **Simon Willard** (1753–1848) From Grafton, MA; Roxbury, MA, after 1783 <br><br> **Aaron Willard** (1757–1844) Roxbury, MA | | | **Augustine Neisser** Georgia (1736–40); Germantown, PA (1740–80) <br><br> **Gawen Brown** (fl. 1749–1801) Boston, MA <br><br> **Valentine Urletig** (fl. 1758–83) Reading, PA <br><br> **Thomas Harland** (1735–1807) Norwich, CT, after 1773 <br><br> **Simeon Jocelin** (1746–1823) New Haven, CT <br><br> **Benjamin Hanks** (1755–1824) Litchfield, CT (1780–90); Mansfield, CT; Albany, NY <br><br> **Frederick Heisely** (1759–1843) From Lancaster, PA; Harrisburg, PA, after 1811 |
| 1800 | **Levi Hutchins** (1761–1855) Concord, NH | **Nathaniel Hamlen** (1741–1834) From Oxford, ME; Augusta, ME, after c. 1780 <br><br> **John Bailey, Jr.** (1751–1823) From Hanover, MA; Lynn, MA | | |

**283.** Seth Thomas "peanut" calendar (after 1863)

# Specialized Clocks

| | Banjo & New Hampshire-style Mirror Clocks | Dwarf Tall Clocks ("Grandmother") | Marine Clocks | Tower Clocks |
|---|---|---|---|---|
| **1800** (cont.) | **David Wood** (1766–c. 1824) Newburyport, MA | **Jonathan Winslow** (1765–1847) New Salem, Warren, and Worcester, MA; Springfield, MA, after 1820 | | |
| | **Paine Wingate** (1767–1833) Augusta, ME, with brother Frederick (1811–17); Haverhill, MA (1817–33) | | | |
| | **William Cummens** (1768–1834) Boston, MA | | | |
| | **Elnathan Taber** (1768–1854) Boston, MA | | | |
| | **William King Lemist** (1791–1820) Boston, MA | | | **Samuel Terry** (1774–1853) Bristol, CT |
| | **Daniel Munroe** (1775–1859) From Concord, MA; Boston, MA (1809–58) | | | |
| | **Nathaniel Munroe** (1777–1861) From Concord, MA; Baltimore, MD (1816–40) | | | |
| | **Abner Rogers** (b. 1777) Berwick, ME | | | |
| | **Samuel Whiting** (b. 1778, fl. 1808–36) Concord, MA | | | |
| | **Joseph Chadwick** (fl. 1810–31) Boscawen, NH | | | |
| | **Samuel Ranlet** (1780–1867) From Augusta, ME; Monmouth, ME, after 1809 | | | |
| | **Frederick Wingate** (1782–1864) From Haverhill, MA; Augusta, ME, after 1804 | | | **Jehial Clark** (c. 1781–1854) Cazenovia, NY |
| **1825** | **Joseph Dyar** (1795–1850) From Concord, NH; Middlebury, VT, after 1882 | | | |
| | **James Collins** (fl. c. 1830) Goffstown, NH | **Reuben Tower** (fl. c. 1825) Hingham, MA | | |
| | **Lemuel Curtis** (b. 1790) Concord, NH (1811–20); Burlington, VT (1820–44) | **Joshua Wilder** (1786–1860) Hingham, MA | | |

284. E. N. Welch "Regulator No. 7" (c. 1885)

# Specialized Clocks

| | Banjo & New Hampshire-style Mirror Clocks | Dwarf Tall Clocks ("Grandmother") | Marine Clocks | Tower Clocks |
|---|---|---|---|---|
| **1825** *(cont.)* | **Benjamin Swan** (1792–1867) Augusta and Hallowell, ME | | | |
| | **Joseph Nye Dunning** (1793–1841) Concord, NH (1816–20); Burlington, VT (1820–41) | | | |
| | **Benjamin Morrill** (1794–1857) Boscawen, NH | | | |
| | **Abiel Chandler** (1807–81) Concord, NH | | | |
| | **Leonard W. Noyes** (fl. *c. 1840*) Nashua, NH | | | |
| | **E. H. Nutter** (fl. *c. 1840*) Dover, NH | | | |
| | **Phineas Parkhurst Quimby** (1802–66) Belfast, ME | | | |
| | **Edward Howard** (1813–1904) Howard & (D. P.) Davis (1842–57) E. Howard & Co. (after 1857) Boston, MA | | | **Aaron Dodd Crane** (1804–60) Caldwell, NJ; Boston, MA, after 1858 |
| | **David Porter Davis** (fl. after 1842) (E.) Howard & Davis (1842–57) Boston, MA | | | **Jacob Detweiler Custer** (1805–72) Norristown, PA |
| | | | **Silas B. Terry** (1807–76) Plymouth, CT (1831–50); Terryville, CT (1850–59); Winsted, CT (1859–67); Waterbury, CT (1867–76) | |
| | | | **Charles Kirk** (fl. *c. 1847*) Bristol, CT | **Edward Howard** (1813–1904) Boston, MA |
| | | | **Mathews & Jewell** (1851–54) Bristol, CT | |
| **1850** | | | | **Seth Thomas Clock Co.** (1853–present) Plymouth, CT |
| | **Harvey Ball** (1818–1902) Westmoreland, NH | | **Noah Pomeroy** (1819–96) Bristol, CT | **Charles Fasoldt** (1819–98) Albany, NY |
| | | | **Samuel Emerson Root** (1820–96) Bristol, CT | |
| | | | **Laporte Hubbell** (1824–89) Bristol, CT | |

285. Seth Thomas "Wardroom" model—marine movement

# Giants of the American Clock
# Manufacturing Industry
# (1850–present)

**Ansonia Clock Co.**
Ansonia, CT & Brooklyn, NY
(1850–1929)

**The New Haven Clock Co.**
New Haven, CT
(1853–1959)

**The Seth Thomas Clock Co.**
Plymouth Hollow & Thomaston, CT
(1853–present)

**The Waterbury Clock Co.**
Waterbury, CT
(1857–1944)

**The E. Ingraham Co.**
Bristol, CT
(1857–1967)

**The William L. Gilbert Clock Co.**
W. L. Gilbert & Co.
Winchester, CT
(1845–48/1851–71);
Gilbert & Clark
(1848–51)—became
The William L. Gilbert Clock Co.
(1871–1964)

**The E. N. Welch Manufacturing Co.**
Forestville, CT
(1864–1903)—became
The Sessions Clock Co.
(1903–68)

# SELECTED BIBLIOGRAPHY AND
# SUGGESTED READINGS

Many books have been written on clocks and watches in the past years. Those listed below are ones that this author feels are of exceptional merit.

Allix, Charles. *Carriage Clocks, Their History and Development.* Suffolk, England, 1974.

Battison, Edwin A., and Kane, Patricia E. *The American Clock, 1725–1865.* Greenwich, Connecticut, 1973.

Beeson, C. F. C. *English Church Clocks, 1280–1850.* London, 1971.

Camp, Hiram. *A Sketch of the Clockmaking Business.* 1893.

Chamberlain, Paul M. *Its About Time.* New York, 1941.

Chandlee, Edward E. *Six Quaker Clockmakers.* Philadelphia, 1943.

Crossman, Charles S. *The Complete History of Watch Making in America* (Reprint). Exeter, New Hampshire, 1971.

Drost, William E. *Clocks and Watches of New Jersey.* Elizabeth, New Jersey, 1966.

Dworetsky, Lester, and Dickstein, Robert. *Horology Americana.* Roslyn Heights, New York, 1972.

Edwards, Ernest L. *The Grandfather Clock,* 3rd Edition. Altrincham, England, 1971.

Hoopes, Penrose R. *Connecticut Clockmakers of the Eighteenth Century.* Hartford, Connecticut, 1930.

——*Shop Records of Daniel Burnap, Clockmaker.* Hartford, Connecticut, 1958.

Hummel, Charles F. *With Hammer in Hand–The Dominy Craftsmen of East Hampton, New York.* Charlottesville, Virginia, 1968.

James, Arthur E. *Chester County Clocks and Their Makers.* West Chester, Pennsylvania, 1947.

Jerome, Chauncey. *History of the American Clock Business for the Past Sixty Years.* New Haven, 1860.

Mercer, Vaudrey. *John Arnold & Son, Chronometer Makers, 1762–1843.* London, 1972.

Miller, Andrew Hayes, and Miller, Dalia Maria. *Survey of American Clocks–Calendar Clocks.* Elgin, Illinois, 1972.

Moore, Charles W. *Timing a Century: History of the Waltham Watch Company.* Cambridge, Massachusetts, 1945.

Roberts, Kenneth D. *The Contributions of Joseph Ives to Connecticut Clock Technology, 1810–1862.* Bristol, Connecticut, 1970.

——*Eli Terry and the Connecticut Shelf Clock.* Bristol, Connecticut, 1973.

Smith, Alan. *The Lancashire Watch Company, Prescot, Lancashire, England, 1889–1910.* Fitzwilliam, New Hampshire, 1973

Symonds, R. W. *Thomas Tompion, His Life and Work.* London, 1951.

Terry, Henry. *American Clock Making: Its Early History.* Waterbury, Connecticut, 1870.

Tyler, E. J. *The Craft of the Clockmaker.* London, 1974.

# BIBLIOGRAPHY

## PRIMARY SOURCES:

Vital records of the following towns: CT: Bristol,
   Waterbury, Watertown, Torrington, Plymouth, Thomaston,
   Harwinton, Litchfield, Milford, Winchester, Burlington,
   Farmington, Preston, Plainfield. RI: Newport, Providence.
   MA: Worcester, Shrewsbury, Grafton, Haverhill,
   Amesbury.
Cemetery records of the following towns: CT: Bristol,
   Plymouth, Waterbury, Milford, New Haven, East Haven,
   Saybrook, New London, Watertown, Southington,
   Farmington, Litchfield, Torrington, Winchester,
   Harwinton, Burlington, New Hartford, Norwich,
   Plainfield, Middletown, Hartford, East Hartford,
   Goshen, Cornwall.
Land records of the following areas: CT: Bristol,
   Burlington, Plymouth, Watertown, Waterbury, Winchester,
   Norwich, Litchfield. NY: Cayuga County, Oswego County.
   MA: Berkshire County.
Bankruptcy suits: Lemuel Harrison (1818); Joseph Ives (1822);
   Northrop & Smith (1836); Silas B. Terry (1859).
Probate records: CT: Thomas Harland (1807); Thomas
   Harland, Jr. (1807); Putnam Bailey (1840); Eli
   Terry (1852); Seth Thomas (1859). KY: Thaddeus
   Benedict (1845).
U.S. military pension records: Norris North, Emily C.
   North, widow.
U.S. federal census records: 1850–80 industrial census
   of Connecticut. Searchers in miscellaneous years 1790–
   1880 and various counties of Connecticut, Vermont,
   New Hampshire, Maine, Massachusetts, Rhode Island,
   New York, Pennsylvania, Ohio.
Original accounting records and manuscript materials:
   American Clock & Watch Museum, Bristol, CT:
      Accounts: E. N. Welch Mfg. Co., Sessions Clock Co.,
      E. Ingraham Co., Elias Ingraham, Andrew
      Ingraham, Ephraim Downs, George B. Seymour
      (Silas Hoadley), Hopkins & Alfred, Samuel
      Terry, Eli Terry, Jr., H. Welton & Co.,
      Smith, Blakeslee & Co. Manuscript materials:
      Joseph Ives, Epaphroditus Peck, Eli Terry,
      Candace Roberts' diary, Edward Ingraham memoirs.
      U.S. patents: Eli Terry (4); Joseph Ives (3);
      Henry E. Warren collection of electric clock patents.
   Mattatuck Historical Society, Waterbury, CT:
      Mark Leavenworth accounts and papers;
      Lemuel Harrison papers.
   Connecticut Historical Society, Hartford, CT:
      Accounts: Alpha Hart, Hoadley & Whiting,
      Daniel Burnap.
   Reading, Massachusetts, Library and Historical Society:
      Daniel Pratt, Jr., accounts and papers.
   Trade catalogs and trade materials:

Hundreds of trade catalogs were searched at the
American Clock & Watch Museum, the Connecticut
Historical Society, and the Connecticut State Library.

## SECONDARY SOURCES:

Printed Genealogies of the following families:
   Leavenworth, Terry, Hoadley, Boardman, Burnham,
   North, Wooding, Tallmadge, Judd, Clark, Hyde,
   Cheney, Ives, Bailey, Blaisdell, Munger,
   Wingate, Benedict, Northrop, Pease, Hart,
   Barnes, Forrer, Willard, Stowell, Ward,
   Sanford, Packard, Hodges, Upson.
Manuscript Genealogies: Harrison, Harland, Pratt,
   Sperry, Roberts, Ives, Hotchkiss, Brace,
   Jerome.
Abbott, Henry G. *A Pioneer—History of the American Waltham
   Watch Company.* Chicago, 1905.
——*Watch Factories of America.* Chicago, 1888.
Anderson, Joseph. *The Town and City of Waterbury, Conn.,*
   3 vols. New Haven, 1896.
Atwater, Francis. *History of the Town of Plymouth, Conn.*
   Meriden, Connecticut, 1895.
Bailey, Chris H. "160 Years of Seth Thomas Clocks," *The
   Connecticut Historical Society Bulletin* (July '73).
Barber, Lawrence L. "The Clockmakers of Ashby,
   Massachusetts," *Antiques* (1933).
Barnum, P. T. *Struggles and Triumphs or Forty Years'
   Recollections of P. T. Barnum.* New York, 1871.
Barr, Lockwood. *Willard Time Pieces, Forerunners of the
   Banjo.* Unpublished manuscript.
——*William Faris.* Unpublished manuscript.
Battison, Edwin. "The Auburndale Watch Company," *U.S.
   National Museum Bulletin* (1959).
*Boston Clock Club.* Research papers (mimeographed):
   Barber, Lawrence L. "The Clock-Makers of Lexington
      and Concord, Massachusetts" (1938).
   Conlon, James E. "The Clockmakers of Newburyport
      (Mass.) and Vicinity" (1937).
   ——"The Roxbury Clockmakers Who Were
      Associated with the Willards" (1938).
   Packard, Donald K. "The Baileys of Hanover,
      Massachusetts, Clockmakers" (1940).
   Partridge, Albert L. "Peter Stretch, Clockmaker."
Boyd, John. *Annals and Family Records of Winchester, Conn.*
   Hartford, 1873.
*Bristol, Connecticut, in the Olden Times New Cambridge.*
   Hartford, 1907.
Bronson, Henry. *History of Waterbury, Conn.* Waterbury, 1858.
Buell, Carleton, and Barr, Lockwood. *Bristol Clockmakers.*
   Unpublished history (1936).
*Commemorative Biographical Record of Hartford County* (Conn).
   Chicago, 1901.

Conrad, Henry C. *Old Delaware Clock-Makers*. Wilmington, 1898.

Devoe, Shirley S. "The Litchfield Manufacturing Company, Makers of Japanned Papier Mache," *Antiques* (n.d.).

Dolan, J. R. *The Yankee Peddlers of Early America*. New York, 1964.

Drepperd, Carl W. *American Clocks & Clockmakers*. Garden City, New Jersey, 1947.

Eckhardt, George H. *Pennsylvania Clocks and Clockmakers*. New York, 1955.

——*United States Clock and Watch Patents, 1790–1890*. New York, 1960.

Fales, Dean A., Jr. "An Early Marblehead Clock," *Essex Institute Historical Collections* (Jan. '63).

Gibbs, James W. *Buckeye Horology*. Columbia, Pennsylvania, 1971.

Hoopes, Penrose R. *Early Clockmaking in Connecticut*. New Haven, 1934.

Howe, Florence T. "Jacob Sargeant, Goldsmith and Clockmaker," *Antiques* (April '31).

Lathrop, William G. *The Brass Industry in the United States*. Mt. Carmel, Connecticut, 1926.

Loomes, Brian. *The White Dial Clock*. London, 1974.

Milham, Willis I. *Time & Timekeepers*. New York, 1923.

Miller, Edgar G., Jr. *American Antique Furniture*, 2 vols. Baltimore, 1937.

Moore, N. Hudson. *The Old Clock Book*. New York, 1911.

National Association of Watch and Clock Collectors, *Bulletin:*

Avery, Amos G. "An Unusual Pillar and Scroll Shelf Clock" (July '48).

——"Heman Clark" (July '48).

Babcock, Harrison F., and Babcock, Mary E. "The Railroad Watch" (Oct. '60).

Babel, Richard B. "The Clockmakers of Cazenovia" (Feb. '74).

Baier, Joseph G. "Mathias Schwalback, His Church and Tower Clocks" (Aug. '73).

——"The Role of Wisconsin Residents in the Early American Clock Industry" (Feb. '72).

Barclay, Miriam A. "Daniel Pratt, Junior—Reading (Mass.) Clockmaker" (Supplement No. 2, Summer, 1964).

Barr, Lockwood. "The Ives Patent Equalizing Lever Spring" (April '56).

——"The New Haven Clock Company" (Dec. '57).

——"Peter Stretch, Philadelphia, 1670–1746" (Dec. '67).

——"Some Kentucky Clockmakers" (Oct. '57).

Barrington, Samuel H. "Early Pillar and Scroll—1788" (Dec. '50).

——"Jacob Detweiler Custer" (Dec. '59).

Berg, Paul. "The South Bend Watch Company" (Aug. '71).

Blackwell, Dana J. " . . . And Regulators in Every Style" (April '63).

Brooks, John G. "The Ithaca Calendar Clock Company" (Dec. '51).

Burns, A. Bruce. "An Isaac T. Pease Wood Movement Timepiece with Notes on Other Makers" (Oct. '69).

——"Eight-Day Wood Shelf Clock Movements" (Feb. '70).

——"Eight-Day Wood Tall-Case Movements" (Feb., April, Aug. '74).

——"Terry Standard Thirty-Hour Wood Movement Contemporaries" (Dec. '70).

Burt, Edwin B., and Forgie, Frasier. "Clockmakers of the Concord, Massachusetts, Community" (Supplement No. 5, Summer, 1967).

Crews, William G., Jr. "Tall Clocks Made by Jacob Craft of Shepherdstown, West Virginia" (Aug. '66).

Francillon, Ward. "Wood Movement Alarms" (Oct. '70).

——"More Wood Movement Alarms: The Groaners" (Dec. '73).

Fuller, Eugene E. "The Priceless Possession of a Few" (Supplement No. 10, Winter, 1974).

Hackett, F. Earl. "E. Howard: The Man and the Company" (Supplement No. 1, Winter, 1962).

Haskell, Henry A. "Grandpa Hinckley's Story" (Oct. '54).

Hauptman, Wesley R. "The American Watch Company" (April '64).

——"Appleton, Tracy & Company" (April '63).

——"The Boston Watch Company" (Oct. '63).

——"The First Waltham Watches—or Are They Howards?" (Dec. '61).

——"J. C. Adams, American Horological Promoter Without Peer" (Aug. '62).

——"Swiss Imitations of Early American Watches" (Aug. '60).

Hollingshead, Paul. "Torrington Clocks and Clockmakers" (Oct. '52).

Ingraham, Edward, et al. "Eli Terry—Dreamer, Artisan & Clockmaker" (Supplement No. 3, Summer, 1965).

Kalish, Charles. "The Ingersolls, The Daniells, and the Dollar Watch" (Oct. '61).

Korten, Elmer C. "An Eli Terry Regulator" (Aug. '72).

LaFond, E. F., Jr. "Frederick Heisely Strikes Again, or After You, Mr. Heisely!" (April '68).

McCollough, Robert L. "Hamilton Watch Company, Lancaster, Penna. U.S.A.—Some Notes on Its Founding and History" (April, Dec. '65, Oct. '66).

McMillan, F. H. "Asa Munger's Shelf Clocks" (Dec. '66).

——"Salem Bridge Clocks" (Dec. '63).

Meader, Robert W., and Gibbs, James W. "Shaker Clockmakers" (Supplement No. 7, Summer, 1972).

Miether, William E. "The Babcocks—Mary and Harrison—and Webb C. Ball" (Oct. '64).

Milham, Willis I. "The First Waterbury Watches" (Feb. '49).

——"The World's Columbian Exposition Watch" (May '48).

Muir, William. "The Problems of Chestnut Street" (Aug. '69).

Nijssen, Gerrit A. "The American Repeater" (Dec. '73).

Palmer, Howard. "Eight-Day Wood Movement Shelf Clocks" (Dec. '47).

Parsons, Charles S. "An Early Clock Made by Richard Manning of Ipswich, Massachusetts" (April '60).

——"Examples of New Hampshire Timepieces" (Oct. '60).

——"Jesse Emory, Clockmaker" (April '61).

——"New Hampshire Strikers" (Dec. '61).

——"William Fitz—Clocks to Fish" (Feb. '68).

Partridge, Albert L. "Some Minor Silas B. Terry Patents" (Dec. '50).

Pelletier, Rene. "An Astounding Discovery" (April '61).

Pritchett, W. F. "The Terry Patent Clock Pre-Standard Production" (Oct. '71).

Roberts, Kenneth D. "Asa Munger Shelf Clock Production at Auburn State Prison" (Aug. '69).

Roberts, Shepard. "Identification and History of Wood Movements in Tall Clocks" (April '70).

Seff, Herman H. "The Lond Wind Waterbury" (June '56).

Shafer, Douglas H. "A Survey History of the American Spring-Driven Clock 1840–1860" (Supplement No. 9, Winter, 1973).

Small, Percy L. "A Discussion of Dr. W. Barclay Stephens' Paper 'The Newark Watch Company and Its Career'" (Dec. '50).

——"Don J. Mozart" (April '57).

——"Napoleon Bonaparte Sherwood" (Feb. '54).

——"The Pitkin Brothers" (Oct. '54).

——"Samuel Curtis" (Dec. '52).

——"Luther Goddard and His Watches" (April '53, Feb., April '54).

Smith, Charles W., Jr. "A History of Clockmaking in Maine from 1750 to 1900" (April '73).

Starkey, C. L. "Humphrey Griffith, Indiana Clockmaker" (Dec. '59).

Stephens, W. Barclay. "J. P. Stevens and His Watch Company and Inventions" (Dec. '54).

——"The Newark Watch Company and Its Career" (Feb. '50).

——"The New York Watch Company" (Feb. '51).

——"The United States Watch Company, Marion, N.J." (June '50).

Stoltz, Victor, and Parkhurst, E. H., Jr. "William Wallace Dudley and His Masonic Watch" (Oct. '68).

Tschudy, Robert F. "Ingersoll—The Watch That Made the Dollar Famous" (April '52).

Wells, J. Cheney. "Silas Burnham Terry, Experimental Balance Wheel Clocks" (Dec. '49).

White, George V. "The Early American Watch—Waltham" (Aug. '47).

Orcutt, Samuel. *History of the Town of Wolcott* (Conn.). Waterbury, 1874.

Palmer, Brooks. *The Book of American Clocks.* New York, 1950.

——*A Treasury of American Clocks.* New York, 1967.

Parsons, Charles S. *New Hampshire Clocks.* Mimeograph (1956).

Parton, James. *People's Book of Biography.* Hartford, 1869.

Ransom, Stanley. "History of the William L. Gilbert Clock Corporation, Winsted," *The Lure of the Litchfield Hills,* Nos. 60, 61, 62.

Rosenberg, Charles. *American Pocket Watches.* 1965.

Smart, Charles E. *The Makers of Surveying Instruments in America Since 1700,* 2 vols. Troy, New York, 1962, 1967.

Stillman, Karl G. "Deacon William Stillman," *Timepieces* (Feb. '49).

——"Reverend Willet Stillman," *Timepieces* (Feb. '50).

Thomson, Richard. *Antique American Clocks & Watches.* Princeton, New Jersey, 1968.

Timlow, Heman R. *Ecclesiastical and Other Sketches of Southington, Conn.* Hartford, 1875.

Townsend, George E. *Almost Everything You Wanted to Know About American Watches and Didn't Know Who to Ask.* Vienna, Virginia, 1971.

——*Encyclopedia of Dollar Watches.* Arlington, Virginia, 1974.

Ward, Andrew H. *History of Shrewsbury, Mass.* Boston, 1847.

# INDEX

Montpelier, VT, 92, *92*
Moravia and Moravians, 33, 78
Mordecai, Thomas, 34
Morrill, Benjamin, *81*, 85–86
Morris, John, 54
Morris, Major, 106
Morristown, NJ, 43
Morse, Myles, 126
Moscow, USSR, 203
Moseley, Charles S., 207
Moses, Thomas, 136–38
Motion train, 19, 20
Moulton, Edward S., 80, *83*
Mt. Holly, NJ, 43, 90
Mt. Lebanon, NY, 39
Movement, 20–23, 47; Cheney-style, 54; east-west wood, 121–22; English imported, 79; horizontal wood, 121–22, *124*; overhead-striking, 144; skeletonized, 169; suppliers, 135–38; tinplate, *131*; Torrington-style, 121–22; uncased, 122; upside-down, 124
Mowrove, Peter, 78
Mozart, Don J., 161, 203–4
Mozart Watch Co., 203–4
Mulliken, John, 47
Mulliken, John (2d), 48
Mulliken, Jonathan, 47
Mulliken, Joseph, 48
Mulliken, Nathaniel, 47, 48, 54
Mulliken, Nathaniel, Jr., 48
Mulliken, Samuel, 47
Munger, Asa, 39, 40, *41*, 52, 124
Munger, Perley, 40
Munger, Sylvester, 40
Munger and Benedict, 41
Munger & Co., Asa, 41
Munger and Gillmore, 41
Munger & Pratt, 40
"Munroe," *59*
Munroe, Daniel, 27, 59
Munroe, Nathaniel, 59
Munroe, Nehemiah, 59
Munroe, William, 59
Munroe & Co., D., 59
Munroe & Whiting, 59
Musical clocks, *19*, 20, 33, 40, 65, 66, *66*, 68, *68*, 79
Mygatt, Comfort Starr, 63, 88

Nashua, NH, 86, 198
Nashua Watch Co., 194, 198
National Watch Co., 202, 204, 205
Negro clockmaker, 73
Neiser, Augustine, 33, 78
Nevins, David, 65
New Amsterdam, 39
New Bedford, MA, 50
New Bern, NC, 77
New Brunswick, NJ, 44
New Castle County, DE, 71
New England Clock Co., *155*, 185
New England Watch Co., *190*, 205, 208, 214; (fictitious), 218
New Hampshire mirror clock, 79, *81*, 85–86, *85*, 96
New Haven, CT, 17, *56*, 60, 61, 62, 63, 104, 108, 109, 126, 131, 150, 152, *157*, 208, 209
New Haven Clock and Watch Co., 170–71, 218

New Haven Clock Co., *157*, *169*, 170–71, 218 *221*
New Haven County, CT, 110
New Haven Watch Co., 208–9
New Lebanon, NY, 39
New London, CT, 67
New Orleans, LA, 67
New Salem, MA, 53
New York, NY, 15, *31*, 44, *44*, 45, 56, 58, 78, 131, 136, 150, *155*, 162, 164, 166, 170, 176, 178, 182, 185, 191, *192*, 194, *196*, 198, 200, 202, 209
New York Chronograph Watch Co., 209
New York City Watch Co., 218
New York Standard Watch Co., 209, *210*
New York Watch Co., 203, 218
New York World's Fair, *208*
New Zealand, 169
Newark, NJ, 44, 200, 201, 202, 218
Newark Watch Co., 200–1
Newberry Township, PA, 35
Newburyport, MA, 45, 47, 48
Newell, Sextus S., 115
Newfield, CT, 106
Newmarket, NH, 47, 80, 96
Newport, RI, 17, 26, *26*, 48, 78, 79
Newtown, CT, 63
Nolan, Spencer, 59
Nolan & Curtis, 128
Non-Magnetic Watch Co. of America, 220
Norfolk, VA, 77
Norristown (Norriton), 33, *37*, 52, 194, *194*
North, Ethel, *120*, 121
North, Dr. Joseph, 121
North, Norris, 108, 110, 118, *120*, 121, 122, *122*, 132
North, Simeon, 69
North & Co., Norris, 121, *132*, *136*
North Bridgewater, MA, 48, 122
North Goshen, CT, *152*
North Yarmouth, ME, 50, 96
Northampton, MA, 80
Northbury, CT, 103
Northfield, CT, 118
Northfield, MA, 91
Northrop, Herman, 138
Northrop & Smith, 135, 138
Norwich, CT, 26, 27, 60, *61*, 63, 65, 66, *66*, 67, 80, *190*, 191, 193
*Norwich Packet*, 65
*Norwich Weekly Courier*, 64
Nottingham, MD, 31, 33, 71, 73
Noyes, Leonard White, 86, 198
Numerals, Arabic and Roman, 25
Nuremburg, Germany, 191
Nutter, E. H., 86
Nutting, Granville, 207
Nutting brothers, 207

Oberlin, OH, 209
Oehl, Henry, 209
Official Bureau of Railroad Time Service, 209
Ogden, Moses, 44
Ohio Watch Co., 218
Olmstead, Nathaniel, 68
One-hand clocks, 47, 48
Organ clock, *143*

"Orwigsburg," PA, 31
Osaka, Japan, 209
Osgood, John, 48
Oswego, NY, 122
Otay, CA, 209
Otay Watch Co., 209
Otis, Frederick S., 184
Owen, Elizabeth, 34
Owen, George B., 182
Owen, Griffith, 34
Oxford, ME, 94, *95*, 99

Paillard, Charles August, 220
Painters, ornamental, 56, 196
Pallets, 19, *24*
Palmer & Coe, 79
Papier-mâché, 182
Paris, France, *49*, 191
Paris, ME, 96
Parker, Charles W., 201
Parmele, Abel, 57, 60
Parmele, Ebenezer, 26, 60, 63, 164
Parry, John J., 34
Parsell, Oliver, 44
Parton, James, 152
Patents, 34, 41, *41*, 44, 55, 56, 58, 62, 63, 104, 106, 108, 109, 113, 118, 119–20, 121–34, 139, 140, *151*, 156, 161, 162, 164, *179*, 180, 193, 202, 203, 206, 210, *210*, 213, 218
Paulus, Eugene, 220–21
Peabody, John, 91
Pearson, Isaac, 26, 31, 43
Pearson & Hollingshead, 43
Peck, Epaphroditus, 149, 176
Peck, Timothy, *62*
Peddlers, taxing of, 117
Peddling, 17, 78, 113, 116–17
Pendulum, 14–15, 19, 46; flying, *169*; rotary, 43, 44, *186*; torsion, 43, 44, *44*
Penniman, John R., 56
Peoria, IL, 207
Peoria Watch Co., 207
Pepperell, MA, 52
Perkins, Robinson, 82
Perry, E. H., 205
Perryville, PA, 37
Peru, IL, 187
Petersburg, VA, 77
Pewter, 53
Phelps, Anson G., 166, 169
Philadelphia, 15, 17, 26, 31, *31*, 33, 34, *34*, 39, *52*, 63, 71, 72, 78, 90, 91, 191, 198, 200, 206, 207, *213*
Philadelphia Watch Co., 220–21
Pillar, 19
Pillar and scroll, 40, 50, 113, 119, *120*, *122*, 125, 171
Pinion, 19, 20, 23; leaves, 23; rolling, 115, 128, 131, 132, *134*; wire, 18, 23
Pitkin, H. & J. F., *193*, 194
Pitkin, Henry, 193, 194
Pitkin, James Flagg, 193, 194
Pitkin, John O., 193, 194
Pitkin, Levi, 68
Pitkin, Walter, 193
Pitkin & Brother, 194
Pitkin & Co., 194
Pitkin brothers, 191, 193–94
Pitman, Saunders, 79
Pittsburgh, PA, 38

# ACKNOWLEDGMENTS

One cannot write a book such as this without assistance from a great many others. They may be previous researchers or authors, contemporary researchers or friends. A complete listing would not be possible, as dozens have contributed in some way, especially members of the National Association of Watch & Clock Collectors, whose assistance has been constant through observations, discussions, and presentations of horological artifacts and knowledge.

I should like to express special thanks to my photographer, John Garetti, who was especially fine to work with; to the officers of the American Clock & Watch Museum for their encouragement and support; to Mrs. Annette Murphy for reading the manuscript; to Charles S. Parsons for his expert evaluation and suggestions; and to my assistant, Mark Menard, for his encouragement.

Thanks also to Edward F. LaFond, Paul M. Walker, Dana J. Blackwell, Edward H. Goodrich, Amos G. Avery, Sheldon Hoch, Paul Hollingshead, Frank H. Murphy, Thomas Manning, George A. Bruno, Ward H. Francillon, Kenneth D. Roberts, Robert D. Schwartz, Mrs. Muriel Harris, Mrs. Carol Smith, Philip Dunbar, Henry Harlow.

And to the Connecticut Historical Society, Hartford, Connecticut; Connecticut State Library Museum, Hartford, Connecticut; Old Sturbridge Village, Sturbridge, Massachusetts; Mystic Seaport Museum, Mystic, Connecticut; Lyman Allyn Museum, New London, Connecticut.